VONNEGUT IN FACT

VONNEGUT IN FACT

THE PUBLIC SPOKESMANSHIP
OF PERSONAL FICTION

Jerome Klinkowitz

UNIVERSITY OF SOUTH CAROLINA PRESS

Copyright © 1998 University of South Carolina

Published in Columbia, South Carolina, by the
University of South Carolina Press

Manufactured in the United States of America

02 01 00 99 98   5 4 3 2 1

Library of Congress Cataloging-in-Publication Data

Klinkowitz, Jerome.
    Vonnegut in fact : the public spokesmanship of personal fiction /
Jerome Klinkowitz.
        p.   cm.
    Includes bibliographical references and index.
    ISBN 1-57003-237-8
    1. Vonnegut, Kurt—Political and social views.   2. Politics and
literature—United States—History—20th century.   3. Literature and
society—United States—History—20th century.   4. Social problems
in literatures.   5. Vonnegut, Kurt—Ethics. 6. Ethics in
literature.   I. Title.
PS3572.05Z748   1998
813'.54—dc21   97–49182

For Bob Weide, Kurt's "Whyaduck"

CONTENTS

Acknowledgments

Kurt Vonnegut has helped me locate copies of his speeches and some of his harder-to-find essays and reviews, for which I am grateful. I also appreciate his willingness to let me quote his work as I have done in this study. Such quotations come from publications of first appearance except where, as in the cases of *Palm Sunday* and *Fates Worse than Death,* the original materials have been employed in the making of a newly coherent work. All of his writing has been ascribed to "Kurt Vonnegut," a recognition that he dropped "Jr." from his name in 1976.

As always, the University of Northern Iowa, through a series of research grants, has been my sole support. Special gratitude is due to Robert Weide, the producer of television documentaries who revived my interest in Vonnegut and redirected it to his public spokesmanship. Julie Huffman-klinkowitz's archaeological skills were employed in organizing what has become a vast midden of Vonnegut artifacts, for which I am ever in her debt.

Introduction

THE PRIVATE PERSON
AS PUBLIC FIGURE

When on November 1, 1993, Kurt Vonnegut spoke to an overflow crowd at Heritage Hall in the Civic Center of Lexington, Kentucky, he was almost certainly motivated by a principle drawn from *Cat's Cradle,* his novel published thirty years before.

At the beginning of *Cat's Cradle* the narrator describes how life has become less nonsensical to him after learning about an honestly bogus Caribbean religion called Bokononism, the central belief of which concerns the notion of karass. Humanity, it is said, is organized into teams who fulfill God's Will without ever knowing what they are doing. Such a team is called a *karass*—and having any intimation of who else may be in one's karass gives a sense of deep purpose to the otherwise chaotic nature of life.

The comic nature of this novel derives from how unlikely and apparently disparate the membership of a karass can be, stretching across generations, geographies, and cultures to form surprising but ultimately necessary connections. As a thematic device, it allows Vonnegut to introduce and synthesize themes as dichotomous as war and peace, hate and love, absurdity and meaning. Philosophically, his prototypical religion lets him explore how people can derive benefit from a belief system based on its own self-evident fabrication. The greatest benefit, however, is to his novel's structure. Modeled as it is on the notion of karass, *Cat's Cradle* ranges as far and wide as a jazz musician's solo, dipping and weaving through apparent impossibilities to form what in the end is as coherent as a harmonic pattern's resolution. The method can be found not just here but anywhere in Kurt Vonnegut's fiction. And shortly after the publication of *Cat's Cradle* in 1963, it became apparent in his essays and public addresses as well.

In connection with his 1993 appearance in Lexington knowledgeable journalists made reference to this notion of karass. It was a seeming contradiction, after all, that an acknowledged atheist should appear on behalf of Midway College, supported as it was by the Disciples of Christ. And how odd that this religiously affiliated school, raising funds for its new college library, should seek the help

1

of our era's most frequently banned author, his *Slaughterhouse-Five* having been the target of Christian militancy since its publication in 1969. Yet here he was, this figure of postmodern innovations and sophistications, entertaining and instructing an audience of fourteen hundred in the heartland and advising them that their library would encourage a subversion of dogmatism more effective than eastern mysticism.

What brought Kurt Vonnegut to Lexington was his perception, at age seventy, of the workings of his karass. Not that one needs a technique of innovative fiction to explain the track of one's footprints in the sands of life. But having one had given this author a handle on otherwise perplexing ideas, on the whole notion of a latter twentieth century in which conventions and values themselves had been eclipsed by as yet inexplicable forces. As a survivor of one of these catastrophies, the World War II firebombing of Dresden, Germany, Vonnegut would have asked the question anyone beating such 1-in-100,000 odds would ask: why me? As a novelist, he had come relatively late to such ponderings, not beginning his career until 1952, at age thirty, with *Player Piano*. It would take another decade and a half before the matter of Dresden was first addressed, about the same time as his personal fictions began expressing themselves in public spokesmanship. Now, as a man in his seventies, Vonnegut would respond enthusiastically to elements in his past, delighting in fortuitous connections and marveling at ironies of correspondence still apparent from distances of fifty years and more.

For Lexington, the first connection was Ollie Lyon. As chair of Midway College's Development Council, Lyon found himself reaching back to the late 1940s for a resource in raising funds. As a publicist for General Electric in Schenectady, New York, Lyon had worked side-by-side with another young World War II veteran who'd begun responding to the brave new world of technology around him with sardonically satirical short stories. When on February 11, 1950, *Collier's* magazine published this fellow's "Report on the Barnhouse Effect," Lyon helped celebrate his friend's good fortune, for Kurt Vonnegut was the first among them to break out of the corporate tedium into something hopefully bigger. So many years later that success would have a happy payback in helping Lyon's work with Midway's fund drive.

Yet for Vonnegut the benefits would be even greater. Reuniting with Ollie Lyon was both a joy for reminiscences and a helpful benchmark for measuring just what purposes had been served in the interim, just what sense life may have made in that half century since these two men had returned from the war and gone to work rebuilding a bombed-out world. They did this work at General Electric, a company so taken with the idealism of such effort that its motto became "Where Progress Is Our Most Important Product." Lyon and Vonnegut were at the forefront of this idealism, publicizing the achievements of GE's Research Laboratory, itself a scientist's dream where investigators could follow their every whim. From civilization's most devastating war, these two young men had returned to embark on not just massive reconstruction but, in technological terms, a virtual reinvention of what humankind could make.

Does the novelist reveal himself when he sits down over morning coffee at a dining room table in Lexington, Kentucky, to talk about the past with a friend of fifty years? In Kurt Vonnegut's case, the answer would be yes, because his artistic talent all these years had been to draw on autobiographical elements in constructing a fictive approach to a world evolving well beyond the old conventions. For the first one-third of his writer's career, these novels had seemed so radically innovative as to defy comfortable explanation; in despair, critics had dismissed them as science fiction, even though their few science-fiction elements existed only as devastating satires of the subgenre. Then, beginning in the late 1960s and corresponding with his first serious recognition, Vonnegut had introduced more discursive elements in his work, references to a history he had shared and which the reader could reliably recognize. From here the author's work would include more and more autobiographical elements, his fiction being supplemented by a growing body of discourse which in the forms of essays and public addresses made instructive use of specific components in that vision. Finally, in what Vonnegut would self-consciously describe as the conclusion of his effort, he could be seen clarifying the importance of these elements—revisiting them, as it were, before taking leave of his spokesman's duty. At Lexington, beginning with Ollie Lyon, one can see much of that clarification taking place.

The novelist as public figure involves himself in much more than speech making. The nature of his booking, as has been seen, is an important part—not just an anonymous invitation from a bureau or committee but, as so often happens, a connection from the past that involves the whole business of coming to speak, meeting old friends, making new ones, and refining one's own view in the process. Sitting around the table with Ollie Lyon and others, Vonnegut could feel transported back over half a lifetime to the publicity office at GE, where he and his colleagues would seek relief from the loneliness of writing by socializing around the coffee pot or water cooler. In such circumstances it is enlightening to see ideas from Vonnegut's speech not just interweave with notions from his fiction, as listeners could hear the night before, but mix as well with comments about his and Ollie's experiences as beat reporters for one of the world's largest and most inventive corporations at the very start of what would become the postmodern era. Here themes from *Player Piano* and *The Sirens of Titan* seem far less science-fictionish than commonly middle-class, as two friends remark how what began as a technological miracle meant to free people from drudgery wound up relegating them to the emptiness of having no meaningful, rewarding work. Yet life's dimensions inevitably outstrip those of simple ideas, whether of philosophy or fiction, and from these same years with GE, Vonnegut and Lyon could also appreciate the joy of their bonding—of how these young professionals away from home and separated from the nurturing culture of their prewar lives drew on each other's support to form a true extended family, not just another idea in Kurt Vonnegut's fiction but an antidote of sorts to the dead end of scientific progress.

Here are not just components being checked off but a fictive vision being constructed. As Vonnegut and Lyon chat over morning coffee one sees the progress of novels taking shape, from the technological satire of *Player Piano* to the coy invention of *Slapstick* and the deeper understanding of *Bluebeard* and *Hocus Pocus*. And it happens among neither the claptrap of low-grade space opera or the intricacies of intellectual metafiction but rather in the context of two eminently familiar men whose backgrounds and subsequent careers have followed the pattern so common to their generation: being educated for the bright world of scientific modernism, seeing it challenged first by wartime destruction and then again by the nature of postwar development, quitting the corporate ideal to strike out more rewardingly on their own, and—after long, successful careers in these endeavors—taking stock of how it had all turned out.

A karass, *Cat's Cradle* suggests, includes someone like Ollie Lyon, bringing Kurt Vonnegut back to ideas and experiences of half a century before. But there are many other players as well, and the author's Lexington visit identified two more. Appearing with him at his press conference were Louis Grivetti and George Bloomingburg, older friends whose bond to the author was sealed by an experience even deeper and more profound than those formative years at GE. Grivetti and Bloomingburg had been prisoners of war with Vonnegut in Dresden and survived with him what has been called the largest massacre in European military history. With him they descended into their underground meat-locker quarters, where on the night of February 13–14, 1945, they listened while one of the world's most architecturally and artistically treasured cities was destroyed above them—destroyed with scientific brilliance and precision for virtually no strategic or tactical purpose. Today Vonnegut is fond of saying that the firestorm raid, controversial even at the time, turned out not to end the war one minute sooner, not to have saved one Allied life or freed one person from a concentration camp. Only one person on earth drew any benefit from the massive bombing, but for him it was a windfall. That person was Kurt Vonnegut, whose *Slaughterhouse-Five* as novel and movie earned him upwards of a million dollars—about five dollars for every man, woman, and child killed that night.

Yet in his reunion with Grivetti and Bloomingburg, Vonnegut would be reminded once again how history itself offers no simple explanation, how as in his General Electric experience the fiction writer's synthesis is needed to contain such apparent contradictions as good and evil, hope and despair. Vonnegut's response had been to dedicate himself to a life of pacificism, speaking on its behalf and writing a novel considered to be a classic of antiwar literature. Yet this type of response need not be the only one, not even the only successful one, for in reuniting with 'Lou Grivetti he had to confront the fact of one POW colleague's opposing strategy, that of continuing in a twenty-year military career and achieving the rank of colonel. Asked whether this bothered him, Vonnegut answered no, not at all—that what mattered was the bonding when he and Grivetti were very young men. That bonding, after all, was what brought them back together today. What happened in between might well appear inexplicable, but in the workings of this world their reunion was obviously necessary. In fretting about discrepancies between the one's pacifism and the other's military professionalism investigators might well be looking for answers in the wrong place.

The war business, in fact, had come to interest Vonnegut more in his advancing years. It had always been a quiet influence on his personal life, showing itself in affinities with writers totally unlike him except for the service life they had shared. Teaching at the University of Iowa in 1966, for example, he had begun a close friendship with Writers' Workshop colleague Richard Yates, a mannerist with a style as fine as Flaubert's and as far removed as possible from the jerky, almost brittle experiments with prose that Vonnegut was crafting into the first draft of *Slaughterhouse-Five.* Yet the two became at once like brothers, simply because they were both infantry privates from World War II's last phase, a phase fought mostly by half-trained, confused youngsters. Afterward, as an internationally famous author, Vonnegut would meet the German novelist Heinrich Böll, the two finding common sympathy as infantry veterans, albeit of opposing armies— having recognized that the immediate enemies of each were officers and that the larger struggle was one against war itself. The Dresden firebombing made its first appearance in Vonnegut's work about this time, in a 1966 introduction (written from Iowa City) to a new edition of *Mother Night,* just at the time Vonnegut was meeting Yates, reviewing Böll's *Absent without Leave,* and making plans for writing *Slaughterhouse-Five.* Yet even through his war novel's best-seller fame the author was loath to credit too many historical specifics, making clear that protagonist Billy Pilgrim was not Kurt Vonnegut himself but rather an Everyman figure in the children's crusade that the latter days of World War II had become.

As time moved on, however, and half-century anniversaries of the conflict turned up on the calendar, Vonnegut joined the trend of reminiscence and began talking in detail about his experiences in the war. Fifty-year commemorations serve a purpose, for they coincide with new phases in the lives of their participants, recently retired as they are with time to look back on these events and measure their importance even as a look forward implies that there might not be too much time left. In May of 1990, while television ran documentaries on the Nazi blitzkrieg five decades before, Kurt Vonnegut spoke at the Smithsonian's Air and Space Museum as part of a series on strategic bombing. Representing the victim's perspective, he repeated many points from his basic public addresses of the time—but also mentioned, in an offhand manner and in response to the news that another POW colleague was in the audience, that one of their buddies had not been so lucky, dying of malnutrition and virtual despair a few weeks before the war ended. This individual Vonnegut identified as Joe Crone, and from the description of his character listeners might have supposed that here was a model for Billy Pilgrim.

POW Tom Jones's reunion with Kurt Vonnegut at the Smithsonian that night provided another contribution: a set of photographs from their final prisoner-of-war days back in May of 1945, when the author and seven buddies wandered free from their quarters, searching the countryside for Allied units. Vonnegut recalled the horse and wagon they had commandeered, and also the peaceful valley through which they'd traveled. Indeed, he had just recently described it at the end of his novel *Bluebeard.* Now he was reminded that one of their group, Bill Burns, had found a camera with film and had, with Jones, clicked off several snapshots. Given copies, he would use them next year as documents concluding his book of essays *Fates Worse than Death,* a technique reinforcing his position as witness. In this same section Vonnegut reprints a page from an Allied intelligence document outlining beforehand the importance of Dresden as a target, which was nil.

Having first established the importance of his wartime experience for the artistic imagination, something he had waited twenty-five years to do, the author of *Slaughterhouse-Five* now, another quarter century later, would speak with candor in a more documentary fashion. Not that he had to research these materials. Rather they would be brought back to him by other longtime partners in his purpose, all of whom had taken different paths to these days fifty years later. Lou Grivetti stayed in the service to become a colonel; Bill Burns went into broadcasting; Kurt Vonnegut wrote *Slaughterhouse-Five.* Now, a lifetime afterward, Vonnegut was pleased to look back through all that past for fragments of what they'd shared in common; for each of them a snapshot of the war could speak volumes.

With the fiftieth anniversary of the war's end approaching, Kurt Vonnegut found that memories long disregarded or trivialized were taking on great importance. And so for the commemoration of the Dresden bombing and then for V-E Day itself he declined invitations to speak as the author of *Slaughterhouse-Five,* preferring to focus attention on the veterans whose stories had for too long not drawn many listeners. That had been his own experience when returning home in 1945, wishing to write a great war novel but finding that no one cared for such a topic just then. When he did get around to it in 1969, the result was read as something as pertinent to Vietnam as to World War II, successful as *Slaughterhouse-Five* was in its methods of fragmentation and indirection. But by 1995 those veterans who remained, whose stories were now more comparatively rare, for the first time took center stage. And as he did with Bill Burns's and Tom Jones's photographs, this was what Vonnegut chose to tell.

Thus the revelation, made in public addresses and correspondence with the association of his old prisoner-of-war colleagues, that the "Joe Crone" recalled so casually with Tom Jones that night in 1990 was more than just an offhand model for Billy Pilgrim. The POW group, whose directory prided itself on tracing careers and listing addresses of those surviving from the group of 121 prisoners housed in Dresden's slaughterhouse number 5, could now hail the literary celebrity of Edward Reginald "Joe" Crone Jr., a quiet young man who had enlisted in the army so he could finish one more year of college (after which he hoped to enter the religious ministry), who'd been trained in the service for work with an engineering battalion but then, in November 1944, had rushed as an ill-prepared infantryman to help fill the massive need for fresh troops on the Ardennes front. Gangly and awkward, innocent and confused, images from his 1940 high school yearbook and snapshots from army boot camp show him to be the perfect picture of what Kurt Vonnegut had in mind for a hapless participant in the children's crusade his war had become. Real-life details and points of character sought out from those who remembered him complement the portrait of Billy Pilgrim in both novel and movie—not historical correspondence as such but rather a reminder of how art and life enhance each other when good narratives work especially well.

From Vonnegut's Dresden group a remarkable number survived the war, and an even more remarkable number lived on through the postwar decades to become honored septuagenarians on the fiftieth anniversary of V-E Day in 1995. According to the list compiled by former POW Ervin Szpek, only two died in the slaughterhouse number 5 prison itself, and both are commemorated in *Slaughterhouse-Five*. Michael D. Palaia is listed as having died in prison, executed by a firing squad—not for stealing a teapot (in the novel) or a Dresden figurine (in the movie) like character Edgar Derby, but for taking food, as Lou Grivetti would clarify during the meeting at Lexington. The other was Joe Crone, who—having despaired of surviving and given away his meager rations of food—virtually willed himself to death on April 11, 1945, just four weeks before the war would end. This was how Kurt Vonnegut recalled Joe's death when chatting with Tom Jones in 1990; to both of them it was a reminder of how odd and yet how necessary the workings of our lives happen to be.

Thus Kurt Vonnegut's public spokesmanship would reflect the quirky nature of that necessity. His message at Lexington and elsewhere would include simple bits of folk wisdom meant to correct misapprehensions and put people more at ease, from such things as understanding the seasonal change of weather to lightening the burdens of misconstrued responsibility. He would speak on major social issues and address himself to concerns as specific as gun control, classroom size, and the need for people to identify in groups. But his approach was anything but dogmatic or deductive. Rather his listeners could hear him amass points of information with the seeming randomness that they had come to him in life—this from General Electric, that from the war, another piece from back home in Indiana—and follow with amused pleasure how the speaker could knit them together into a surprising inevitability that not only resolved the issue but did so with the shock of unsuspected necessity. It was the same unsuspected necessity that had the author sharing coffee one hour with Ollie Lyon from GE and the next swapping POW stories with Lou Grivetti and George Bloomingburg, regretting only that Kentuckian Bill Burns, who'd found that camera forty-eight years before, was sick today and couldn't be with them to reminisce over his photographs.

Did this reunion mean that the author's karass was complete? Not at all, for life was continuing and with it humankind's need to discern a sense of import. By now Vonnegut knew that the act of coming to deliver a speech could influence its subject—seeing Tom Jones in his Smithsonian audience and learning now that Lou Grivetti had become a military careerist were just two more examples. But the business of arranging a speech at the Lexington Civic Center's Heritage Hall meant more than crossing paths with Ollie Lyon and Lou Grivetti. It involved helping with a poster for the event, not just to advertise his speech but to be sold for additional Midway College fund-raising. For this he was brought together with a local printmaker, Joe Petro III, with whom Vonnegut prepared a design similar to the line drawing of himself on the last page of his 1973 novel, *Breakfast of Champions.*

Since introducing such drawings into his work Vonnegut had continued dabbling with other semiabstract renderings, going so far as to have a small show in 1980 at New York's Margo Feiden Galleries. But in meeting Joe Petro the author discovered both a new medium and a congenial printer with whom to work. With Petro, Vonnegut could apply india ink to acetate and have anywhere from a dozen to fifty prints pulled with fine detail in exceptionally brilliant color. Stimulated by the poster-making experience and delighted with Petro's work habits, Vonnegut began an association that would occupy his future while once more gathering purpose from his past. His father and grandfather, while working as architects, had been artists, and the entire Vonnegut family, especially Kurt's sister and his daughters, enjoyed great talents for drawing and painting. He himself appreciated how working with Joe was a relief from the isolation of writing, and also a reprieve from the task of producing work that bore the responsibility of articulated meaning. Yet even in their self-apparency his artworks shared a similarity with his novels and his speeches: that correspondences need not be one to one, and that in the spontaneity of radically combined elements could be found a pattern to life not otherwise so readily discerned.

It is the need to find such patterns, Vonnegut believes, that distinguishes humanity as a species. Men and women, he has learned—both as a trained anthropologist and practicing novelist—are the only creatures in nature whose lives seemed bedeviled by having to find a purpose for things, a meaning for existence that in natural terms would rather follow its own rhythms of being. Such self-imposed responsibility is itself vexing and can distract one from the pleasures of life. But the drive becomes problematic when humans attempt to impose their own notions on the nature of existence. On the one hand, such impositions cause one to focus on what might be unimportant things; on the other, they almost inevitably lead to frustration when life itself refuses to work out according to plan.

Not just Kurt Vonnegut's work but all postmodern thought addresses this problem. A more useful endeavor is not to impose assumptions but rather deconstruct them, revealing the arbitrary side of what has been assumed to be natural. Once this deconstruction has taken place, one's thoughts can then be restructured to accommodate what may have been otherwise censored out. Vonnegut's own method, implicit in his fiction and explicit in his public spokesmanship, is to organize ideas and images so that a space can be opened for a freedom of fresher thought. Thus does he loosen the claims of convention and open the possibilities for surprise, all the while keeping himself ready for innovations of the occasion—whether they be Ollie Lyon raising funds for a church-supported school or Lou Grivetti turning out to have retired as a colonel.

Sometimes criticized as an apparent nihilist, Kurt Vonnegut in fact brings a message that is hopeful. If life seems without purpose, perhaps it is because we have tried (and failed) to impose a purpose inappropriately. The quest for meaning can be self-defeating, especially when pursued with the rigidities of conventions that in truth no longer apply. The radicalness of the author's own propositions seem so only because of the persistence of those conventions he so successfully interrogates.

Kurt Vonnegut's first such interrogation was in the form of a short story, "Report on the Barnhouse Effect," written with the encouragement of Ollie Lyon and his other coworkers at General Electric in 1949. For the next two decades he would write in obscurity and seeming anonymity. But from those conditions arose both the need for and the techniques of a public spokesmanship that would influence his manner of expression in fiction and nonfiction alike. Once perfected, that manner would make Kurt Vonnegut one of the most popularly received and happily heeded novelists of his age.

Chapter One

EMERGING FROM ANONYMITY

At the beginning of 1969 Kurt Vonnegut was forty-six years old and the author of five novels, two short-story collections, forty-six separately published short stories (in magazines as familiar as *Collier's* and the *Saturday Evening Post*), and twenty feature essays and reviews. However, he was almost totally unknown—unknown in public terms, that is. With his more than half a million words in print, editors knew him—but as a professional pigeonholed as doing science fiction or selling to the slicks rather than as a major voice in American culture. True, much of his production was undertaken, by necessity, in commercial fashion. Rejected stories with a technical theme were shuttled off to the nickel-a-word venues of *Argosy* and *Worlds of If;* when the family magazine markets dried up, he found he could make the same money by outlining paperback originals, which is how some of his most important novels were conceived; and to support himself and his large family by his writing he undertook review assignments on far from literary topics. But compared to other major writers at similar stages in their careers, Kurt Vonnegut at midpoint was laboring in virtual obscurity, writing fiction and fact alike that were not having any public impact beyond a moment's entertainment and another month's expenses met.

Beginning in March of 1969, all that changed. With the publication of his sixth novel, *Slaughterhouse-Five,* Vonnegut found himself in unlikely places: as the lead item in the most prominent national book reviews and as a major presence on the best-seller lists of these same newspapers and journals. Quality alone is rarely the distinguishing factor in such attention. In Vonnegut's case, subsequent scholarship has shown that *Cat's Cradle* and *Mother Night* are as significant achievements as *Slaughterhouse-Five,* yet the former never outsold its first printing of six thousand copies and received just a few passing reviews, while the latter's debut as a paperback original meant no media coverage at all, a fate shared with *The Sirens of Titan,* another work now considered central to the Vonnegut canon. Rather, as any publicist will testify, getting reviewed by major critics on the front pages of book sections is a privilege mostly reserved for the country's best-known authors. Getting there as an unknown is a rare achievement indeed, the reasons for which merit close study.

A correlation exists between the first two major reviews of *Slaughterhouse-Five:* each was written by a critic who had heard Vonnegut speak to audiences, and who had been, moreover, deeply impressed by the personal voice in the author's fictive statement. Not that public speaking was Kurt Vonnegut's chosen profession; rather, his talk at Notre Dame University's Literary Festival (as heard by Granville Hicks) and his two-year lectureship at the University of Iowa (where Robert Scholes was a colleague) were stopgap measures to generate some income after his customary publishing markets had either closed (as in the case of *Collier's* and the *Post*) or ceased to respond. Those who have met him know he is a quiet person much protective of his privacy; for him, public speaking is a nervous chore. More than once he has observed of a lecture that instead of courting laughs and easy applause he should be at home doing his real work, writing novels. But with the relative failure of his fifth novel, *God Bless You, Mr. Rosewater,* to make much headway in 1965, novel writing was no longer an option, and so Vonnegut accepted a teaching position at the University of Iowa Writers' Workshop and booked speeches at literary festivals and library dedications around the country as ways of matching the modest income his short stories and paperback originals had generated before.

This was what was known to Granville Hicks in 1969, when the venerable old critic (who had made his initial mark as a commentator on socially radical literature of the Great Depression era) was faced with introducing an unknown author to his readers in the *Saturday Review.*[1] The new novel itself, *Slaughterhouse-Five,* was an equally difficult topic, for its innovative format was worlds away from the realistic, sociologically based fiction Hicks had championed for nearly half a century. Therefore the critic began discussing what he *did* know: that the year before he and a student audience at Notre Dame had heard Kurt Vonnegut deliver "as funny a lecture as I had ever listened to." Given what Vonnegut then had in print—a few paperback editions gaudily dressed as space opera—his audience might have expected the wooly ruminations of a science fiction writer. But after hearing him speak, no one present could mistake Kurt Vonnegut for a Harlan Ellison, Isaac Asimov, or even for his affectionately drawn portrait of the perennially misunderstood SF hack, Kilgore Trout. "What he really is," Hicks announced, "is a sardonic humorist and satirist in the vein of Mark Twain and Jonathan Swift." Twain and Swift, of course, are remarkable as two of the English language's great public writers, spokesmen who addressed the crucial issues of their day in the most direct manner and in the most personably appropriate voice. There was much of that same quality in Vonnegut, Hicks learned in the audience that night, and he encountered it again in the pages of *Slaughterhouse-Five,* in which the same real-life person speaks directly to the reader in chapters 1 and 10.

Science Fiction, Hicks realized, was at least a tangential concern in the author's earlier work: *Player Piano, Cat's Cradle,* and *God Bless You, Mr. Rose-*

water had made great fun of the worship of science and technology; misfunctions of both were responsible for catastrophes of plot and hilarities of incident, not to mention a dim overview of human strivings toward a mechanical ideal. But *Slaughterhouse-Five* was more autobiographically revealing. "Now we can see," Hicks revealed, "that his quarrel with contemporary society began with his experiences in World War II, about which he has at last managed to write a book." From here Hicks went directly to Vonnegut's most personal statement to the reader, his confession that "I would hate to tell you what this lousy little book cost me in money and anxiety and time." From Vonnegut's admission of problems in writing his book, Hicks proceeds to the second key factor: that "All this happened, more or less," another personal confession that violates even more seriously the convention that an author must maintain a certain distance from his or her work. It is this personal relationship that makes the novel interesting. It is, in fact, the only thing the book truly has, since its purported subject, the fire-bombing of Dresden late in World War II, is something "Vonnegut never does get around to describing." What matters is that "Like Mark Twain, Vonnegut feels sadness as well as indignation when he looks at the damned human race," and in *Slaughterhouse-Five* he has found a vehicle for expressing that very personal view. "There is nothing intelligent to say about a massacre," the author tells his publisher; yet as Granville Hicks reads what Vonnegut offers in place of such conclusive statements, "I could hear Vonnegut's mild voice, see his dead pan as he told a ludicrous story, and gasp as I grasped the terrifying implications of some calm remark." The reaction, then, is to a public spokesman: one who not only addresses himself to a topic of great common interest, but who fashions his own reaction as an expression of what he feels should be the socially and culturally responsible view.

Even more instrumental in presenting Kurt Vonnegut's new novel to the public was Robert Scholes's front-page coverage in the *New York Times Book Review*.[2] Personal articulation of a common cause was the first thing Scholes pointed out—"Kurt Vonnegut speaks with the voice of the 'silent generation,' and his quiet words explain the quiescence of his contemporaries"—and, like Granville Hicks, the reviewer was familiar with the author, having been his colleague at the University of Iowa as recently as the 1965–1967 academic years. To Scholes, Vonnegut's message was a simple one, its testimony an act of witness. The novel's speaking voice is plain and simple, suiting its message that one had best be kind and unhurtful because "Death is coming for all of us anyway, and it is better to be Lot's wife looking back through salty eyes than the Deity that destroyed those cities of the plain in order to save them."

Because he sees himself in his act of witnessing as Lot's wife, the author of *Slaughterhouse-Five* judges himself a failure. Robert Scholes thinks not, but feels that "Serious critics have shown some reluctance to acknowledge that Vonnegut is among the best writers of his generation" because he is "too funny and too intelligent for many, who confuse muddled earnestness with profundity." Yet it is his plain and honest approach, which cuts through the obscuring technicalities of morals and philosophies, that allows "the cruelest deeds" to be "done in the best causes," while writers whose language and approach are immensely more sophisticated find it impossible to convince their readers that "our problems are not in our institutions but ourselves."

Accompanying Robert Scholes's review was a background piece on Vonnegut himself by another former Iowa colleague, C. D. B. Bryan.[3] Like Scholes, Bryan made much of the author's personal qualities, especially his "quiet, humorous, well-mannered and rational protests against man's inhumanity to man" as forming "an articulate bridge across the generation gap." Bryan reinforced this personal sense by crowding his piece with intimacies, including references to Vonnegut struggling to support his family by selling what he could to the commercial magazines and reportedly earning "what I would have made in charge of the cafeteria at a pretty good junior-high school," another folksy comment intended to make the reader feel as familiar and comfortable with the man as Bryan did.

Getting page 1 of the *New York Times Book Review* is no small accomplishment; having page 2 devoted to a personality piece is even more impressive, prompting one to ask why a generally unknown author such as Kurt Vonnegut would receive such treatment by the nation's leading review medium. One reason was the author's own persistence in making those commercial sales that kept his family supported by at least middle-class standards. One of the publications for which Vonnegut undertook relatively servile duties was the *Times Book Review* itself, reporting not a fancy best-seller or important intellectual work but rather one of the greatest challenges to a reviewer's imagination possible, *The Random House Dictionary.*[4] What does one say about a dictionary, Vonnegut might have asked himself. In fact, his response is generated by a series of questions he asks himself as he pages through the volume's front matter and ponders what linguists argue about when debating each other's standards for inclusion or exclusion. "Prescriptive, as nearly as I could tell, was like an honest cop, and descriptive was like a boozed-up war buddy from Mobile, Ala."—such was his way of putting the editors' theoretics into terms simple and familiar enough for himself and his readers. To emphasize the shared nature of this discovery, Vonnegut reported how it emerged from conversations with two of his coworkers at Iowa, Bob Scholes and Richard Yates. But rather than sounding academic, Vonnegut's quest seemed no more complicated than simply pondering the problem, asking the guys at work about it, and then presenting his conclusion in as clear and simple and personally meaningful a way as possible.

"I find that I trust my own writing most, and others seem to trust it most, too," Vonnegut recalled several years later, "when I sound most like a person from Indianapolis, which is what I am."[5] Such is the persona he used in the dictionary review and in most other essays he was writing at the time. One, "Science Fiction,"[6] also appeared in the *Times Book Review* and was reprinted by its editor in a volume of especially convincing personal statements. Here Vonnegut made sense of SF enthusiasts' mania to include everyone from Kafka to Tolstoy as a science fiction writer by remarking that "It is as though I were to claim that everybody of note belonged fundamentally to Delta Upsilon, my own lodge, incidentally, whether he knew it or not. Kafka would have been a desperately unhappy D.U." As in the dictionary piece, Vonnegut ranges far (by mentioning Kafka and Tolstoy as SFers), brings things back in (by talking of his own fraternity), and then makes his point by unexpectedly uniting the two (Kafka making a wretched brother of Delta Upsilon). Like the approaches of other great public speakers in the American vernacular vein—Abraham Lincoln, Mark Twain, and Will Rogers—Kurt Vonnegut makes his point by shaping his public message in the most personally familiar terms.

That Vonnegut's public spokesmanship had an infectiously personal quality to it extends to his circumstances of publication, even as those circumstances, in the case of his breakthrough book, *Slaughterhouse-Five,* encompass all that business with his friends in Iowa City and folksy appearances in the front pages of the *New York Times Book Review.* The novel itself begins with the author' own commentary on how he came to write the book, including not just its struggles of composition but the role of publisher Seymour Lawrence in bringing it to press. For his part, Lawrence revealed that what caught his attention and prompted him to buy this unknown author's next three books sight unseen was *The Random House Dictionary* review—and not just because it was brightly and amusingly written, but because it had some of its fun at the expense of Random House's Bennett Cerf, for whom Lawrence had once been a rather exasperated vice president.[7]

The circle becomes complete when Vonnegut delivers the typescript of *Slaughterhouse-Five,* in which an actual occurrence in the book's production becomes a moment in the reader's experience of that same text. But what lies within the larger sweep of this circle, this arc of experience that stretches from an Indiana childhood through wartime service and a writer's career on the East Coast all the way back to a temporary teaching post in the Midwest where not just *Slaughterhouse-Five* but also those essays on science fiction and *The Random House Dictionary* were conceived? Before reaching the best-seller list (for the first time in his life) in Spring 1969, Kurt Vonnegut left abundant evidence of where he was heading: five novels plus all those short stories, essays, and reviews provide much for the reader to consider. But just as it was the supposedly mundane occasion of a dictionary review that brought him to the attention of Seymour Lawrence and includes so many clues to the nature of his literary genius, so does a surviving lecture from these years indicate what it was in his speaking style that impressed Granville Hicks and actually forecast the structural mode of *Slaughterhouse-Five*.

On November 21, 1967, Vonnegut appeared at Ohio State University to deliver a talk entitled "Address: To Celebrate the Accession of The Two Millionth Volume in the Collections of the Libraries of The Ohio State University." Later on, there would be many such speeches, all of them getting major media attention—on June 29, 1970, in the wake of his bestsellerdom and campus fame (during days of massive campus unrest), his commencement speech at Bennington College was reported as the lead item in *Time* magazine.[8] But in 1967 Kurt Vonnegut was yet to be discovered, and was in fact often misunderstood—in this case by the ceremony's organizer, Professor Matthew J. Bruccoli, who was following William F. Buckley's lead at *National Review* (where Vonnegut's short story "Harrison Bergeron" was reprinted on November 16, 1965) in assuming that the author was an outspoken political conservative.

Kurt Vonnegut, of course, was and is anything but a right-wing activist, and at Columbus one finds him taking great delight in confounding expectations.[9] He begins, just as he would in speeches after he had become famous, by warning listeners not to expect a coherent, conventionally delivered lecture. He explains that this is because he has found out there is a world of difference between sticking to a written text and interacting with a live audience. Therefore, he cautions, his audience should be ready for anything and everything, his lecture notes being just one of several texts to be flipped through and referred to in the manner of comedian Mort Sahl paging through a daily newspaper and improvising comments at random. This contrast between the formality of presenting a university lecture and the casualness of Vonnegut's approach suggests another dichotomy, one that becomes both the theme and structure of his address: the irony of having him, a college drop-out, speaking at such an august academic occasion in honor of the library acquiring its two millionth book.

It was World War II that took Kurt Vonnegut out of college, but the speaker prefers to show himself as a fugitive from the rules of formal education. Instead, he says, he wound up having to educate himself. This meant that he did his browsing for books in bus stations instead of university libraries, something that gets him his first big laugh: that it would be more appropriate, as he suggests, for him to be dedicating a new Greyhound terminal today. On such newsstands he discovered what the times had branded as tawdry fare: gaudily packaged paperbacks by D. H. Lawrence and Henry Miller, respectable editions of which continued to be banned until the Supreme Court decisions just the year before. This fascination with "dirty books" will make several appearances and is an early indication of how what the author introduces as an offhand joke seemingly tangential to the topic will become absolutely central to his enlightening argument and surprising yet convincing conclusion.

The first legacy of such an apparently shabby self-education, however, is the

15

irony of this self-styled college dropout becoming a professor in the University of Iowa's postgraduate creative writing program, something he had been for the past two years. How did this person without so much as an undergraduate degree manage to teach master's and doctoral level students? His hope was to follow a friend's advice and not tell the class everything he knew in the first hour. An hour proved not to be the problem—after three minutes, Vonnegut explains, he was out of material. What that material was he now repeats at Ohio State, giving a quick chalk talk on the nature of storytelling derived from his anthropology thesis on the fluctuation between good and evil in simple tales—a thesis that had been rejected by the University of Chicago after the war, preserving his degree-less status.

The trick is to draw two axes and between the vertical of "good fortune/bad fortune" and the horizontal of the hero or heroine's progress to map the rise and fall in conditions. The result is comically reductive: that narratives as simple as "Cinderella" and as complex as Kafka's "The Metamorphosis" work essentially the same: that is, by measuring the protagonist's experiences in trying to distinguish the good news from the bad news. The moral is a simple one but effective in reflecting back on the speaker's situation—not just that high and low literature share the same structures, but that such patterns can be explained by a dropout chemistry major who had studied anthropology on the G.I. Bill.

As Vonnegut would refine this speech in future years, the nature of fluctuations in narratives would assume a critical dimension: that while the greatest tales, such as Shakespeare's *Hamlet,* have a relatively flat development in common with primitive stories, it is the sensationalistic crowd pleasers that take their readership on roller-coaster rides of almost hysteric highs and lows. This will be the lesson he himself learns in writing *Slaughterhouse-Five,* as Mary O'Hare cautions in the novel's first chapter: that he must resist the temptation, encouraged by Hollywood, to dress up his story in false heroics with roles tailored more for famous actors than for the haplessly common men like Kurt Vonnegut and her husband.

At Ohio State vulgar literature consisted of "Cinderella" and bus-trip abridgments of banned novels. While on the subject of vulgarity, the author pulls another of his Mort Sahl tricks, reaching for a copy of *Cosmopolitan* and citing a report that says novelists, dirty or otherwise, make lousy lovers. This draws more laughs, but Vonnegut turns them to a serious point: that these supposedly dirty books do not sell like hotcakes or sell very well at all. He names *The Rosy Crucifixion* by Henry Miller as the most sex-packed novel he knows, and then confirms that its sales are poor. What sells is not sex itself but sex stories about famous people, preferably of the gossip column variety. And even here the motive is less for stimulation than for group membership, to read what everyone else is reading and thus be able to share in conversations. In the novel he would begin soon afterward, *Breakfast of Champions,* Vonnegut would brand ideas themselves as mere badges of friendship, their conceptual content being second-ary to their function as signs of human commerce, what he calls in this speech "a cheap way of saying hello."

But still there is the titillation at the idea of sex in literature, and his listeners' own awareness of that fact gets him his biggest laugh so far. "Two million!" Vonnegut marvels, crediting the number of books the Ohio State University Libraries house. "I wonder how many of them are dirty?" Before they can recover he shares another thought: "Which is the dirtiest?" Obviously meant as a joke, this question is impossible to answer—it is not meant to be answered, and knowing that they are absolved of such responsibility allows the audience to laugh along in relief. But then he turns the tables and gives them some answers, valuable in their specificity even as their checklist fashion underscores the speaker's confidence. Which is the greatest of those two million books? *Ulysses.* The noblest: *The Brothers Karamazov.* The most effective? *The Catcher in the Rye.* The most humane? *The Tenants of Moonbloom.* The most important? As Vonnegut would say in the first chapter of *Slaughterhouse-Five* in less than two years, *Death on the Installment Plan,* an important book which just now was teaching him how to handle the unspeakable nature of death—a problem that had kept his Dresden book unwritten for so long. But he had found Céline's novel without finishing college, just as he had learned similar lessons from Joyce, Dostoyevsky, Salinger, and the others. His own experience had been something like James Thurber's, who had dropped out of this very university in order to spend time reading books he cared about. Which leads to one last question: who had won the lottery, as it were, by writing the two millionth book to be acquired? Could it have been Thurber himself?

Whoever it was, it almost surely was not Kurt Vonnegut. For at this moment in his career it would have been easier to find copies of his novels at the Columbus Greyhound Terminal than at the Ohio State University Library. But maybe that was not so bad after all. As taught in college, reading great literature was turned into a version of hell week lasting all semester long, novel after massive novel being plowed through on a weekly basis until students were bleary-eyed and professors were drained of enthusiasm and ideas. What matters is his own engagement with literature, in bus stations and elsewhere—an engagement that he replicates and shares with his listeners here today.

So much of *Slaughterhouse-Five*'s method can be found in this Ohio State address: the author's introductory acknowledgment of his own insufficiency, based on the impossible nature of his assignment; the apparent digressions into seemingly unrelated subjects, only to bring those subtopics back into a mainstream argument all the stronger for its elements of surprise; his humor at the expense of himself; and yet the triumph of that self as a measure of wisdom and integrity. Just as the contradictory nature of having to say something about an unspeakable event—a massacre—generates the true subject of *Slaughterhouse-*

Five, the struggle of its making, so does Kurt Vonnegut seize upon the specific problems of presenting an address on a library accession of its two millionth volume to make salient points about what that accomplishment really means. In both cases, the mode of public address is used to make his commentary possible. Indeed, because more literary approaches have proven not to work, Vonnegut must speak to his audience and readership directly—personally, and yet wearing the mantle of an otherwise unspeakable experience in a way that makes his achievement a shared occasion.

What public spokesmanship Kurt Vonnegut engaged in before the mid-1960s related more to his personal circumstances than to the profession of authorship. Yet each example relates to how public fact would become a shaping element in the way he crafted and presented his personal fictions. In the commentaries on his childhood that can be found within his works, two formative elements emerge: his pride in being instructed in old-fashioned American civics, where citizenly resourcefulness and accountability were taught not just as ideals but as practical realities, and the role that classic radio and film comedians such as Jack Benny, Fred Allen, and Laurel & Hardy played in relieving some of the personal dismay over trials and deprivations in the Great Depression. College meant life in an extended family; wartime service was another exercise in collective action; afterward, his first serious career was as a public relations writer for General Electric, explaining and promoting the idea that scientific abstractions and technological advances were in everyone's interest—and in being able to justify this interest in layperson's terms, in words everyone could understand. Behind this all stood the model of his family in Indianapolis: pioneering, large and well established, involved in the community's arts and culture as well as its business, and providing the extensive support that only a seemingly limitless group of close and affectionate relatives can. Combined with Vonnegut's studies in anthropology at the University of Chicago immediately after the war, this upbringing had shaped an individual who knew how much of his life depended upon finding and exercising his role in the community, within a functioning social group.

During this initial period of obscurity as a writer, dating from his first published story in 1950 through his lead-up to fame in 1965–67 with the University of Iowa lectureship and the beginning of his essay writing and public speaking, Vonnegut was still a public spokesman, albeit under more limited circumstances. His family life during these years has been outlined in loving detail by his first wife, Jane Vonnegut Yarmolinsky, in *Angels without Wings.*[10] Her specific focus is the way she and Kurt exercised their sense of social responsibility within the form of an extended family: when Kurt's sister and brother-in-law died within days of each other, he and Jane at once adopted their children, turning a family of five into a family of eight overnight. But during these same years Vonnegut was balancing his extremely private profession as a writer (including days alone with his typewriter, when the only person he would see was the mailman bringing either acceptances or, more often, rejections) with public actions: involving himself and his wife in amateur theatrical groups, teaching in a school for emotionally disturbed children (those who had fallen beyond the reach of conventional strategies of education and socialization), and for a short time picking up needed cash by doing some public relations work (specifically translating the masterly achievements of an iron-casting firm into terms the general public could appreciate). That so many of his short stories were drawn from everyday middle-class concerns is unremarkable, given his relatively unwriterly interest in so many mundane activities.

Vonnegut's fiction of the 1950s, as will be seen, remains of a piece with his novel writing of later years thanks to a common dedication to the way the author sees himself and so positions himself in his work: as an individual with a very personal history addressing the public multitudes, conveying to them needed information but in a way that makes it acceptable as friendly, almost intimate advice. That his speaking style itself remained unchanged by fame is evident from a typical appearance during his decade of greatest celebrity, the 1970s. The occasion here is a visit on March 31, 1977, to the University of Northern Iowa—where a former Iowa City student had hosted his appearance eleven years before and where she and several other friends and former students now taught. In those eleven years Kurt Vonnegut had gone from an unknown writer of bus station paperbacks and stories for family magazines to one of the country's best-selling and most eminent authors. Whatever he wrote now received national acclaim, Broadway had hosted his play, and Hollywood produced a major film of the book that had made him famous, *Slaughterhouse-Five*. At the decade's turn he had been treated, much against his will, as a guru to disaffected youth of the student revolution; now, in 1977, he had more willingly assumed the role of public spokesman on a host of much larger issues, issues he felt were of ultimately global importance.

Yet despite the gravity of these issues, which included the political and ecological disasters the author felt were consuming these times, it is the same Kurt Vonnegut who speaks in 1977 as in 1967. At Ohio State University, he had played his own supposedly vulgar status against the solemnly academic nature of the occasion and the audience's intellectual expectations. At Northern Iowa, he starts with the same approach, only transposed to accommodate his change from obscurity to fame. He picks, for example, a title that exploits his listeners' expectations, "Kurt Vonnegut: A Self-Interview."[11] Here, they might suppose, is the zany author of *Cat's Cradle* and *The Sirens of Titan,* ready to reinforce his position as the font of mystic wisdom and offer them subversions of convention and authority. But once again the author uses his technique of catalyzing this relationship with his audience to generate the participatory attention a good speech must have to succeed. As at Ohio State, a good way to do it is by confounding their expectations.

19

"How many of you," he asks his listeners, "believe in the superiority of meditation, of the inward contemplation recommended by the great Eastern religions?" Around the auditorium hands shoot up as hundreds of eager students among the audience of nearly two thousand seek to identify themselves with him.

"Well, you're all full of crap," Vonnegut tells them, at once deflating their pretensions and correcting one of the more superficial, even inane aspects of his fame. The hand-raisers are shocked, while those who kept their hands in their laps are now both laughing and applauding this only slightly cruel joke played on the less serious among them. The speaker takes part in the laughter, but in a warmly forgiving rather than judgmental way, as if to remind himself that for many years in the late 1960s and early 1970s the joke had been on him. Then comes his justification for this little bit of harmless criticism: that meditation is too passive to produce much good, and that the simpler practice of reading books—and reacting to them imaginatively—is a much better way to grow and learn, even about oneself.

Kurt Vonnegut, of course, is famous for his books—specifically for writing *Slaughterhouse-Five* and seeing it made into a major motion picture. But just as with his misconstrued notoriety as a partisan of meditation and other countercultural practices, he pauses to lament how bestsellerdom and film success contradict his beliefs in how societies best operate. The ideal, he recalls from his studies in anthropology, is to organize in a folk society of about two thousand people. Coincidentally, that is the size of his audience tonight, but it offers a good example of the point he wants to make. Here they are, all two thousand of them, listening to one author—a reminder of the vast national and international audience he serves. Far better than this global community would be smaller yet coherent groups in which there would be a role and meaningful work for everyone, including artists, musicians, and even a few storytellers. But now, in the mass-market culture America must produce, a single musician performs on records and on television for 200 million people. For writers it becomes a case of being a best-seller or going bust. There are just a few who can publish in such circumstances, he says, adding "Thank God I'm one of them!"

For movies it is even worse. A writer hoping for best-seller status can at least get writing on his own; all he or she needs is a pencil and paper, and ultimately the use of a typewriter to get it looking professional enough for a publisher to consider. But for film, the prerequisites are overwhelming. Here the whole process, even once under way, remains so expensive that it is almost impossible to make room for individual expression. In turn, the product is viewed passively by audiences being shown what to imagine. Almost completely lost is the generative power that creates great literature and rewards imaginatively active reading.

At this point the author takes up the printed portion of his text, the "Self-Interview" soon to be published in the *Paris Review* and eventually collected in *Palm Sunday*.[12] The text itself is a patchwork of others, with bits and pieces drawn from four separate interviews done over the years by several different people, none of whom had captured the essence of Kurt Vonnegut's art. From these scraps the speaker assembles a coherent narrative that, as if made to order for this occasion with his audience, explores the nature of interrogating himself. Listener reaction to this process is essential, as the National Public Radio tape of it reveals: Vonnegut using two voices, a normal one for the interviewer and an absurdly choked one for his "own," a comic situation that at once has the audience howling. As he did in Ohio, Vonnegut works his audience by working himself, in each case taking a point of difficulty in public delivery of his material and then making that struggle both a joke and his speech's point. Once more he makes art from his response to life, then tests it and perfects it by trying it out in public, the "audience of strangers" he had always told his writing students to face.

The next decade would be less kind to Kurt Vonnegut. Somewhat like F. Scott Fitzgerald in the 1930s, the conservative 1980s were less fond of Vonnegut's sometimes revolutionary attitudes from an era which had seemed to run its course. Audiences were still at capacity, applauding whichever work-in-progress he would conclude with—*Slaughterhouse-Five* in 1967, *Jailbird* in 1977, or *Bluebeard* later in the 1980s—and such recurrent devices as his story-line chalk talk continued to prompt delight and understanding. The books themselves would be best-sellers, but critics were more hostile than ever. Not surprisingly, the author chose this time to write a requiem mass. Yet even here his intentions were meliorative, transposing the hellfire and damnation of typical sixteenth-century works into happier attitudes of peace and repose. To seal his accomplishment in formal terms he had his *Requiem* translated into Church Latin and set to choral music, the premier performance of which became the occasion for what would be his representative speech of these times.

The speech's title is one used for most of his appearances here and afterward: "How to Get a Job Like Mine." Producer Robert Weide, assembling raw film for a planned documentary on the author, captured it on March 12, 1988, when in preparation for the *Requiem*'s premier by the Buffalo Symphony and choir of that city's Unitarian Universalist Church.[13] For this occasion Vonnegut delivered his talk the night before as a fund-raiser for the musical event. Presented from the cathedral's altar where the *Requiem* would be performed the following evening, it is much the same lecture he would give a year later during his third appearance (in three different decades) at the University of Northern Iowa.

Twelve years older and presumably even wiser, Kurt Vonnegut now comes on as more the grandfatherly type than a father, bringing gentle rather than caustic knowledge to his listeners in hope of making them more comfortable. It was March in Buffalo and early April in Cedar Falls, times of the year when better weather is promised but not yet at hand, and it is this vexation to which the speaker addresses himself. Why does the weather always make us unhappy? Why

then repeats the process (in Panama) as a manageable amusement ride, when in fact the proper role of government is to keep things securely stable.

Thus Kurt Vonnegut's public spokesmanship takes the same course as his fiction: indicating the assumptions that lie behind our most firmly held convictions. As such, he qualifies as a deconstructionist, sharing the habit of thought common to our age. The roots for this disposition can be traced back to the firebombing of Dresden, where many scientific and cultural principles of his education were dismantled in an orgy of physical destruction and moral contradiction. Such were the matters Vonnegut spoke about on May 3, 1990, at the Smithsonian Institution's Air and Space Museum for its program of lectures and films on "The Legacy of Strategic Bombing."[14] Here he appeared not only as the author of *Slaughterhouse-Five* but as a victim of aerial bombardment, just the opposite role of the next month's speaker, bombing strategist Gen. Curtis E. LeMay. The novel had been conceived as an act of witness to the Dresden event, and the difficulty of articulating such unspeakableness had determined its structure and generated its ideas—just as the professed difficulties of speaking at Columbus, Cedar Falls, and Buffalo had set the formats and bridged understandings with his audiences there. At the Smithsonian the same thing would happen.

For this new decade of activity Vonnegut would move to integrate his roles of writing and public spokesmanship. Increasing mention would be made of such issues as politics and the environment even as they assumed thematic importance in the novel being worked on at the time, *Hocus Pocus.* Dresden is given repeated emphasis as something not just central to his fictive canon but pertinent to such concerns as the invasion of Panama and the ecological catastrophe of global warming. Yet even as Kurt Vonnegut approaches the podium with these and other matters in mind, the specific occasion of delivering this speech intrudes and determines his strategy for all that follows.

The circumstance is one of surprise, being informed that in attendance tonight, sitting in the second row, is his colleague from prisoner-of-war days in Dresden's slaughterhouse number 5, Tom Jones. This remarkable coincidence, reaching back to events forty-five years past and yet on the docket for tonight's appearance, lets Vonnegut transform his lecture into something well beyond its printed text. He is able to do so by relying on what has come to be his customary manner, improvising a public talk the same way his personal fictions are constructed and then tested out. In each case his method has been to involve the audience, posing questions and challenging assumptions. With a bonafide participant from Dresden in this audience, the speaker is able both to strengthen existing points and improvise new ones, discovering fresh truths in the process and sharing them with listeners who are themselves witnesses to Vonnegut and Jones's reunion. This process is similar to the way he was cross-referencing historical materials in *Hocus Pocus,* and it anticipates how he would use Tom Jones's material in *Fates Worse than Death* the next year.

"You're still alive!" Kurt Vonnegut exclaims as he reads the note and spots Tom Jones down in front. "How nice!" As a spontaneous and inevitably offhand remark, this confirms the speaker's thesis even before he had a chance to state it: that there is nothing intelligent to say about a massacre. In *Slaughterhouse-Five* the response is to listen to the birds chirping; here, it is what any old-timer might say to another he has bumped into after many years. More than 150,000 human beings were wiped out at Dresden; Tom and Kurt were not; and as for finding a reason for this, there is nothing much more to be said than "So it goes." As Vonnegut will explain, strategic bombing works much like germ eradication, with any chance for individual consideration about surviving the disinfectant being lost in the greater general purpose—a purpose that even in military terms often lacks meaning beyond the reflexes of anger and revenge. It was a pure accident that Kurt Vonnegut survived, just as it is an accident now that both he and Tom Jones have lived so many years afterward and meet here tonight. Such meeting can only prompt a similar reflex—"How nice!" But like the *"Poo-tee-wheet?"* of birdsong after the Dresden firestorm, it is the most sensible appraisal of strategic bombing that can be made.

What does survive is the human bond, and with Tom Jones present Kurt Vonnegut has a perfect example of what he means. Throughout the speech that follows Jones will be called upon for a witness's confirmation. He begins with his familiar joke with the first rule of public speaking, that one must never apologize, and adds that this is probably the first rule for strategic bombing as well. Then he explains that because he has been a critic of Allied bombing, it is always necessary to prove how he was as opposed to Nazi aggression as any patriotic American. In the past Vonnegut would mention how he served in the army and was taken prisoner at the Battle of the Bulge. Now he can look up from his text and say he is glad that Tom is here to tell what a brave soldier he was, "how hard I fought before being subdued," something that encourages his listeners to break into laughter at this obvious ploy of old buddies exaggerating their war stories. Later, after detailing the Dresden raid and what he saw there, Vonnegut departs once again from his script to say "So was Tom. See, this is all true! I could be snowing you. This is the truth, isn't it, Tom?" From this point on Tom Jones becomes part of the speech, every "I" becoming a "we," every "me" now an "us."

Such extension helps make Vonnegut's point about how the Dresden raid's victimization is related to subsequent bombing in Cambodia, in Vietnam, and most recently in Panama, in reference to which the speaker mentions a casualty figure of four thousand. He asks how many others in this audience have been bombed from the air and sees several hands go up, proving his point that "it is not a very exclusive club." Yet it is a club of individual people and not just statistics. Vonnegut describes the attack on Libya's Muammar Qaddafi that wound up killing his adopted daughter, "the same age and degree of innocence

25

as my own adopted daughter"—who, like Tom Jones, is present tonight and can be pointed out. Here is where individuality lies: not in strategic bombing's symbol of national pride, "like the Liberty Bell," but rather as a practice that kills real people, most of them haplessly innocent.

But simply to protest against war does no more good than protesting against a glacier, as Vonnegut himself was reminded when writing the first chapter of *Slaughterhouse-Five*. His listeners need something practical, and so just as at Ohio State when he checklisted the best books they could read, he now evaluates which cities should and should not have been bombed. "No" for Dresden, as has been credibly established. "Yes," to his audience's surprise, for the other German city destroyed in a firestorm, Hamburg—a defensible answer because the target did have military importance. By the same manner of thinking Hiroshima is checked off "Yes" while Nagasaki rates a "No." After that, through America's subsequent wars, every other city is judged "No" because they were inappropriate targets, from Hanoi and places in Cambodia to more recent attacks on Libya ("That was show biz") and Panama ("That was more show biz").

In both his fiction and his public speaking Kurt Vonnegut begins as very much the personalist. But never is mere confession or simple autobiography his method; rather, his way is to engage this personal self in larger issues. In *Slaughterhouse-Five* that issue is not just the book's subject but his own struggle in finding a way to write about it, just as in all his speeches he makes use of his present circumstances (at Ohio State, obscurity; at the University of Northern Iowa, misconstrued celebrity; at Buffalo, grandfatherly wisdom; at the Smithsonian, encountering Tom Jones) to involve his audience with what is made of this occasion. By the 1990s, with Vonnegut in his sixth decade as a writer and fourth as a public speaker, he comes full circle to the matter of Dresden, not just identifying Joe Crone as the model for Billy Pilgrim but visiting the grave in Rochester, New York, to which Joe's parents had brought his remains. Talking about this at the University of New Orleans on the fiftieth anniversary of V-E Day, the author shared his experience with novelist Joseph Heller and historian Stephen Ambrose, telling these fellow veterans what it meant: "I was deeply moved, and it finally closed out the Second World War for me completely."

Vonnegut's novels are much like his speeches, built on the implications of an audience attending to the author's foibles and weaknesses as well as taking cues from his strengths. With a real, live audience present, one can witness Vonnegut proposing and responding, acting and reacting, drawing on his own experience to meld it with the experiences of his listeners in order to create a work that succeeds as performance. In each speech one hears the vernacular American voice that first became a literary mode with Mark Twain, but which performed national service as well for Abraham Lincoln and Will Rogers as those great public spokesmen counseled the country through its two greatest crises, the Civil War and the Great Depression. Like the finest of American art in all genres, his speeches are improvised and even a bit cobbled together—yet based on an individuality of character and delight in personality that audiences are forever willing to share.

Reminded of Granville Hicks's comments twenty-one years after they were made, Kurt Vonnegut remarked that "It really makes a difference, I find, if people hear me speak."[15] His governing tactics and strategies as a writer have been to make his readers hear, an ideal approach for conveying in his personal fictions what turn out to be urgently public messages.

Chapter Two

SHORT-STORY SALESMANSHIP

"Let me begin by saying. . . ." These are the first published words of Kurt Vonnegut, fiction writer—phrased, appropriately enough, in the terms of public spokesmanship. Then, as would be an effective trick later on in actual public speaking, he breaks one of the form's first rules by making an apology: "that I don't know any more about where Professor Arthur Barnhouse is hiding than anyone else does." In the process a second rule is broken, as the public speaker not only apologizes but surrenders any claims to authority, obviating any reason for his audience to listen. Yet Vonnegut's first published story, "Report on the Barnhouse Effect,"[1] continues anyway; though further disclaimers follow, readers become caught up by one of the oldest ploys of salesmanship, the claim that buyers really would not be interested in the product. But because these dissuasions continue for more than the story's first page, readers wonder why there is so much protesting. Obviously there is something controversial to the Barnhouse Effect, whatever on earth it is—obviously something important, for it has been given a name, capital letters and all. Thus by the end of page 1 the reader is hooked, and another sale is made: to *Collier's,* who bought the story, and to the readers who, having purchased the magazine, have chosen to spend their time with this story.

Nor is Vonnegut's choice of forms a sign of mere amateurism, for the mode of public address continues through his heydays as a regular not just in *Collier's* but also in one of the era's most popular magazines, the *Saturday Evening Post.* "Ladies and Gentlemen of the Federal Communications Commission," begins "The Euphio Question,"[2] "I appreciate this opportunity to testify on the subject before you." Through story after story Vonnegut's narrators find themselves compelled to speak: sometimes to groups, sometimes in open letters to historical individuals, and most often in the guise of what the real Kurt Vonnegut was during the 1950s, a salesman working out of his home in West Barnstable, Massachusetts, marketing fictions just as his neighbors were selling everything from insurance policies to storm windows. The occupation is always mentioned in the narrative's first line, a way of establishing credibility and tempting the reader with inside knowledge picked up in the process of making a sale. His epistemology is much like the reader's, as the story's unfolding reveals how he himself acquired this knowledge. And it is all told emphatically from his own mundane point of view. "The farthest away from home I ever sold a storm window," his narrator in "The Hyannis Port Story,"[3] begins, "was in Hyannis Port, Massachusetts, practically in the front yard of President Kennedy's summer home." Glamorous as the Kennedys were at the height of their celebrity, Vonnegut's tale takes its measure in its distance from home—not just in mileage but in customs and values, all of which depend for their effect on contrast with the narrator's unassuming practicality.

Above all, this mode of address enables Vonnegut to place himself (or someone just like him) inside the story, functionally relating the strangeness of his topic to the audience of strangers in a personally affirmative way. And as his talents grow, it is a style he devlops and deepens. When making an initial gathering for his 1961 collection, *Canary in a Cat House,*[4] he began with "Report on the Barnhouse Effect" and added five others (of a dozen total) in this mode. By 1968, when reharvesting these plus other stories for *Welcome to the Monkey House,* nine such pieces were included, plus his personally confiding review of *The Random House Dictionary,* an essay written for *Venture* called "Where I Live"[5] that opens the collection by describing the author's position from which he observes the world, and—most significantly of all—a "Preface" that marks a new feature in almost all his novels that follow: an autobiographical introduction stating his own role in the fictive work.

It is worth noting how many of these features exist in Kurt Vonnegut's first published story. Like the publicist he then was at General Electric, Vonnegut creates a protagonist who works side-by-side with scientific researchers with the task of explaining their complex discoveries to the public. In this case the subject is *"dynamopsychism"* (p. 157), surely a term in need of definition—a device Vonnegut uses to justify the narrator's presence in novels such as *The Sirens of Titan ("chrono-synclastic infundibula")* and *Cat's Cradle ("karass," "foma,"* and the religion to which they pertain, *"Bokononism"*). Its popular name is the Barnhouse Effect, and its nature is the stuff of which makes science popular, along lines stretching from the *Scientific American* to *Popular Mechanics:* that a commonly accepted randomness, in this case luck, is actually a measurable (and hence controllable) force. Such a discovery might well generate a traditional story, just as a certain hysteria among the press and public in response to this breakthrough yields opportunities for satire. "Report on the Barnhouse Effect" exploits these formulas; doing so surely helped its previously unpublished author get through the magazine's editorial doors. But what makes the story so characteristically a work by Kurt Vonnegut, the future author of *Slaughterhouse-Five,* and so representative of his peculiar genius—sufficiently representative to survive the 64 percent attrition rate when stories were culled in the making of his first collection and to survive again in his second—is how the mode of public address and especially public statement determines its effect.

Although incidents of plot and messages of theme contribute to the public spokesmanship mode, it is primarily Vonnegut's attitude toward this material that makes its presentation anticipate that of his most innovative fiction. Having to begin with an apology and follow up with a disclaimer of technical ignorance are key features of his narrator's technique. Far from being a simple storyteller, Vonnegut's spokesperson is a witness to something that defies reductive explanation. Instead, he must expand upon the subject, taking it beyond the confines of rational intelligence and into realms where empathy and emotion can fill in the blanks and approximate a sense of what Professor Barnhouse and his breakthroughs mean. The newspapers surely do not have it right; neither do the misinformed people who have run off in search of bogus religions to explain the phenomenon. The phenomenon itself is simple science, just as the nature of Dresden's firestorm was scientifically understandable to the young American prisoner of war who experienced it. But just as the actual firebombing never appears in *Slaughterhouse-Five,* the Barnhouse Effect is far less important than the narrator's report on it. Instrumental to his presentation is that he has seen the hysterical reaction it has produced; and as far as revealing anything about the Professor's work itself, much less is known about the secret formula than about its inventor's utopian hopes for it. "I think maybe I can save the world," our narrator reports hearing from him. "I think maybe I can make every nation a *have* nation, and do away with war for good. I think maybe I can clear roads through jungles, irrigate deserts, build dams overnight" (p. 162).

Such indeed has been the Professor's discovery, that such accomplishments may be possible. But according to the formula that generates popular magazine fiction, his gift—one that could end wars forever—is in danger of being stolen by politicians and militarists as a weapon in the games of power and domination. Stating this makes Vonnegut a public spokesman, but hardly one of any originality. His story takes life when his narrator's role turns back upon itself; while preparing this report, the Professor sends him the secret to controlling acts that would otherwise be chance: not so that it may be revealed (and hence probably misused), but so that the narrator himself may guard it after the Professor's death and use it covertly to destroy the world's military arsenals. Having this knowledge has shaped the narrator's report, not simply in keeping the science secret (and hence forever generative of curious stories) but motivating all the descriptions of Professor Barnhouse's utopian hopes and dystopian fears. Stated flat out, such fears would be familiar and simple; dramatized by means of a transformation of the very text readers have before them, they take on a life of their own, one that the narrator brings as a consequence of his own acts of witness and testimony.

Between this first published short story in 1950 and the end of his tenure with

Collier's and the *Saturday Evening Post* thirteen years later, Vonnegut develops and extends this narrative mode to the point that it leads directly into the autobiographical way he will begin initiating and enfolding his novels just as the magazine markets close. "EPICAC,"[6] his third story, adapts the mode to one of confession and confidence. "Hell," his narrator begins, familiar and vernacular from the start, "it's time I told somebody about my friend EPICAC," another textual game in that it takes the normal patterns for an employee talking about a coworker and transposes them to a computer operator discussing his machine. As with "Report on the Barnhouse Effect," it is the mode of address itself that reflects action transpiring in the story. Why is the tale a publicly responsible one? Because EPICAC has wasted nearly a million dollars of taxpayer money, and taxpayers "have a right to know." But it is moreover a personal one because of the narrator's special relationship to this creation he describes as "The best friend I ever had, God rest his soul" (p. 268). The narrator himself has much in common with his counterpart in "Report on the Barnhouse Effect": working at the same small college ("Wyandotte College"), responsible to spiritual as well as technological matters, and above all figuring out the import of his story even as he tells it. And there is indeed much to figure out: in the earlier story because of the Professor's mysterious effects; here because the intelligence with which we interface is fully artificial.

How full can artificial be? The epistemology for deciding begins with a perfect null set—or rather a tabula rasa, considering what will be learned. The plot compilation begins when the narrator confides to EPICAC that "My girl doesn't love me" and is answered with the questions "What's love?" and "What's girl?" (p. 271). Having to start with such basics causes the narrator to rephrase (and hence reexamine) the entire nature of his relationship; in the act of expressing it for the machine, he sees his love and the object of it as he never has before. The problem is that his methodology is too perfect, too complete—with the result that EPICAC itself falls in love with the young woman. That the story incorporates a sentimental formula, with EPICAC destroying itself in a fit of heartbreak but nevertheless producing a lifetime supply of poetry with which the narrator can romance his loved one, does not detract from the larger fact of the narrator's self-discovery through his public account.

EPICAC's legacy is a text, just as The Barnhouse Effect is most noteworthy not because of itself but because of the report it generates. In each case the story is structured less as a fabrication by the storyteller than as a document he delivers with a witnessing report. In "The Manned Missiles"[7] Vonnegut asks a text to speak for itself, in the shape of open letters exchanged between the fathers of Russian and American astronauts killed in space. The exchange is initiated by the Russian, who wishes to reach out to the similarly bereaved parent in America. To do so, he not only writes a letter but tells a story, a seemingly offhand joke about how the initial Soviet space capsule carried not a dog but a dairy manager arrested for petty crimes; his correspondent replies with another innocent narrative from his own son's childhood. Here are stories, but ones existing because they are placed inside the larger and more obvious text of letters. The stories are told, then, within the vehicle of direct address; that they carry meaning at all is not because of anything in their content but because the fathers are telling them to each other, the act of public speaking empowering the narrative rather than the other way around. In each case attitudes toward the lost children are expressed indirectly, as texts about them make the point. As in "Report on the Barnhouse Effect" and "EPICAC," it is the act of personally addressing an audience that shapes the story, with the occasion for such an address being a significant part of the narrative structure.

More conventional are Kurt Vonnegut's short stories that give his narrators an intermediary role. So that they may become functional in the central characters' lives, these individuals are presented as salespersons: of anything from investments to storm windows, as long as it gets them through the door and into peoples' homes where their doings may be observed and, in a most subtle manner, commented upon. In "The Foster Portfolio"[8] the narrator, "a salesman of good advice for rich people" (p. 53), once again shares an epistemology with the reader as he tries to fathom why a low-paid and ill-treated worker in a dead-end job would wish to let windfall earnings from an unsuspected source lie unused. As with "EPICAC," the ending itself is formulaic, contrived, and mechanically added on as a way of inverting the narrator's expectations. New riches should allow their beneficiary to do anything his heart desires; at the very end we learn that he has been doing this all along, using his dire financial straits to justify an otherwise unacceptable part-time job, playing jazz piano in a low-down dive on weekends. Yet the very artificiality of this ending highlights the more innovative nature of Vonnegut's tale, that during all the time between the commencing act of discovering the wealth and the conclusion that Herbert Foster must avoid drawing upon it in order to maintain his secret happiness, the "salesman of good advice for rich people" is undergoing an education himself. What is the good of money, especially in such large and unexpected amounts that it would utterly change one's life? And what does good advice in using such circumstances mean? In presenting his case as a financial counselor, Vonnegut's narrator should be answering questions; but instead he asks them, at times to the point of browbeating his client over why he does not want to make use of these new riches. In doing so, the storyteller becomes less a contriver of devices and imparter of knowledge to his readers than a reader himself, honestly stumped (as perusers of *Collier's* would certainly have been) as to why Herbert Foster is not gleefully cashing in on his fat portfolio. This is why, in fact, he has come to the readers: not to give an answer, for the story's "answer" is reductively simplistic, but to share his experience of coming to this knowledge. Because his client's wishes defy simple words of explanation, he must do the same thing Vonnegut does in

Slaughterhouse-Five: make the matter convey his own struggle to understand and express it. What the narrator *can* articulate makes no sense, neither that the socio-economic details of Herbert Foster's shabby home (a jerry-built crackerbox with expansion attic, furnished in pathetic suites of discount furniture) should make him unhappy nor that the contrasting appurtenances of wealth (sports car, filet mignon, exotic vacations) should provide welcome new pleasures. The truth is just the opposite, confounding the narrator's standards of measure and forcing him to restructure his own sense of values, just as the narrator of "EPICAC" learns the depth of love not by expressing it directly but by running it past a coworker, in this case the computer, whose artificiality of intelligence and need to learn love as a mechanical problem emphasize the spokesman's own concern.

Selling advice is the job of two other Vonnegut narrators, those of "Custom-Made Bride"[9] and "Unpaid Consultant."[10] In each the focus is on women, the first telling of a client whose overenhancement of his wife's beauty has produced an alienating effect, the second dealing with the husband of a famous and wealthy television star who feels compelled to create a worthwhile identity for himself. As in "The Foster Portfolio," much is made of the clients being far richer than the narrator, and of how their atypical behavior at first stumps him, prepared as he is to begin from offering alternatives of seeking income or growth. Like Herbert Foster, these customers want neither—or rather have entirely other things on their minds. But even more so than in the Foster story, it is the narrator's act of witnessing these events that contributes to their outcome. In "Custom-Made Bride" customer Otto Krummbein's finances are in disarray, but even more desperate are circumstances with his new bride, a young woman he has redesigned to outward perfection but with whom he is unable to share anything truly personal. Fixing money matters is a simple matter of opening a bank account and renting a safe deposit box; more strategically helpful is the way Vonnegut's narrator, momentarily implicated in one of the customer's design schemes himself (and thus appreciating how captivating such schemes can be), arranges that Krummbein and his wife spend an evening alone. This is the first such quiet night since their wedding, and it forces them to face the issues Krummbein's makeover has covered up. "Unpaid Consultant" shows the narrator similarly being taken in by a husband's grand plans for himself but then exposing them (through another customer) and inviting the man to admit he is happiest as his own simple self. Without such narrative involvement the stories would be flatly pious, somewhat as are two similar tales that lack this spokesmanship device: "Poor Little Rich Town,"[11] a third-person affair in which judgments do not arise out of the narrative experience but rather are spoken in moralistic fashion by one of the bystanding characters; and "Hal Irwin's Magic Lamp,"[12] in which the action lacks such stimulating involvement not just because the investments counselor strikes it rich himself but because his tale is one of narrative omniscience rather than testimony.

Vonnegut's finest salesmanship story comes near the end of his story writer's career, just as he is about to begin incorporating a participatory role in his novels. "The Hyannis Port Story" exploits an even greater gap between normal life and great riches, as its narrator not only sells storm windows but installs them as well, a combination that prompts him to remark (just at the point when confronted with the first great absurdity practiced by his wealthy customer) that his own class status is at best uncertain. Yet in simple, noncomparative terms, he knows who he is and where he is from, and for most of the story he tries to remain inconspicuous as he installs a full set of combination storms and screens at the Hyannis Port mansion of Commodore William Rumfoord.

Even his approach to public spokesmanship is much like Kurt Vonnegut's: apologizing, self-deprecating, and offering any number of excuses for why he really should not be speaking, or at the very least wondering at the irony that has placed him on the platform and in the spotlight. From the start, his attitude is one of *what am I doing here?*, a mode of self-interrogation that, much like Vonnegut's speech at Ohio State (given just four years later), shapes his presentation and contributes to its theme.

There are two major reasons why the story's narrator does not belong in Hyannis. For one, the Commodore has only purchased this expensive and probably unneeded home improvement job to reward the narrator for defending his son after the young man's speech to a Lions Club meeting back in North Crawford. But before that comes another reason: what the Commodore has interpreted as a spirited defense is actually the narrator's heated argument with a friend and customer (who has only incidentally debated the son's politics) over some problems with a self-installed bathtub enclosure that has developed a leak. In this year (1963) of extreme political contrasts, the narrator is anxious to maintain his neutrality—he has not made up his own mind about Barry Goldwater's candidacy yet, he admits to the reader, making sure that the same mistaking of allegiance does not happen again. But as a businessman he makes the most of it, taking on the job, however ironic, just as four years later his creator would accept the task of rededicating a university library despite his having dropped out of four different colleges.

Although its meaning does not become apparent until much later, there is a parallel indifference expressed by the Commodore's son Robert (as in Robert Taft Rumfoord), who seems unimpressed by the politics he speaks about to the Lions Club—"He would say strong things," the narrator notes, "but they came out sounding like music on a kazoo" (p. 134). Yet he does it to humor his father's enthusiasm, much as the narrator accepts the contract for all those storms and screens that Commodore Rumfoord offers in the same feisty spirit. In time the son's disinterest will cross paths with the narrator's, pausing for a while to form a common avenue toward values and beliefs of an entirely different order from the Commodore's. But before that it is necessary for Vonnegut to establish the (apparently) full Other world of Hyannis.

Even driving into town is an adventure. The Kennedy craze has drawn crowds that jam the roads, causing traffic stalls and overheating. This leads to the narrator's first brush with celebrity, as Ambassador Adlai Stevenson's limousine is stuck alongside his car. But as did Kurt Vonnegut at Ohio State, the storm window salesman democratizes the affair, asking Stevenson how things are going as casually as he might the guy next door (and receiving an answer just as mundane). As things begin to move, he finds himself in another New England small town, albeit one somewhat cornily transformed by the Kennedy popularity, and the narrator finds himself passing "the *Presidential Motor Inn,* the *First Family Waffle Shop,* the *PT-109 Cocktail Lounge,* and a miniature golf course called the *New Frontier*" (p. 136). There is a clear progression here into absurdity; and, like the narrator's, our impulse as readers is to bail out. As in his public speeches, however, Vonnegut saves the day, having his narrator check into a degree of silliness he can handle (the waffle shop) and there once more democratize the affair, passing up entrees named after Jackie, Caroline, and Arthur Schlesinger Jr. in order to have the less offensive sounding *Teddy* accompanied by that old-time standby, "a cup of *Joe*" (p. 137).

Yet thematic waffle shops with cutesy menus are less than half of it, as far as "The Hyannis Port Story" is concerned. After lunch and as the narrator closes in on the Rumfoord mansion, matters only become more bizarre, climaxed by what the Commodore has installed in full view of the neighboring Kennedy compound: a massive portrait of the rival presidential candidate, Barry Goldwater. "It had bicycle reflectors in the pupils of its eyes. Those eyes stared right through the Kennedy gate. There were floodlights all around it, so I could tell it was lit up at night," the narrator remarks. "And the floodlights were rigged with blinkers" (p. 137). Here, approaching the midway point of his story, the narrator finds himself returned to the misconstrued reason that landed him the job in the first place; having thought he could sidestep the problem of right wing politics, it now hits him squarely in the face. And so it is no surprise that as he begins his work the Commodore treats him to a nonstop stream of vituperations against the Kennedys. This time there is no way to stay out of it, forcing the narrator into an interesting role, considering the circumstances: that of a tacit spokesman for common middle-class values.

The challenge of those values comes, as it were, from the audience—in this case from the tour guide aboard a sight-seeing boat who, as a sidelight to the Kennedy highpoints, indicates the Rumfoord mansion as an emblem of wealthy irresponsibility and indolence. Not having had a job for over thirty years, Commodore Rumfoord compares poorly to the only person around employed at anything: the narrator, who in the face of all this bluster has simply been doing his job. At this point his partner in political disinterest, young Robert, shows where his enthusiasms lie: in a romantic match with Sheila Kennedy, the president's fourth cousin. At first devastated by the news, Commodore Rumfoord is slowly brought back to equilibrium by the story's obvious lessons of how love and hard work are matters of much greater substance than outdated cultural and political animosities. But there is still the matter of that egregious Goldwater sign, which even though turned off looms in the darkness as a reminder of all the trouble that has gone before. In this case it is not the narrator's role to act but rather someone behaving much like him: President Kennedy himself, who surprises everyone by acting like nothing more than a next-door neighbor, asking that the sign be turned on to show a visitor and be left on so "I can find my way home" (p. 145).

That Kurt Vonnegut is more interested in public spokesmanship than in specific narrative situations is clear from his adaptation of materials. Unique as the doings of "The Hyannis Port Story" seem, his narrator was not invented for that tale. Two years earlier he exists, plying the same storm-and-screen trade from North Crawford, New Hampshire, in "Who Am I This Time?"[13] Here the circumstances are entirely different; he is no more tailored for them than was Kurt Vonnegut himself for the occasion of addressing the students and faculty at Ohio State. Instead, just the opposite happens, as in each case the circumstances are transformed by the speaker's idiosyncratic approach to them. In "The Hyannis Port Story" Vonnegut accomplishes what no other writer of the era could do: write about the Kennedy family's presence without making them the focus. Instead, the reader's attention is directed to the narrator's response, especially as he presents that response to an audience presumably in it for the glamor. Because the narrator remains a most reliable measure of things, the glamor begins to seem foolish—and at this point the solid probity that has remained the center of this tale takes over to direct the Commodore and his family to a happier ending, one that familiarizes President Kennedy and establishes him as a friendly neighbor after all. "Who Am I This Time?" has the same narrator in a more apparent role, not just as the narrator of faraway adventures but as the director of an amateur theater group. This dual presence allows him both to recount the wonderful problematics of a situation and contribute to its resolution. The matter itself is unexceptional, a story of two people so utterly lacking in identities of their own that each seems destined for a life of isolation, loneliness, and rootlessness. Those features—or rather lack of them—are what necessitate a convincing role of spokesmanship, for without the narrator's expressed interest the reader would be likely to have none, certainly not enough to merit attention to a third-person, omnisciently told story. But because the narrator is their director, their problems become his—and ours, for as his partisan we are interested to see how he resolves this business and gets his play staged. Good stagecraft demands arranging things so that the two can become lovers, not just in the play but in real life, happily ever after. In "The Hyannis Port Story" it was the narrator's common values that led the way to resolution. Here it is his naive talent as a theatrical director. But in each case it is his act of testimony to his success, rather than the success itself, that makes for interesting fiction.

Though unnamed, Vonnegut's storm and screen salesman is as solid and familiar a person as the author himself, as comfortable a presence in North Crawford as Vonnegut himself is in West Barnstable—both are New England villages of about the same size and distance from Boston and with the same day-to-day happenings. This presence gives a narrator a position from which to speak, to represent issues; it is no accident that he is used four times between December 1961 and November 1963, years which not only saw Kurt Vonnegut peak as a fully mature and technically confident short story writer but also saw him moving more toward novels and personal essays even as the markets for his short fiction began to close. The first thing he says about himself is always the same: that he not only sells and installs combination storm windows and screens but handles the occasional bathtub enclosure as well. Characterizing himself in terms of his function, it is that role that brings him into the narrative; and just as tub enclosures are the somewhat bohemian side of his business, so, too, do they prompt the more bizarre actions, such as the argument over Hay Boyden's installation leading by misdirection to the Rumfoord job in Hyannis Port and a customized shower door giving him a window from which to observe the life of another rich and famous person, Gloria Hilton of "Go Back To Your Precious Wife and Son."[14]

The Gloria Hilton story is a good example of how Vonnegut uses his sense of narrative presence to enhance a story whose formula would otherwise be so thin as not to merit retelling. As with the same person's tale of working "practically in the front yard of President Kennedy's summer home" (p. 133), there is much fun with the nature of celebrity; the narrator is good for plenty of jokes with his friends and his own family about what it is like to be working in the home of a famous person. Because Ms. Hilton is on her fifth marriage and only living in town briefly, there is even more gossip about, and here is where Vonnegut's tub enclosure man centers his story. The woman has ordered a custom-made shower door accenting her notoriety for beauty and seductiveness; but when putting it in, the narrator becomes an innocent audience to a fight between her and husband number five, thanks to a heat register that relays the sound of their argument from the room below.

The formulaic part of "Go Back To Your Precious Wife and Son" anticipates the penultimate resolution of "The Hyannis Port Story," when the narrator resolves the husband's problems with an alienated son from his previous marriage by recommending the simplest of emotional responses: giving the recalcitrant kid a kick in the pants, just as the tradesman threatens his own son at the end. But neither tactic is the resolution alone; instead, just as the example of work's dignity not only restored Commodore Rumfoord's equilibrium but set the stage for President Kennedy's magnificent punch line, so the narrator's presence allows the husband to escape his confining world of celebrityhood and get roaring drunk in a most engagingly egalitarian way: "Somewhere in the course of this conversation, a fifth of a gallon of Old Hickory's Private Stock Sour Mash Bourbon was evaporating, or was being stolen, or was otherwise disappearing fast" (p. 103). As the liquor flows, so do Gloria's husband's metaphors, as he struggles to transpose his own situation into one the tradesman could experience. The two wind up rolling around drunkenly on the front lawn, after which the narrator returns home to regale his wife with a surrealistic montage of these metaphors before passing out—a situation which does indeed place him in the other husband's alienated position. From here the narrator's advice takes on added authority— from a colleagueship of harmlessly shared tipsiness that objectifies their problems and gives a wife at least something specific to forgive. The silliness of their jokes corresponds to the humor Kurt Vonnegut introduces in his public speeches: amusing little analogues to the more serious but otherwise less graspable problems of life.

Within a month of being contemporaneous with "The Hyannis Port Story" is "Lovers Anonymous,"[15] a self-styled report from what the narrator calls his age group in general and from his unique little club in particular. The club, Lovers Anonymous, consists of former suitors of the town's most strikingly intelligent young woman, Sheila Hinckley; what bonds them is not just their affections for Sheila but their common mistake of thinking she would never submit to a marriage of dull housewifery. In marrying Herb White she has surprised them by doing just so, and now their role is to console one another in played-up misery at losing her.

From here, the plot becomes more integrally connected to the narrative device, for just about every member of the club has become a home improvements tradesman of one sort or another. And when Herb White responds to some presumed marital trouble by adding a self-contained addition to his and Sheila's home, the guys of Lovers Anonymous find themselves doing not just storms and screens but carpentry, wiring, and finish work on the project, giving them all the type of narrative access only the storyteller has enjoyed heretofore. But it is not just Herb's addition, where he intends to live and housekeep alone so that Sheila may concentrate on her own self-development, that the club members discuss. In addition they argue over a feminist text on the oppression of women's intelligence, one that has prompted Sheila herself to admit that her brainy reputation as a student was all a sham—that she had not cared for it then and only values such things now.

Thus are the more diffuse narrative factors in Kurt Vonnegut's earlier stories sharpened in effect and focused in presentation through the character of his storm and screen salesman. Along the way, a repertory of devices has built up: having a subject's cover blown by the narrator's phone call to what turns out to be a humbling place of work, as happens in "Any Reasonable Offer"[16] as well as at the end of "Unpaid Consultant"; a similar sense of discovery in reporting on a subject's oddities, including the exposure of a abstract (rather than concretely real) mania for interior decorating in "More Stately Mansions"[17] that corresponds to the narrator's discovery of his client's true motives in "The Foster Portfolio"; and any number of reports on the future (such as "Unready to Wear"[18]) or the apocalyptic present ("HOLE BEAUTIFUL: Prospectus for a Magazine of Shelteredness"[19]), in which curiosities of behavior provide a forum for the narrator's revealing testimony.

When these stories are gathered together, a coherent personality emerges from within them: of an unassuming, middle-class trades professional who only speaks up when he has something to say—and when he does speak up, it is to bear witness to some curious phenomenon that puzzles others and indeed has puzzled him until he looked it over and put it to the test of his own vernacular standards. That this prototypical narrator is much like Kurt Vonnegut becomes apparent from the way *Welcome to the Monkey House* is organized and presented: a personal essay about the author's life in West Barnstable, Massachusetts, serves as the first selection, following an even more candid preface reporting on the nature of his work as a fiction writer. This preface marks a major new development in Vonnegut's literary art and is a key factor in his sudden leap to fame the next year with *Slaughterhouse-Five,* which also begins with a personal statement about the author's methodology and autobiographical involvement with his story, setting the tone for the work that follows; it is a practice he would continue in almost all of his novels afterward.

"Where I Live," published near the end of Kurt Vonnegut's career as a short story writer and initiating the series of essays on science fiction, *The Random House Dictionary,* and other odd topics that would add up to the collection *Wampeters, Foma & Granfalloons* by 1974, is in fact a summation of nearly all the authorial attitudes he had developed in the much earlier material assembled in *Welcome to the Monkey House.* Indeed, it seems as if Vonnegut's narrative voice was just waiting to be developed in the workshop of popular magazine fiction before facing the world directly through personal essays and highly personalized novels. Appropriately, it begins with a salesman—not doing the talking but raising a problem that Vonnegut himself must now solve. The question is one an outsider would ask: how can this tucked away village be so out of touch? And his product line, encyclopedias, allows him to challenge the locals with the issue of knowledge itself, since their library's most recent reference set is a 1938 *Britannica*—"backstopped," as Vonnegut wryly notes, "by a 1910 *Americana*" (p. 1). In most of his own short stories, Kurt Vonnegut fashioned the narrator as a salesman intruding on some questionable affair and both explaining it to the reader and moderating its resolution for the other characters. Here, in the virtual climax to his story writer's career and at the commencement of his next phase as a personal essayist (and ultimately personal novelist), he places himself at the confident center of the action, a holder of knowledge unique beyond the most exhaustive encyclopedia. And it is this knowledge that, roused to attention by the salesman, he now reports to his audience of readers.

What readers learn is that Vonnegut's little village of Barnstable is built on a series of ironic but idiosyncratically appropriate contradictions: that the library, in the oldest such building in the United States, is a quarter-century out-of-date in terms of information; that the Yacht Club, where library directors with such eminent names as Cabot and Lowell convene, is a small shack looking as if transplanted from the Ozarks; and that the only restaurant in this supposedly booming tourist town is a lunch counter at the news store. That the salesman perceives these as "indignities" is accountable to his own limitations, "strangling on apathy" being "an affliction epidemic among casual visitors to Barnstable Village" (p. 2). Thus he seeks relief in what are banalities of Hyannis, including the preposterous miniature golf course from Vonnegut's "Hyannis Port Story."

Against the shabby commercialism of Cape Cod's south shore stands the time-lessness of Barnstable, where changes are "about as fast as the rules of chess" (p. 3). When innovation beckons, villagers resist as long as possible, such as rejecting tuna as a fishing catch for years, dismissing it as "horse mackerel" and preferring to "chop it up and throw it back into the bay as a warning to other horse mackerel" (p. 3). But eventually things happen: tuna is found to be not only edible but, properly grilled, delicious, spawning an annual festival; a long-secret balance in the bank account of the dramatics club is spent lavishly on a new curtain; and the bay harbors an abundance of bass, mussels, and clams which, once discovered, promise another boom that may threaten the town's integrity.

Will Barnstable Village survive? Perhaps so, because of its nature as a coherent society:

> For one thing, it is not a hollow village, with everything for rent, with half the houses empty in the winter. Most of the people live there all year round, and most of them aren't old, and most of them work—as carpenters, salesmen, masons, architects, teachers, writers, and what have you. It is a classless society, a sometimes affectionate and sentimental one. (p. 4)

It is, in short, the community where Vonnegut's fictive narrator lives; where in anthropological balance everyone has a role, a task to perform in terms of meaningful work. Meaning itself is derived from such work and its usefulness to the community—think of all the Vonnegut short stories in which this has been the moral on which the narrator has reported, the message he has brought to the piece's readers. And note the equality of trades: carpenters, salesmen, masons, writers. Hence the interchangeability of roles—salesman-narrator of the other tales and writer-narrator of this one, the "I" of "Where I Live." As an introduction to the collection, it presents Vonnegut's spokesmanship role fully formed, inviting the reader to continue on and see how that formation happened.

Even more revealing is Vonnegut's preface, a brief three-page affair that marks a crucial turning point in his approach to writing. There are hints that it was coming: the fact that he wished to name his narrator "Vonnegut" in *Cat's Cradle* and was only dissuaded by the conservative traditionalism of his publisher; that in 1966 for a second edition of *Mother Night* (published by Harper & Row), he added an introduction (dated from Iowa City) explaining his personal role in the otherwise fictional account to follow; and his own decrease in short story production in favor of a new emphasis on the personal essay, taking the public spokesmanship of his salesman-narrator a step further toward direct commentary, albeit commentary based on his idiosyncracies of observation and attitude. In this volume's preface Vonnegut is more idiosyncratic than ever, presenting himself in much the same style as at Ohio State and other lecture stops: disclaiming any expertise, apologizing for having to be just himself, and breaking all the rules an author's foreword would normally have to follow.

A preface, after all, should attract the reader's notice and win his or her confidence—to buy the book and continue reading it. Here Vonnegut fractures convention by saying he is a self-taught writer with no theories about writing that might help authors: "When I write I simply become what I seemingly must become" (p. xiii). With this frankly honest, take-it-or-leave-it attitude, he proceeds to tell about himself and his background in ways that break further rules—for instance, by revealing the secret ingredient (coffee) in his grandfather's award-winning brewing recipe, and by admitting that if comedy is to be a standard (as his publishers have indeed advertised this collection) then readers should know that his brother, a physicist, is much funnier than Kurt himself. As for expertise, the author holds it in two fields, public relations and science fiction, that higher authorities consider to be inferior forms of expression. As far as stability and hope, he has considered suicide—and though rejecting any such overt actions, continues to smoke, knowing it will kill him. He says his marriage has worked and that his wife is still beautiful—but that "I never knew a writer's wife who wasn't beautiful" (p. xv). To finish, he even quotes a bum review from a leading magazine, one that is the standard for excellence in American short fiction, the *New Yorker*.

Yet as for his public speaking occasions, Vonnegut makes these disclaimers for a very specific reason. Like his storm window salesman from the short stories to follow, he does not wish to be received as an eminent authority; instead, from his much more humble position he will show how much uncertainty, unhappiness, and disappointment are due to an unwarranted respect for what experts have tried to impose. Standing before the awesome library at Ohio State University, a collection totaling two million books, Vonnegut can ask an otherwise unanswerable question—"How many of them are dirty?"—and then proceed to demonstrate how such supposed dirtiness is boring and beside the point, given the imaginative powers good literature can inspire. Greeting audiences locked in the foreboding March weather of upstate New York and the Middle West, he can correct the conventional meteorological wisdom of measuring four seasons by revealing that there are in fact six, and that everyone has been so unhappy because they have been expecting a spring that is still six weeks beyond its announced calendar arrival. In his preface to *Welcome to the Monkey House,* he is in similar manner announcing that readers will be finding here something quite different from stories that appear in the *New Yorker.* Self-taught, he has no great technical secrets to reveal (not that secret ingredients ever turn out to be much more than putting coffee grounds in beer); trained in science and experienced in public relations, he brings to fiction writing talents the experts deplore. His brother, we are told, is funnier, and his sister more gracefully expressive. And so the question remains, why read him?

This is the question Kurt Vonnegut himself has been pondering, and his answer comes from reviewing two lines quoted previously from his siblings, the first on the occasion of bringing a new baby home from the hospital, the second during the final ravages of a death from cancer. His brother's reflection on new fatherhood is funny, and his sister's dying words strike Vonnegut as good ones: "And I realize now that the two main themes of my novels were stated by my siblings: 'Here I am cleaning shit off of practically everything' and 'No pain.' " (p. xiv).

For such themes to be effective, they need to come from a familiar source. Vonnegut has established that familiarity by disclaiming expertise and speaking of himself and his family background instead. It is important to him that readers receive him not as a posh *New Yorker* stylist or as a precious dabbler in the more refined techniques of fiction. Rather his antecedents are closer to his general readers', in the world of popular fiction; as far as professional writing, he has done that where most of his readers work, in the office. Now, with what wisdom he has been able to absorb from a background almost everyone else has—their families—he wishes to address himself to some themes of mutual concern.

There follow twenty-five stories from *Collier's,* the *Saturday Evening Post,* and other popular weeklies and monthlies as likely to have entered the reader's home as any salesman of life's necessities. In writing the stories, Vonnegut has spoken with no more pretense than any of his narrator-salesmen. He even admits that the stories were marketed in salesmanlike fashion to finance the writing of his novels—"Here one finds the fruits of Free Enterprise" (p. xiv). But like the clients and customers who allowed Kurt Vonnegut's salesmen and tradesmen in the door for a look at their financial portfolios or bathtub enclosures, readers of these short stories would find themselves addressed in a most personally compelling manner.

Chapter Three

THE ROAD TO *WAMPETERS*

Kurt Vonnegut came to essay writing near the end of his career as a short fictionist and well after his intentions as a novelist had been established. His most apparent motive for doing such pieces was the same as for his stories: to buy time for writing those novels, since only after seventeen years and on the sixth try would one earn him a living wage. With *Collier's* defunct, the *Saturday Evening Post* shutting down, and the other family magazines reducing or eliminating fiction, doing essays was one way to generate a positive cash flow. Reviewing was even quicker, and while the pay was not as good (measured in hundreds of dollars at most compared to the $2,500 earned for a *Post* story at Vonnegut's peak), the range of topics and frequency of publication were much greater. Between 1965 (when his short story publication had virtually ceased) and 1971 (when *Slaughterhouse-Five* appeared in paperback and sold to the movies, making personal income no longer a month-to-month problem) Kurt Vonnegut placed twenty major reviews of widely various titles in such venues as *Life*, *McCall's*, and the *New York Times Book Review*. Among these reviews would appear the occasional personal essay, always in feature format and thus meeting the pay scale of those stories from *Collier's* if not the *Post*.

Rereading them now, one sees a logical continuation of Vonnegut's interests from the short stories and an anticipation of themes and even techniques that would characterize his subsequent novels—especially once those novels were no longer written in anonymity for an extremely slim readership but became instead a factor of their author's immense fame. In both the essays and the reviews Vonnegut was getting a taste of writing as a personally responsible figure. Rather than fictions presented in the guise of a storm window salesman from North Crawford, New Hampshire, his writings were now judgments and opinions signed by a very real person, a person who to make his point would often mention where he lived and what he had done. There is an obvious sense of accountability to such a task, and a very real sense of influencing one's readers—not indirectly, through the pretense of fiction, but most immediately by engaging the issues in other writers' works and in the world at large.

Soon to be an item in popular culture himself (through the fame and notoriety

43

of *Slaughterhouse-Five* and the counterculture's response), Vonnegut begins his reviewer's career with a *Life* magazine piece on pop psychologist Eric Berne's *Games People Play*.[1] In future pieces he would comment on similar phenomena, including Tom Wolfe's jazzy pop style and the Maharishi's trendy success with such celebrities as Mia Farrow and the Beatles. For an evaluation of Eric Berne's contribution to the popular mainstream, however, the reviewer looks beyond facile trends to study this man's true importance: it lies in his acknowledgment that people have an "anguished need for simple clues as to what is *really* going on." As a psychoanalyst, Dr. Berne observes common behavior patterns and names them, according to their rules, as games; but what he actually does, Vonnegut notes, is to provide "story lines that hacks will not exhaust in the next 10,000 years" (p. 15). This certainly explains the book's success as a best-seller because "Most people read the games first, I suspect, skipping the body of theory Dr. Berne carefully builds before them"; the storylike games are appealing, for they have "the queer 'There's Aunt Louise!' charm of Abner Dean cartoons" (p. 17). But behind this fascination lies a practice that gives people answers, which is why *Games People Play* is a true contribution to popular culture rather than just one more curiosity within it.

Much more a product of popular culture himself is Tom Wolfe, who as Vonnegut reviewed him[2] in 1965 was savoring his first fame as a wildly overexpressive and blatantly self-taken commentator for *Esquire* and the New York *Herald Tribune*. Where Dr. Eric Berne had used storytelling techniques to solve riddles for his anxious readers, Wolfe functions more like a confused reader, whose techniques of reaction Vonnegut understands quite well: "Wolfe has proved to himself and to some others that teen-age culture is becoming dominant, so he casts himself as a teen-ager, a razzer of old folks and old establishments, the better to describe that culture. But he sounds hooked to me," because, like all teenagers, he is "terribly annoyed by almost anything an American grownup not associated with automobiles may wear or say or do" (p. 38). As he does with *Games People Play*, Vonnegut can translate apparently bizarre notions (best-sellerdom for a work of psychotherapy, notoriety for the almost preposterous prose of a romantic age dandy) into terms familiar enough that they are used on a daily basis in people's lives—which is, it turns out, why Berne and Wolfe and their doings are so popular in the first place.

Who else was wildly popular back in 1965 for writing a very unlikely book? After Eric Berne and Tom Wolfe, the leading candidate was Bel Kaufman, a New York City high school teacher who cleverly assembled the detritus of her school day—administrative memos, student compositions, notes passed in class, and other items otherwise destined for the wastebasket—into a charming, comic work titled *Up the Down Staircase*. Reviews of the book, which grew from quiet publication and word-of-mouth endorsements to top rankings on the sales charts, were almost uniformly fulsome in their praise for Ms. Kaufman's wit and dedication, with no small appreciation for all she had achieved in the difficult circumstances of Calvin Coolidge High. Given his review assignment by *Life* magazine[3] rather late in the game, when not only the book but reactions to it had taken on a life of their own, Vonnegut wisely chose not to speak out for or against the book and its reputation. Instead, he adopts the voice of *Up the Down Staircase* itself, writing not a word in his own name but rather adopting the volume's method and concocting seven little texts similar to those combined by the author to form her own book. A student writes an egregiously misspelled and grammatically fractured letter praising his teacher and wondering how much she will make from the movie sale; the preciously inspired class poet, "Snowbird," writes an emotive little quatrain; and so forth, through a "Circular #101" from the principal warning that all such circulars should be saved, lest they fall into future authors' hands. The review ends with a much more serious letter that engages the book's deeper issues and offers what serves as a reviewer's response: that while method of assembly is "kind and brilliant and shrewd," made of materials that "could not fail to pluck the heartstrings" (p. 9), *Up the Down Staircase* in fact conveys something more substantial than many sentimental observers have been willing to note, an undertone that eventually wells up into "a piercing scream about the neglect and destruction of children's minds" (pp. 9–10). This last letter is signed "Your Replacement at Coolidge High" and is obviously spoken in Vonnegut's own voice—here his voice of public spokesmanship, because his final words draw a serious point from the book's sentiment and his own fun with it: "As a man, I am bound to be suspicious of your seeming advocacy of more love on the high school level. But I sure agree with you that, until the New York public schools have more dollars and fewer chowderheads, their failures will continue to be ghastly" (p. 10). The message about school funding is one Vonnegut would continue to make in his speeches three decades later, including specific remarks about the need for smaller class sizes. That the editors of *Life* had a spokesmanship role in mind is clear from the usual practice of their headnote to the review: a paragraph remarking that not since 1871 and the publication of Edward Eggleston's *The Hoosier Schoolmaster* had a book on education made such a popular impact, and that therefore they were asking a Hoosier and schoolmaster to "appraise this phenomenon" (p. 9). That Vonnegut had not lived in Indiana for twenty years and had only taught private school on Cape Cod for a brief period did not discourage him from taking on the spokesman's role; and it is significant that he signed himself as Bel Kaufman's replacement, for in a relatively short time he would be prefacing a book of high school underground writing and be adopted as a guru for this age group and beyond.

In 1965, of course, there was scant evidence that Kurt Vonnegut would become a best-selling author and great celebrity by decade's end. Instead, with his short story markets closing and novels rarely selling beyond their initial small first printings, he was forced to take the first full-time day job away from writing since he had quit General Electric back in 1950, moving in fall 1965 to Iowa City and a low-paying instructorship at the University of Iowa. Nevertheless, book review editors sensed his affinity for the popular, and along with titles by Eric Berne, Tom Wolfe, and Bel Kaufman they continued to send him volumes whose currency and reputation among the nonliterary public were just as much subjects of interest as their own topics. Yet Vonnegut would show some pre-science himself, not only noting certain figures quite early in their careers but grasping from the start just why the populace found them so fascinating.

One of these figures is Carl Sagan, famous throughout the 1970s and 1980s as a televised popularizer of astronomy and the wonders of space. In 1966 Kurt Vonnegut encounters him as the co-author, with the Russian astronomer I. S. Shklovskii, of an appealing book called *Intelligent Life in the Universe*.[4] Looking over their collaboration, he is struck by its being "a comedy of the most pleasant sort"—language one would use for reviewing a Neil Simon play or James Thurber book, but curious indeed for a work of science. The comic element is not necessarily one that was intended, but which Vonnegut finds instrumental in the book's popular success. The collaboration itself was something that evolved between the two authors: Shklovskii writing the book for readers in Russia, Sagan annotating the American edition "so enthusiastically" as to merit co-author status, and then Shklovskii making comments on Sagan's commentary. Because the two astronomers are of contrasting moods and personalities, Vonnegut finds amusement in the mix they provide:

> Of the two collaborators, it is the American astronomer who is the more humane writer, who, with friendly, wry little asides, acknowledges that the reader might, for good reasons, be nauseated and scared stiff [by the intellectual seasickness of contemplating the immensity of space]. Dr. Sagan has seen fit to include as illustrations, along with flabbergasting photographs of galaxies and double stars, cartoons by Charles Schulz and Charles Addams which relate human beings (and Snoopy) to the universe humbly. Dr. Shklovskii, on the other hand, is a sort of heedless Tom Swift with trillions of rubles to spend.

Vonnegut's method is here the same as in his *Random House Dictionary* review, sorting out the theories of linguistics by rummaging through his own catalog of life's little values and finding one theory reminding him of an honest cop while its rival seems like a boozed-up war buddy from Mobile, Alabama. Here he finds a good comparison provided by Carl Sagan himself, in the form of illustrative cartoons; but it is Vonnegut who adds the gratuitous (though hilarious) reference to Snoopy and then extends it by comparing the eminent Russian scientist to another fantasy figure, Tom Swift.

This technique, cartoon characters and young adult literary heroes and all, will soon become a factor in Vonnegut's public speeches, where the exotic is cleverly downscaled and made intellectually manageable by relating it to something comfortably familiar in the listener's life. If that downscaling can be made comic, all the better—hence the author's interest in the "pleasant comedy" Shklovskii and Sagan provide. But as he would do in his lectures, Vonnegut not only takes what the subject has to offer but adds something of his own, pushing what may have been mildly amusing in the astronomers' book into the realm of the ridiculous:

> Man's intelligence, by the way, has already effected a radical change in the solar system. Earth has suddenly become a powerful source of radio energy. "Thus," says Sagan the humanist, "the characteristic signs of life on Earth which may be detectable over interstellar distances include the baleful contents of many American television programs." It is a sobering thought that Gomer Pyle and the Beverly Hillbillies may be our only interstellar emissaries.

Thus it is the reader's great fascination with Sagan's subject—that intelligent life does exist elsewhere in the universe and by mathematical probability visits Earth every thousand or two years—that gets turned around into the review's greatest comedy of all, that instead of alien cultures sending awesome visitors to us, we are exporting something familiar and preposterous all at the same time.

If space was one hot topic of the 1960s, another was the lingering fear of nuclear Armageddon, a question now posed more thoughtfully with more sophisticated views of scientific weaponry and made immediate by President Kennedy's brinkmanship in handling the Cuban missile crisis. Given a very serious book to review,[5] a collection of essays by international scientists on the perils of future weapons of mass destruction, Vonnegut adopts a pose he would use not just in speeches but in two subsequent editorials for the *New York Times*[6] on similar topics: that of comparing the whole business to behavior typical in high school or junior high. Here the discussants would not be eminent authorities from the United States, United Kingdom, and France, but rather "Tony Hinkle and Bob Forslund and Jack Ottinger," the author's classmates from James Whitcomb Riley School in Indianapolis. These kids, Kurt Vonnegut among them, would spend their afternoons devising what they called "neat tortures" to practice upon people who were bad. Who were these people? Just "a guy" or "these guys," as in "You take these guys, see . . . and you tie 'em back to back and you cut off their eyelids, see, and you hang 'em upside down from an airplane over the Sahara Desert. . . ." That Vonnegut is not just reviewing but editorializing (and thus engaging in public spokesmanship on the issue) is clear from where he takes this allusion. Sitting in this junior high school named for a poet whose most famous line reads "The Goblins are gonna *git* you if you don't look out," he and his classmates anticipate the methods of today's cautionary scientists, whose essays in the book under review make pretty much the same statement.

What Vonnegut regrets, however, is that whereas "Most people stop thinking up neat tortures after they get out of junior high," enough others persist that the author rallies support for asking them an obvious question: "Are you out of your *minds*?" In any other context such a question might be considered too silly, too reductive of the topic's immensity to be of any intellectual use. But in his review's first half Vonnegut has established how such simplicity not only befits the topic but circumscribes its moral dimensions: for anyone beyond junior high idleness to be discussing such devices eclipses all responsibility and even practicality, given that existing weaponry already provides the equivalent of a hundred tons of explosives for every person on earth and that technology itself, once unleashed, has surpassed any human ability to control it.

Given his first popularity among high school age and collegiate readers, it is understandable that editors would send Vonnegut books putting that age group in the news, particularly when authors chose to study its countercultural revolutions supposedly in Vonnegut's mode. Such was the case with reporter J. Anthony Lucas's *Don't Shoot—We Are Your Children*, assigned to Vonnegut by *Life* magazine in 1971, at the height of his student-readership fame.[7] Effective public speaker that he was, he approached the topic by inverting the rhetoric that had been so successful for his commentaries on the foolish risks of military weapons. For that concern, he had taken the supposedly adult business and turned it back into the rather ridiculous stuff of high school; for the Lucas book, he chooses just the opposite tack, encountering statements on youth and responding to them not as a promoter of youthful revolt but rather as a somewhat skeptical adult.

"I heard Rollo May the psychiatrist say in a lecture the other night that one historical era was ending and another one beginning," Vonnegut tells his readers at the start of this review. "The changeover, he suggested, was giving us the heebie-jeebies and the generation gap." How great a change? According to May, it was as "jangling" as took place between the Middle Ages and the Renaissance. *Heebie-jeebies* and *jangling* are slang words, but of Kurt Vonnegut's own middle-aged generation, not of the differently speaking generation on the campuses and in the streets. Thus when the slang makes the topic seem familiar, it is familiar to those of the reviewer's age (a likely readership for *Life* magazine). Underscoring this somewhat skeptical maturity is Vonnegut's own response. "What exciting arguments they must have had back in olden times," he ponders, "when the parents belonged to the Middle Ages and the children belonged to the Renaissance." At once the topic is transformed into something comically familiar, reduced to the manageable dimensions of another generational squabble back home. In a way, it even mocks the rhetoric of youth—not of radically empowered youth with its language shaped by politics and economics, but of the typical teenager who considers his or her parents benighted relics of the Dark Ages. And from the slang and the humorous posture toward it all, it is clear on what side Vonnegut is placing himself.

This placement, however, is for more than comic effect. The point of Rollo May's statement was not just that change was afoot, but that it was proceeding in a specific direction: not outward into the inhospitability of space or the depletion of the earth but rather inward. "My own guess is that inward adventures are bound to disappoint all but our most listless citizens," Vonnegut objects, "and the striking characteristic of the new era will be a mania for sharing everything." That is the lesson he draws from Lucas's book, reviewing the enthnographically told stories of ten figures from the counterculture.

No less than half of Kurt Vonnegut's early reviews are of such popular culture items—an amazing percentage, given the dominance fiction holds in review space and that novelists are customarily given other novels to review. But of the fiction Vonnegut did cover, most of it prompts far less literary commentary than spokesmanship of public issues. This is remarkable, given the almost exotically literary figures with which the *New York Times Book Review* started Vonnegut off. Faced with interpreting Friedrich Dürrenmatt's *Once a Greek . . . ,*[8] he seizes upon the corniest of leads, that this Swiss writer rigs his narratives like "pretty and queer Swiss clocks":

> There are no mechanical mysteries or flaws. The intricately twinkling, twitching works can be admired through cases of glass, and they make little dolls act our jerky little scenes of human love and greed and stupidity and murder and politics and hope. The dolls are frankly dolls, doing what the machinery says they must. There is one human soul at which to marvel— the soul of the inventor.

What saves Vonnegut's opening from banality is its rhythm of speech, all of those serial "ands" that in their ongoing lack of discrimination suggest the clockwork functioning of Dürrenmatt's art. As a public speaker might, Vonnegut hammers home his point by extending the metaphor a bit further at each turn. The fictional city Dürrenmatt creates is "HO-gauge," his protagonist a "leading doll" whose message is "a lesson that Nelson Eddy tried to teach during the Great Depression, that love alone is worth looking for"; simplistic and even toylike as this message is, it finds resolution "because the clockwork" says it must.

That something can be wrong with this approach becomes Vonnegut's issue— not that Dürrenmatt is not fascinating in the way he builds his remarkable factory in his book that produces everything from tanks to obstetrical forceps, but that "he doesn't give a damn about what modern factories are really like, or what modern industrial jobs are really like." The storyteller is so far off base, Vonnegut laments, that when he wishes to flatter his hero's grand success by giving him a glamorous car, "God help us, it is a red Studebaker." Slipping in a vulgar term to express his own exasperation, Vonnegut explains Dürrenmatt's tale as a dream, "private, Kraut, mythological." The book is not, as its jacket claims, satire. At most, "The colors and the buildings and the costumes are as lovely as anything you will ever see."

Three months later Vonnegut was reviewing another book translated from the German, Heinrich Böll's *Absent without Leave*.[9] Here the reviewer adopts an even more apparent technique of public speaking: bearing witness and offering personal testimony of not just an encounter with the book but a change of heart about it. That his involvement with Böll's subject, a German protagonist's experience soldiering in World War II, was personal is a strategy attested to in the biographical note appended, which states, "Mr. Vonnegut is now at work on *Dresden Left, Slaughterhouse Five*, a commentary on his experiences as a prisoner in Dresden during World War II." Later on Vonnegut would cite this Böll novella as one of the key examples he found for coming to terms with his material. The other was Céline's *Death on the Installment Plan*. The prevalence and inevitability of death in Céline's work taught him that it was fruitless to fall apart at each mortal passing and to assume the dignity of saying "so it goes" instead. From Böll the author learned that one of the best ways to portray war is to not portray it, as happens in Böll's work where the hero is seen setting off to war and then returning, with all the events in between left blank.

In this present review Vonnegut is still several years away from devising his approach to *Slaughterhouse-Five;* during his coming semesters at the University of Iowa he would go so far as to toying with the idea of having lines of print run closer together as the firebombing scene approached, turning the page an indecipherable black for the event itself, and then allowing the text to become gradually distinguishable as events moved on. Dealing with Böll's work now, the future author of *Slaughterhouse-Five* begins by surprising his readers with an apparent hatchet job on *Absent without Leave*, calling it "a royal pain, a mannered, pretentious, patronizing, junky sort of *Notes from the Underground*. It seemed a sophomoric piece of work to me." As with his surprisingly blunt vulgarity in the Dürrenmatt review, Vonnegut foregrounds his disgust by reserving even the most damning terms of literary criticism in favor of the teenage slang term "royal pain" (p. 4). Then, to show how truly mad the book made him, he adds some comments about the protagonist being a lousy soldier, a coward, and a fool of the Nazis, and announces "So I threw the book across the room" (pp. 4, 54), just about the crudest reaction a reviewer can have. As part of Vonnegut's public testimony, even this is shared.

Because it is testimony, the act is shared as a point of revelation: *Absent without Leave* is so unsatisfactory about its protagonist's wartime experiences because there were so many things the character dare not remember. What they are the reader has to guess, making it a book formed out of nothing:

I approve. Does anybody really need to go over the nauseatingly familiar details of World War II yet again? Why not call the era "X," or do what Böll has done, which is to leave a blank, and then go on to the more profound business, as Böll does, of what the effects of "X" or blank were on various human souls? (p. 54)

It is when Kurt Vonnegut can not write as a public spokesman that his reviews fall flat, largely because he is bored with them. Having taught for a year (and facing another) at the University of Iowa, literary topics now become tedious. Given the 1966 volume of O. Henry Prize stories[10] and asked by a student if the American short story is changing, he has to judge that the collection might as well be dated 1937, and that the true innovations in fiction take place far away from the conventional behavior needed to appear in such company (and away from the university as well). Reading Richard Condon's *Any God Will Do*,[11] he hears echoes of the German language writers he has been reviewing, but he has to admit that the book is simply boring. By the time Goffredo Parise's *The Boss* appears in the mail,[12] he has to ask himself what is going on:

> Years ago, when I worked as a public-relations man for General Electric, I was rated by three of my co-workers every six months—anonymously. Then I had to go over the comments with my boss, promising to improve. One comment about myself that sticks in my mind for some reason: "No personality." This may be why I am now being sent so many novels about depersonalized people for comment and review.

And so Vonnegut rescues the assignment by making it anecdotal, paralleling Parise's story with his own as a G.E. employee enduring similar problems with his boss.

Disinfatuated with reviewing books he does not like, Vonnegut earns his pay and sustains his own interest by using such devices as anecdote and humor to liven up the story. In so doing, he develops the techniques that as a personal essayist would make the longer pieces collected in *Wampeters, Foma & Granfalloons* possible. In both cases the key practice was one shared with his public speaking: the construction of an appealing persona, a self-characterization audiences and readers could laugh at but also identify with, and from which could be devised a system of values helpful for understanding the apparent chaos at hand.

Consider his way of handling Len Deighton's novel *Bomber*,[13] "a book nearly as long as *The Brothers Karamazov*. It is a humorless chronicle of collisions during a single fictitious air raid by the British over Germany—during World War II." As with the Parise review, Vonnegut looks back to his own past for a useful comparison, and finds one in the collisions of obsolete steam locomotives staged at the Indiana State Fairgrounds as cheap entertainment during the Great

Depression. It cheered people up, the author recalls. "The folks enjoyed the suspense and then the crunch and the steam. They marveled at the wreckage, picked up pieces of steel which had been bent like taffy, saying reverently, 'My God—looky there.' "

For Vonnegut, the vernacular phrase is everything, a reminder that for these unsophisticated minds "Collisions have always been popular—and never mind what causes the objects to collide." In a reprise of his own "The Scientific Goblins Are Gonna Git Us" and in the manner of his *New York Times* editorial pieces on the perils of mass warfare, he remembers how his grade school classmates would ponder what would happen if an irresistible force hit an immovable object: "Nobody knew the answer, but everybody sure wanted to be there when it happened. And it finally happened, and everybody *was* there, and everybody loved it. We called it 'World War II.' " Thus are not just the locomotive collisions and Deighton's war action linked together, but so are the popular natures of each. "His collisions are lulus," Vonnegut admits, but then reduces the process to manageable proportions by quoting some of Deighton's most serious writing, a description of a German night fighter colliding with a sea gull at two hundred miles per hour, and adding the tag line "Looky there." To be fair, Vonnegut then cites another passage detailing what happens to a turret gunner when struck by a 10.5 centimeter anti-aircraft shell, before reducing it all to hickish wonder with another "Looky there."

The phrase is repeated a total of three times, pulling together the five-hundred-word review and nicely unifying its theme. It is the same method Vonnegut used in reviewing Parise's *The Boss*, beginning with the anecdote of those counseling sessions with his own boss, Griffin at G.E., and carrying the parallel forward through several humorous variations. Parise's character suffers from an employer who wishes his employees to behave like happy idiots—"Griffin was something else again." Next, the character is forced by his boss to marry a Mongolian idiot and submit to hideously painful megavitamin injections—"Griffin and I had our troubles, but nothing like that." Finally, when Parise makes a point about how coworkers gossip, Vonnegut recalls how "We used to dish the dirt like that all the time up in Schenectady. It is the kind of talk you hear around water coolers in every corner of the world." As a result, Vonnegut's own life story sounds a lot more entertaining than Parise's novel, and at a far less creative expense.

For *Bomber*, Vonnegut follows the same pattern of repeating parallels building toward a climactic point. Reminding his readers that before any of Deighton's descriptions of aerial warfare it was collisions of machines that were being talked about, the reviewer chooses what he feels is the writer's best passage. Here a German radar unit sweeps the skies, senses the raider's approach, and indicates a contact. "And so," Deighton notes, "the battle began: three groups of men using every device that science could invent began to grope around the blackness like gunmen in a sewer." Vonnegut's concluding tag? Not "Looky there" but rather "Beautiful," his proof that in stories of collisions "Machines steal the show."

Personal essays are the third of Vonnegut's roads to what would become three major collections of nonfiction prose. Though not published until 1955, the first dates from his time at General Electric in the early 1950s while still at work on his novel published in 1952, *Player Piano*, according to his contributor's note. Appearing in the *Atlantic Monthly*, "Der Arme Dolmetscher"[14] is also the author's first published account of his experiences as a prisoner of war, the topic that would generate *Slaughterhouse-Five* and much of his public commentary during his days of national spokesmanship. In this first response Vonnegut takes the familiar approach of having fun with old time army incompetence. The occasion is his designation, as he moves to the front, as the battalion *Dolmetscher*, or translator, even though the only German he knows is a stanza from *Die Lorelei* memorized phonetically for a college drinking song. That such a cockeyed assignment is not atypical of army procedure is evident from the chain of command Vonnegut cites, including a colonel who is a hotel detective from Mobile and an executive officer who was (and still sounds like) a dry-goods salesman from Knoxville.

Similar incompetence dictates the action that follows. The author is placed in a unit with three other interpreters—Pennsylvania Dutchmen, whose antiquated dialect will prove useless. He himself is housed with a Belgian burgomaster, according to the colonel's belief that it is the Belgians his army has just defeated. Given a German-English phrase book, Vonnegut finds that all of its pages detailing domestic circumstances have been ripped out for cigarette paper, leaving him with just a front-lines vocabulary regarding military commands and inquiries. Once introduced and billeted, he struggles to fall asleep by constructing a little fantasy out of the only language provided, which translates thusly:

DOLMETSCHER (to BURGOMASTER'S DAUGHTER): I don't know what will become of me, I am so sad. (*Embraces her.*)

BURGOMASTER'S DAUGHTER (*with yielding shyness*): The air is cool, and it's getting dark, and the Rhine is flowing quietly.

(DOLMETSCHER *seizes* BURGOMASTER'S DAUGHTER, *carries her bodily into his room.*)

DOLMETSCHER (*softly*): Surrender.

(*Enter* BURGOMASTER.)

BURGOMASTER (brandishing Luger): Ach! Hands up!

DOLMETSCHER and BURGOMASTER'S DAUGHTER: Don't shoot! (pp. 87–88)

Yet all is not lost, for the interpreter begins grilling his host, forcing him to admit where his howitzers are and how many grenade launchers he has. "Johann Christoph Friedrich von Schiller couldn't have done any better with the same words," Vonnegut boasts, "and they were the only words I had" (p. 88). It is the same practice the author has followed in his Parise and Deighton reviews, taking a minimal element from their works and running it through an anecdotal narrative from his own life, doing with it the best he can—with hilarious results. In terms of style, it is the vernacular American way of improvising along, doing the best with what one has, and in the process deflating any of the material's previous pretensions. One finds it in Mark Twain, in Will Rogers, and even in Abraham Lincoln's speeches: a self-effacing honesty and strong simplicity that win readers' confidence by making them like and trust the writer's personal voice.

As a justification of Vonnegut's method, he shows how the story comes full circle. Despite all of the officers' boasting that the Germans will be whipped, the essay ends with a formation of Tiger tanks and a squad of German soldiers surrounding battalion headquarters. "Say sumpin'," his colonel orders, and Vonnegut consults his phrase book for the line "Don't shoot." To this the German leader responds with his own line, "Where are your howitzers?" (p. 88), taken from a similar pamphlet in his hand.

Given the makings of a hopeless situation, Kurt Vonnegut has fiddled with them until they produce something interesting. It is the method he would use in his personal essays of the middle and late 1960s that distinguish *Wampeters, Foma & Granfalloons*, dealing with everything from his own mislabel as a science fiction writer to his misadventures reporting on the Maharishi Mahesh Yogi and covering the Apollo XI moon launch. When the subject itself is not fascinating in itself as popular culture (Dr. Eric Berne's psychotherapy, Tom Wolfe's flamboyant prose), Vonnegut finds a way to relate it to something he recalls as a curious popular phenomenon (steam locomotive collisions, personally invasive job practices back at G.E.). It is a primary technique of public speaking: to make the audience like you and trust you as you make the subject, especially a presumably dull or complexly confounding one, interesting and informative. And though in the preface to *Welcome to the Monkey House* the author disclaims having any theories to share regarding his success, one recalls the admonition he would put on the chalkboard at the beginning of every writing class he taught at the University of Iowa: "Face the audience of strangers." His essays show him doing just that, facing them with the understanding that they are not friends and allies ready to accept every word but total strangers who must be given a reason to listen and agree.

Before the end of 1969, however, the conditions of Kurt Vonnegut's spokesmanship would change. With the great success of *Slaughterhouse-Five*, the audiences for anything he would say or write or do were no longer strangers. Like it or not, he was now a well-known public figure whose opinion was sought by the media and attended to by people not just in the United States but around the world. Beginning that year he was asked to address meetings that ranged from high school and college graduations (all reported nationally) to the International

P.E.N. Congress in Stockholm. Once perfected, these addresses would be included in *Wampeters* and subsequent collections. But several earlier speeches, prefaces, and introductions remain, with the earliest reviews, uncollected, and provide a measure of Vonnegut's progress toward self-consciously public authorship.

The first such example remains the rarest: "Let the Killing Stop," an address Vonnegut was asked to give late in 1969 at his own community's Barnstable High School.[15] The occasion was one of the era's many popular moratoriums against the Vietnam War, and Vonnegut begins with an acknowledgment that "This is no time for a long and glorious speech." Presence alone speaks words, he counsels, referring to the numbers gathered with him, although he would be forced to admit beyond modesty that now his own endorsement of causes carries weight. There is much, of course, that can not be said, for Vonnegut finds no room for "hatred for the brass hats and for the corporations who are making big money out of this war"; words against them might be thrilling, but they would not bring happiness, for the only statement that would—that peace has come—cannot presently be made.

What can be said? That every country makes mistakes, but that only "profoundly free and honorable nations can admit they make them. Dictatorships never do. In Vietnam, we have made a lulu of a mistake. Tonight we are telling the world: 'We have made a lulu.' "

Vonnegut's use of the vernacular defines an important part of his speech. In a war famous for its misuse of language, he delves even deeper into the ways we have of saying things, such as that "Hanoi" does something, as if the city itself were an agent of evil. Elsewhere, he notes, "Washington" is cited as an evil being. Once upon a time, Vonnegut recalls, Rome, Berlin, and Tokyo were considered the same way. Now they aren't. Why not? Because in their cases the killing has stopped, and nothing else. To break through obscuring linguistics, one must think of the individuals involved, such as when it comes to body counts:

> This is how we measure victory, since we have no other way of doing so. We announce each day: "So and so many communists killed." Perhaps the other side counts the bodies of our young men and announces, so and so many capitalists killed.
> The dead soldiers were barely out of childhood.
> They're dead capitalists or communists now.
> How ridiculous and untrue and gruesome.

From here he digresses to remind his listeners that Barnstable, like the places most Americans lived at the time, is a rural area, and that in rural areas one witnesses "acts of unselfishness and bravery every day," notably in the work of volunteer fire departments. It is patriotic to serve in such a capacity, he notes;

going to war is not the only way to show it. In fact, when hearing how self-styled patriots talk about warfare, it sounds more like cheering on a football team. "My God—Vietnam is no football game," the speaker has to exclaim. "It's a slaughterhouse! They're keeping the score with bodies!"

And so Vonnegut's speech is rounded out the same way as his reviews and personal essays, looking at the problem until he can find a few simple coordinates to something in his own background everyone can share, and then repeating those coordinates in a way that resolves the problem. He even finds a way to reuse his vernacular term: "Speaking of lulus: Hanoi certainly made one when they officially praised this moratorium. Thanks a lot, Hanoi. Well—they're people too. Everybody makes lulus."

In 1970 Kurt Vonnegut found himself again on the high school platform, this time talking about his own experiences back at Shortridge High in Indianapolis for *Esquire* magazine and editor John Birmingham's anthology of writings from the high school underground.[16] The Shortridge experience is an especially pertinent one—not just an analogical, anecdotal return to the author's past, but instead a strong example of how important high school writing could be, for Shortridge High "was and still is one of the few American high schools with a daily paper. It was fashionable to write." Now, in times so different from those of the class of 1940, Vonnegut ponders not just his school paper ("the *Echo*, which is an honest name for an officially sanctioned student newspaper") but its yearbook, class poem from 1940, and present-day list of graduates. "Where go the years?" asks that poem, and ponders whether in "the dust of old hall clocks" or to "ride forgotten moonbeams / To the sky?" Vonnegut does not mock any of these sentiments: not the name and institutional policy of his old paper because during those hard, late-Depression days "the smartest people in town had turned to teaching"; and not the poem because as an adult approaching age fifty he really does wonder where the years have gone.

There is, in fact, one more text from Shortridge High School, one that prompts the anecdote that Vonnegut has been leading to all along. Answering the class poet, he confides:

> I will tell you where a lot of our classmates are: they're in soldiers' graves. When I go back to Indianapolis, I sometimes stand beneath the great bronze casualty lists which are bolted to the walls in the entrance of Shortridge, and I read all the names, and I marvel silently, "My God—so that's what became of him . . . and him . . . and him . . . and him." It's easy for me to imagine that all those dead young men are lawyers and realtors and insurance salesmen and teachers and engineers and so on. And they're not.
>
> I reread those casualty lists again very recently, made old friends and

56

enemies stop mowing lawns and barbecuing steaks in my imagination, made them climb back into their graves.

This becomes the author's method of testimony: taking abstract figures and making them real, taking a high school memory and, nearly thirty years later, making it terribly, almost horribly current. Thirty years is a generation, and at the time of this essay it constituted a generation gap. But note how Vonnegut spans it, even if it takes graveyard imagery to do it.

But the gap can be spanned among the living as well. Having complained in the *New York Times* about the current secretary of defense ("Good Missiles, Good Manners, Good Night"), Vonnegut recalls that the man's wife, Mrs. Melvin Laird, is a former Shortridge classmate. This only goes to prove that another old friend's judgment is true:

> When you get to be our age, you all of a sudden realize that you are being ruled by people you went to high school with. You all of a sudden catch on that life is nothing *but* high school. You make a fool of yourself in high school, then you go to college to learn how you should have acted in high school, then you get out into real life, and that turns out to be high school all over again—class officers, cheerleaders, and all.

Vonnegut's point is that high school is "closer to the core of the American experience than anything else I can think of," which means "the mere striplings" who write in high school during these troubled times (of Vietnam dissent and domestic unrest) are as worthy of being listened to as the authors of *The Federalist* papers. Whereas this is not something readers might be willing to grant from any arguments Vonnegut might make based on the content of their own writings, they have been taken step by step through the author's own background and experience, with riveting examples, to accept such a judgment now.

In Kurt Vonnegut's nonfiction prose one finds, of course, a more direct progression toward public spokesmanship than in his stories, but also a more profound anticipation of his later novels. Beginning with *Slaughterhouse-Five*, almost all of them would feature an autobiographical opening not just relating the author to the fictive work but doing it in a manner reminiscent of his essays from the later 1960s and early 1970s. Those statements, be they personal essays, forewords, or book reviews, follow the same methodology as would characterize the openings to *Breakfast of Champions*, *Slapstick*, and the other novels following through the later 1970s and 1980s.

The method itself is anecdotal, but not reductively so. Vonnegut never tells a story about himself for its own sake, but because its structure corresponds with and enlightens the more contemporary (and otherwise impersonal) matter at hand. Speaking in New York City's Bryant Park for the 1970 Earth Day ceremonies,[17] he summons up a picture of President Richard Nixon not as an alien figure but as someone familiar for small things as well as large: for being a fan of sports events as vowing never to be the first American president to lose a war. As for the sports events, Vonnegut guesses Nixon is watching one even now, and he worries that "if we don't get our president's attention this planet may soon die"; and as for the fear of losing a war, the author counsels that "He may be the first American president to lose an entire planet."

Thus is a notably adversarial presidential figure made to seem almost homely in relation to Vonnegut's issues. He uses the same method when forewording Anne Sexton's poems.[18] Not the easiest of poets, Sexton challenges the author to find an image for the power and appeal of her work. He does so by making a seemingly offhand mention of how he met her, at a book party celebrating Dan Wakefield's novel "about the tacky and bleak love life of a young man in Indianapolis after the Korean war" (p. vii). How casual and utterly tangential, we think, until Vonnegut quotes one of her startlingly vivid love poems and observes that "There wasn't any woman as alive and appreciative as all that in Dan's book about Indianapolis. I, too, was from Indianapolis" (p. viii). Not that this alone will suffice as his introduction, for he adds another apparently digressive story of how, to entertain her at the party, he went through his little chalk talk of good fortune versus bad in the tale of Cinderella. Why so? To work in the charming story of learning from a supermarket encyclopedia that the Cinderella tale itself turns upon a mistranslation of the French word *vair* as *verre*, making the magic slippers glass (in our English version) rather than fur (as in the original French). What has happened in the fortunate mistranslation is an extension of language, which is what Vonnegut has begun by saying poets do.

Talking about himself in a clarifyingly structural way is how Vonnegut makes sense of the public matters under review and of the fictive matters facing him in his novels. One sees this happening as his most characteristic approach, on the surface a deflation of sorts but on further investigation an insight into both himself and the issue being raised. Asked by the *New York Times Book Review*[19] which of his own novels he would enjoy rereading, Vonnegut answered, None of them: "I can't stand to read what I write. I make my wife do that." What he calls his favorite, *The Sirens of Titan*, was written euphorically in the belief that no one else would ever read it, a candid and cogent statement on the trials of public spokesmanship. Quizzed by *Playboy*[20] on this consequent peril of success, he tries again to demystify things, making his own career seem just a biographical inevitability:

I think I've had a reasonable career. It seems like a perfectly straightforward business story. I didn't have many alternatives to writing, because I was never a good employee of institutions, so obviously, I had to enter some kind of wildcatting operation. My parents and grandparents were in the arts, so this didn't seem like a high-risk thing or an activity outside of society. I sort of took over the family business and it's been an orderly development.

By rescuing his own life story from the trivialities of fame, Kurt Vonnegut accomplishes the same goal as when he reminds readers and listeners that the supposedly radical pacifism of the Vietnam era is nothing more than the standard civics lesson he was taught in public school during the 1930s. Whether turned into celebrityhood or elevated into a radical issue, the point risks being lost in abstraction. His method is to return it to concrete reality, as personally familiar as possible: unexceptionable but telling all the same.

Chapter Four

WAMPETERS, FOMA & GRANFALLOONS

Characteristically, Kurt Vonnegut begins his first collection of nonfiction prose with a preface. And in it he makes the same type of disclaimers that distinguish the preface to his selected short stories, *Welcome to the Monkey House*. There he had said he was self-taught and could claim no secrets or share any theories about how to succeed in the genre; when writing stories, he simply became what he must become. The thirteen pages of remarks that begin *Wampeters, Foma & Granfalloons* are almost nonstop complaints about how he prefers fiction to nonfiction, especially how the best nonfiction aspires to the form of fictive writing itself.

Not that his novels and short stories as written please him more—just that he prefers doing them. "I am not especially satisfied with my own imaginative works, my fiction," he offers. "I am simply impressed by the unexpected insights which shower down on me when my job is to imagine, as contrasted with the woodenly familiar ideas which clutter my desk when my job is to tell the truth" (p. xxvii).

The key, of course, is how much imagination shapes and fills a typical Vonnegut essay. He admits that the personal essays distinguishing this collection were written during the heyday of the New Journalism, that hybrid form pioneered in the 1960s by Tom Wolfe, Gay Talese, Joan Didion, and Vonnegut's own close friend Dan Wakefield. Their style of writing used the techniques of fiction for conveying information that conventional reportage would miss. More crucially, it encouraged reporters to forego the pose of objectivity—only an illusion, postmodern theory would teach—and help the reader comprehend a strange subject by putting themselves at the center of it and writing about their personal experiences as such. With not just fiction's techniques but its very spirit thus employed, the result could be as imaginatively creative as any short story or novel. By the time of Hunter S. Thompson's great success with *Fear and Loathing in Las Vegas* and *Fear and Loathing on the Campaign Trail '72*, the genre could be said to have eclipsed conventional fiction itself, paralleling as it now did the radical innovations of metafiction and the experimental novel.

As far as the mixing of forms, Kurt Vonnegut had done it when selecting materials for *Welcome to the Monkey House*, passing over two dozen uncollected stories to include a book review ("New Dictionary") and a personal essay ("Where I Live"), two of his earliest nonfiction works. By 1974, when *Wampeters* was published, the author's only recently begun nonfiction had already exceeded nearly two decades' short story production, and eventually the ratio would approach three to one. This happened necessarily because Vonnegut's customary short story markets had closed. And in the wake of his great fame, spokesmanship provided many more opportunities for expository prose; as he would rue in the volume's preface, "Among the many queer things about the American economy is this: A writer can get more money for a bungling speech at a bankrupt college than he can get for a short-story masterpiece" (p. xvi). Writing reviews and essays and giving speeches was now, for better or for worse, what the author was doing with the far greater part of his writing time. This was where his imagination was being exercised. That the personal essay itself was an amenable form had been evident since 1966, when he used it to begin prefacing his fiction and soon incorporating it within the novel's very structure and fabric.

Vonnegut's arrangement of pieces in *Wampeters* is chronological, but his method of selection highlights the combination of imaginative and spokesman-like qualities that are the key to his nonfiction work. As with *Welcome to the Monkey House*, he passes over about half of what is available; and once more he mixes forms, including a short play, "Fortitude," among the essays, speeches, and reviews. Most but not all of his book reviews are discarded; all but one of his personal essays are included. And because spokesmanship is an issue, the book concludes with the author's interview from the July 1973 issue of *Playboy* (just as a later *Paris Review* interview would reappear in his next collection, *Palm Sunday*). If there is a specific trend to the selections, it is the emergence of American national politics as a concern—a factor of both Vonnegut's emerging fame and the country's increased state of turbulence from the earlier 1960s through the Vietnam era and the years of Richard Nixon's embattled presidency. But on the whole it is Kurt Vonnegut's intellectual action that carries things along. Even at his angriest with the Nixon administration's policies, he has time for a joke; and even when pushing an obviously frivolous topic toward further hilarity, such as when lamenting the initiation fees his wife and daughter have cost him in learning about the Maharishi, he can incorporate the most serious observations. By the volume's end Vonnegut has constructed an imaginative structure that is able to engage the most troubling and confusing topics in a manner both entertaining and enlightening, all in an eminently personal way.

Although it is an accident of chronology that places one of Vonnegut's most aesthetically revealing essays first,[1] "Science Fiction" serves well as an introduction to Kurt Vonnegut, person and writer. Like so many of his book reviews, especially those whose subjects gave him trouble, the author begins with a story of working back at General Electric, "completely surrounded by machines and ideas for machines" (p. 1). Thus when he wrote a novel, it was about machines, something that gave reviewers the chance to label him as a science fiction writer. The label has stuck, despite all Vonnegut has done to escape it. And so, rather than filling up his essay with complaints about that, he uses his imagination to play with the fact and see what he can devise with it. This includes pondering why science fiction is despised while at the same time many writers seek the label for themselves and aficionados strive to include so many divergent talents within the fold. Unlike a simple complaint, it makes a fascinating story, one that justifies even the jokes made at science fiction enthusiasts' expense.

In this first of his canonical personal essays, Vonnegut establishes both an orientation and a method for dealing with his subject. While that subject is indeed literary, his key to it is not. Rather, he uses his understanding of anthropology to explain the human behavior motivating all this controversy over the science fiction crowd—writers, readers, and critics alike. "They are joiners," the author notes. "They are a lodge. If they didn't enjoy having a gang of their own so much, there would be no such category as science fiction." That is why the very question of its identity, though endlessly debated, is not at all a literary matter. "They love to stay up all night, arguing the question, 'What is science fiction?' " he observes of these lodge members. "One might as usefully enquire, 'What are the Elks? And what is the Order of the Eastern Star?' " (p. 2).

Vonnegut's anthropological orientation leads to the methodology for his major joke, that of running his thoroughly respectable thesis through the fractured logic of a deliberately improper syllogism. The occasion is the penchant for SF fans to include almost any form of literature as their own, making such claims as that George Orwell and Ralph Ellison and even Franz Kafka are part of their fold:

They often say things like that. Some are crazy enough to try to capture Tolstoy. It is as though I were to claim that everybody of note belonged fundamentally to Delta Upsilon, my own lodge, incidentally, whether he knew it or not. Kafka would have been a desperately unhappy D.U. (p. 4)

Such comically intended illogic is a dirty trick on the SFers, of course. Readers are now laughing at them because of the picture Vonnegut has drawn of Franz Kafka as a rah-rah fraternity brother, not as a science fiction writer. But the faulty syllogism has done its work, empowered by the lodge metaphor that the author, winning the reader's trust, has so carefully built up before.

Further demystification of another favorite target follows in "Brief Encounters on the Inland Waterway,"[2] a companion piece to the author's Barnstable essay also published in *Venture—Traveler's World*. The piece combines the hometown interests of "Where I Live" with the Kennedy glamor of "The Hyannis Port Story" and actually draws upon more of the short story's techniques for moving the action and making its point. "The Hyannis Port Story" had been told by the unassuming storm-and-screen salesman from North Crawford, New Hampshire, an interloper among the rich and famous as he strives to get his installation job done. The Inland Waterway essay is Vonnegut's own narration, and he posits himself in much the same way as a practical, simple person thrust amid the glories of the famous presidential family and one of its most expensive play-things, the fifty-one-foot yacht *Marlin*. Like "The Hyannis Port Story" again, the narration is motivated by a professed desire to simplify all this grandeur. Vonnegut accomplishes this by sustaining the action on an egalitarian note, such as when a registry check revealing the owner as Joseph P. Kennedy, Hyannis Port, Massachusetts, fails to elicit any recognition from the registering official. "Street address there?" the *Marlin*'s captain is asked; the reply is, "It's just a little country town. Everybody knows everybody" (p. 12).

The captain himself, Vonnegut's friend and neighbor Frank Wirtanen (readers of *Mother Night* will recognize the name as one used for that novel's spymaster), carries the burden of this demystification. His initial identifying comment is just the opposite of glamorous. "I don't think a man without children of his own, without a real understanding of children," he confides to Vonnegut, "could hold this job very long without going bananas." To underscore the irony, a brief biography follows:

> Captain Wirtanen is a graduate of the Massachusetts Maritime Academy. He used to command tankers, both in peace and in war. He now has the Kennedy yacht fitted out with a system of rubber mats and scuppers that make it possible for him to hose away the remains of chocolate cake and peanut-butter-and-jelly sandwiches in a fairly short time. (p. 8)

This contrast, between grave significance and frivolous use, structures the entire essay, built as it is on the irony that such a famous and expensive ship is hardly ever used by its larger-than-life owners. Instead, its occasions consist of children's parties and a seemingly pointless routine of empty runs along the eastern seaboard, something most yacht captains experience, as one they meet complains. "Take the ship up to Bar Harbor," he quotes the owner. "Take her down to Miami. Take her through the Strait of Magellan and paint her sky blue" (p. 15). Such disuse is the most glamorous feature encountered. Otherwise, Vonnegut is faced with the most common images. He has told how the topside has been rigged for washing away cake and sandwiches; the main cabin is a narrow affair fitted with a tiny gas range, old-fashioned icebox, bellied glass doors, "and a sink with a bowl the size of a derby," all of which prompts him to complain that "this would make a wonderful set for a Clifford Odets play about the Great Depression. 'The curtain rises on the kitchen of a railroad flat on the Lower East Side' " (p. 9). The Inland Waterway, which Vonnegut sails with his friend all the way from Hyannis to West Palm Beach in Florida, is just as reductive an affair, "marked as plainly as the aisles of a well-run supermarket" with signs such as "Slow—Congested Area" and "All Credit Cards Honored at Bill and Thelma's Sunoco Marina, 8 miles" (p. 10).

The point of it all is that the trip is nothing glamorous, something Vonnegut admits to another captain at the end. "I'd like to take it a lot slower next time," he wishes. "I'd like to explore and fish, anchor in creeks, wake up with the birds all around. A very beautiful life is certainly possible on the Inland Waterway for anybody who has the time." But first, the captain warns him, "get yourself a yacht" (p. 19).

With this similar twist to logic "Brief Encounters on the Inland Waterway" joins "Science Fiction" in establishing the style of Kurt Vonnegut's spokesmanship. For his first book of nonfiction prose, it is clear that he wants his style to be one of familiarity, with only a slight sense of superiority gained from the corrective information he has to supply. And that information is conveyed not in a hectoring or otherwise belaboring manner, but by playing the reader along in a little narrative game. Kafka as a D.U., owning a yacht making one too busy to appreciate its possible pleasures—these are manipulations similar to those Vonnegut undertakes when asking his listeners how many seasons there are or teasing them about how many of the two million books in the library he is rededicating are dirty. Answering those questions takes his audience into realms of logic and information they would never otherwise explore, thus bringing to light the insight they would have denied themselves. What superiority these initial essays boast is not of an alienating variety. Rather it is an invitation to take a different perspective, to cross a syllogism deliberately in order to see what kind of data results. It is the author's manipulation, of course, that brings them to the point of information he has wished to convey all along, such as the silliness of literary lodge joining among the science fiction crowd, but which to be convincing needs first the image of Franz Kafka outfitted with beanie, pennant, and fraternity paddle.

With Vonnegut's next selections, one sees this benign familiarity reinforced with obvious intent. By discarding his earliest essay, "Der Arme Dolmetscher," in favor of a running start with "Science Fiction" and the Inland Waterways pieces, he had avoided any impression of foreign and remote subjects. Now, selecting only "Hello, Star Vega" from several available book reviews and rewriting an important part of a personal essay on writers' conferences, "Teaching the Unteachable," he rounds off some nasty corners and polishes the somewhat abrasive surfaces of his earliest style of commentary in order to make it fit more comfortably with the friendliness so important to the success of *Wampeters, Foma & Granfalloons*.

What does Vonnegut's review of the Carl Sagan / I. S. Shklovskii book, *Intelligent Life in the Universe*, have that his passed-over pieces of Dr. Eric Berne, Tom Wolfe, Heinrich Böll, Richard Condon, Friedrich Dürrenmatt, Bel Kaufman,

Goffredo Parise, and the O. Henry Awards lack? A richness of expression that allows the reviewer's insight to be conveyed from his language alone. Recall how Vonnegut approaches the book not as a foreboding astronomical treatise but as "a comedy of the most pleasant sort" (p. 21), how Shklovskii is contrasted with Sagan's humble folksiness as "a sort of heedless Tom Swift with trillions of rubles to spend" (p. 23), and especially how the book's thesis that Earth has become a source of radio waves broadcast into space is transformed by Vonnegut into the image of extraterrestrials tuning in to reruns of Gomer Pyle and the Beverly Hillbillies. As an attention getter, it is as startling as Kafka pledging Delta Upsilon and just as revealing of the otherwise serious point the reviewer wants to make.

The reviews discarded are Vonnegut's literary ones, in which he was generally bored with the topics and forced to devise anecdotal material in order to make his treatment interesting and entertaining. As a book, *Wampeters* would suffer no such lapses; with himself and not a book review editor in control, the author could choose his occasions. One literary occasion, however, survives near the volume's start, albeit with some doctoring to remove what can only be called some genuinely cutting remarks. "Teaching the Unteachable" appeared as a page 1 feature in the *New York Times Book Review*[3] as a byproduct of Vonnegut's need, before the fame of *Slaughterhouse-Five*, to make whatever money he could by almost any respectable means. The rub of his experience at the West-Central Writers' Conference, however, is that the conference was an unpleasant affair for him, especially when its conduct no longer seemed respectable. In responding, he produces one of his most effectively animated essays. Beginning with a generously understanding summary of what writers' conferences are, he proceeds to let the damning details build until the purposefulness of the affair completely self-destructs. And then, in the uncut *Book Review* version, he unleashes the most ungenerous comments imaginable.

But first there is Kurt Vonnegut's fairness to the idea of such conferences themselves. Given that good writing cannot be taught, the whole idea of college programs and sponsored conferences is a bit suspect—but harmlessly so, because these affairs are able to multiply like rabbits but without consuming much beyond the participants' goodwill. "They are harmless," Vonnegut admits, and he reaches back to a "Li'l Abner" cartoon from the 1950s for an apt image: "They are schmoos" (p. 25). Describing how one was started by preachers' wives in his own Cape Cod community and has grown in five years from twenty-six to almost one hundred students, he looks forward to one of his own works to coin a phrase for it all: "So it goes."

But then comes the story of one writers' conference he just visited, and the details are no longer nonjudgmental. Hosted by Western Illinois University in Macomb, Illinois, its opening reception is held at a motel "between the Coin-A-Wash and the A & W Rootbeer stand," a ghastly location chosen to evade the campus prohibition of liquor. The director is described as "the only teacher at Western Illinois who has published a book," and as being sad, complaining "over the Muzak and the sounds of drag races out on Route 136" (p. 27) that only a handful of students have registered.

The shabbiness of these details prepares the reader for the unpleasant statement that comes next, one that Vonnegut cleverly allows to be stated not by himself but by an even more dejected participant: "You know why more people didn't come?" she offers, then explains "Because 'Macomb, Illinois' sounds like such a hell-hole, and because 'Western Illinois University' sounds like such a jerkwater school" (p. 28). The author seconds her by confiding that a conference sponsored by Harvard or Oxford and located in Acapulco would draw much better; the unstated truth is that most successful conferences, such as the one already described on Cape Cod, are indeed set in more attractive locations. Then, in a paragraph dropped from the essay's reappearance in *Wampeters*, he describes what a good conference needs and how Indiana University provides it, not the least by allowing grown-ups to drink booze.

This is not the only part of Vonnegut's essay dropped for its reprinting. Missing is an amusing anecdote about the author's first encounter with academic critics at the University of Iowa, plus the essay's conclusion, an important passage that rounds out the opening thesis (of writers' conferences multiplying like shmoos) and sympathizes with the ongoing plight of the director:

> To return to the Macomb experiment one last time: I hope they get more people next year than came this year. If the conference dies, it will be the first one that ever did. What they need to make things merrier is a sort of master of the revels, a graduate of some hotel school like Cornell University.
>
> And they must stop telling staff members that they have to sign loyalty oaths or they won't get paid. Poor E. W. Johnson was humiliated when that happened in spite of all he tried to do to prevent it. A little touch like a loyalty oath can lead a visiting writer to suspect, rightly or wrongly, that he is employed by hicks.

Together with the reference to adults being allowed to drink, this omission figures as an important characteristic in Vonnegut's personal essays of the time. As in the "Science Fiction" piece and in company with "Brief Encounters on the Inland Waterway," part of his appeal is just that: to make an appeal to the reader as a somewhat aggrieved party—being mislabeled as a science fictionist, being taken on a yacht cruise that is anything but glamorous, and being run through a dull writers' conference where he is denied a drink and forced to sign a loyalty oath at the same time. The technique itself is comic, one in vogue since Henny Youngmann and further popularized by Rodney Dangerfield and Woody

Allen—not just victimization, but victimization in a comic way, based on one's own insufficiencies and yet bringing much larger issues into play.

It is the method that the author uses in one of his finest essays, an *Esquire* feature on the Maharishi given the marvelously deconstructive title "Yes, We Have No Nirvanas."[4] Almost entirely anecdotal, it pushes New Journalism's methodology to an extreme by forsaking any objectivity whatsoever about this most exotic of subjects in favor of simply writing about—in this case, *complaining* about—one's personal experiences with the man. "Is he a fake?" Kurt Vonnegut is asked by a Unitarian minister, and in defending the transcendental meditation leader from this charge the author effectively condemns him—not because of anything the Maharishi himself does, but because of how people act in response to him. These actions are the cause of Vonnegut's complaints, because two of the individuals involved are his wife and daughter. This places the writer as far as possible from the standards of conventional, objective journalism. But so is the Maharishi, who, like so many other phenomena of the American 1960s, is off the scale of customary judgment.

The key to the Maharishi's honesty is that he demands very little, and even that is "easy as pie" (p. 31), a phrase Vonnegut finds useful as his own mantra for creating an aura of simplicity about the man. If any fault is involved, it is that his followers "get hooked" (p. 31), another term the author uses repetitively for the same effect. Everything about getting involved with transcendental meditation is described with bright language: *bliss, cheer, ease,* and *delight* are the terms used most frequently. Initiates bring gifts for their teacher, including such things as handkerchiefs, fresh fruit, flowers, and the like, but also seventy-five dollars—or thirty-five dollars for students and housewives.

It is with the money that Vonnegut becomes a complainer. Thanks to his wife and daughter joining the movement, he can note, "So I have seventy dollars invested in this new religion so far," a factor that by paragraph's end assumes the language of complaint, as "at cocktail parties every so often, I can be heard to say sulkily, often within earshot of my wife or daughter, 'I've got seventy goddamn simoleons in this new religion so far' " (p. 33). Underscoring the aural nature of his presentation is Vonnegut's careful contrast of language: airy and light and preciously ethereal for the Maharishi, crudely vernacular and harshly material for himself. Such harshness extends to the author's reportorial manner; for a work of classic New Journalism, he sees fit not so much to practice as to imitate, exaggerate, and thereby satirize the digging-out-the-truth methods of an investigative reporter. This allows Vonnegut to be relentless in his questioning, which in terms of the essay's greater movement has the intent of Socratic rather than reductive development. And every time a practice of transcendental meditation is explained, he challenges it with more popular skepticism. Hearing an account of how intoning a mantra allows one to dive into one's subconscious, Vonnegut admits that "There is rapture in those depths," but only to the extent that he can compare it to a narcotically induced "jag," which prompts him to mention another advantage: "And the fuzz can't bust you."

As his essay proceeds, Vonnegut restricts his judgments to what language itself provokes. If indeed TM is destined to "sweep the middle classes of the world," it will do so as something else "sweeps the planet": the pollution of air and water of which the earth "is surely dying" (p. 34). Told of how the power of meditation will save the world, he wonders how this will work for the politicians responsible for war and racism—"You expect to get *them* to *meditate?*" And what if TM fails? For this stickler, he turns his inquiring technique on an unlikely subject, a middle-aged lady whose mind seems as attractive for mantra-diving as "dogpaddling across Cleveland's Cuyahoga River," who tells him there is no such thing as failure—"The worst that can happen is that you might be disappointed." To this Vonnegut responds with a comment that turns his essay toward its central thesis: "That's a long way from being hung up on a cross or thrown to the lions" (p. 35).

Implicit and explicit comparisons with Christianity now pepper Vonnegut's prose. Transcendental meditation is not a doctrine but a technique; fine, but in what does one then believe? Does TM preach doing good works to others? Yes, but the emphasis is on improving one's own condition, including material good such as being better at one's job. As for really tough questions about social problems, the Maharishi dodges them quite amiably, living up to the author's description of him at their meeting, "a darling man—small, golden-brown, a giggler with a gray beard and broad shoulders and a thick chest" (p. 37). Though the author pledges to listen sincerely, what he hears is the same old public relations line put out by General Electric in the 1940s, that "it was ridiculous for people to be unhappy" (p. 38) because there were so many neat little techniques available for improving things; any comparisons the TM leader might make to other organized religions were those of the marketplace, one he felt confident he had cornered, thanks to what Vonnegut calls his "sugar pills" (p. 39).

Following his journalistic encounter with the Maharishi, having done all the things required—closing his eyes, waiting "to be wafted to mysterious India by the poetry of this holy man" (p. 37)—Vonnegut gives up any pose of open-mindedness to exercise a bit of self-indulgence, revealing in its implied sarcasm:

> I went outside the hotel after that, liking Jesus better than I had ever liked Him before. I wanted to see a crucifix, so I could say to it, "You know why You're up there? It's Your own fault. You should have practiced Transcendental Meditation, which is easy as pie. You would also have been a better carpenter." (pp. 39–40)

Comments such as these fit the author's tactics of complaint; beforehand he has been lamenting his lost seventy dollars, and now he can chastise Christ for his own presumed failures—failures, that is, according to the techniques of TM. Complaining influences one's mode of speech, for in positing an audience to listen sympathetically Vonnegut gives tenor to his own voice. It is evident in his vernacular approach to lost funds and the tone used in complaining to the crucifix, each a sure sign that the speaker's routine is exaggerated for comic effect and that what he means is just the opposite. That an even more reductive view of money rules the practice of transcendental meditation is clear from one last charge. "I can see where influential people would like Maharishi better than Jesus," he concludes. "My God, if The Beatles and Mia Farrow went to Jesus, He'd tell 'em to give all their money away" (p. 41). A telling point, one that lets the author's original suspicions about his "seventy goddamn simoleons" win true.

One recalls that part of Kurt Vonnegut's stump-speech routine as a famous author in the 1970s would be to ask his audiences, many of whom would picture him as a similar popular phenomenon of the 1960s, whether the great mystic religions of the East were superior to such occidental practicalities as Christianity and Judaism. To the many hands that shot up in agreement, the speaker would mock them with a reminder that the human imagination inspired by something as unmystical as reading was infinitely superior to the hocus-pocus concocted from Eastern beliefs in shams like the Maharishi's. Though transcendental meditation itself is left behind after the "Yes, We Have No Nirvanas" essay, a continuing interest in the proper power of imagination motivates several of the pieces that follow. "Fortitude,"[5] drafted in the form of a playlet, is closet drama to the fullest, not needing to be staged because its message is one of straightforward statement: that the techniques of science are vastly inferior to the simple spirit of life, a spirit that suffers comic reduction whenever one tries to translate it into measurable (and hence controllable) forms. There are also matters too large for human imaginations, such as the motives for mass murder. " 'There's a Maniac Loose Out There' "[6] details the public reactions to a murderer/mutilator apprehended in the author's own community on Cape Cod, reactions that range from morbid jokes (Vonnegut catalogs several) to a staunch refusal by people to believe that the culprit could have been anyone *they* knew (one such naive soul is Vonnegut's own daughter, who may well have been an intended victim). These reactions and others, such as tourists eager to dig for buried body parts and entrepreneurs who package and sell sand from the seaside crime scene, are attributable to the imagination's inability to fathom such terror; unable to contain such ghastly images and unsettling ideas, the mind simply turns off in favor of giddy laughter, something the reader can appreciate as a factor in the reductive scientism made fun of in "Fortitude."

Challenging events do tax the imagination, and technology can fall victim to its own hucksterism in exploiting human fascination with matters otherwise beyond its appreciative scale. This is what Vonnegut sees happening in another of his strongest essays, "Excelsior! We're Going to the Moon! Excelsior!,"[7] a product of his journalistic involvement with the Apollo XI moon launch. CBS Television had hired him as commentator, innocently expecting him to marvel in approval; instead, his broadcast commentary got cut off when he began to editorialize about how earthbound social improvements were a better place for the money (one notable exchange has Vonnegut being challenged over whether such applications could ever be effected and replying that "I thought Napoleon III did a pretty good job with Paris").[8] Expanding his approach for the *New York Times Magazine* to include anecdotal as well as editorial material, he demythologizes the matter of space launches by consistently comparing them to matters of childhood. As a thrill, blastoff is compared to setting off fireworks as a kid; as for the marvels of astrophysics, Vonnegut bypasses the lavishly sophisticated literature supplied by NASA and quotes instead *The Look-It-Up Book of the Stars and Planets*, a piece of children's literature with even more suitable enthusiasms ("We are flying through space. Our craft is the earth, which orbits the sun at a speed of 67,000 miles an hour. As it orbits the sun, it spins on its axis. The sun is a star"); making himself childish in response, he comments that "If I were drunk, I might cry about that" (p. 78).

The adult side of Vonnegut's moon launch essay tends toward the sarcasm evident in the more put-upon sections of "Teaching the Unteachable" and "Yes, We Have No Nirvanas." As for the benefits of technology through history, something NASA publicists cite frequently in their literature, he wonders if they are thinking of rocket bombardment of civilians and DDT poisoning of the environment; as far as advances in civilization, he asks if that includes the Spanish conquistadors' torturing of the Indians for gold. "Most of the tales of masterfulness in new environments with new technologies," he responds to NASA's claims for what humankind will achieve in space, "have been cruel and greedy," a consequence of "The concepts of reality held by the masterful people" being "customarily stupid or solipsistic in retrospect" (p. 79). Today the case for greed is evident even in the rapturous accounts of Arthur C. Clarke, which Vonnegut notes are published in *Playboy*. "*Playboy*," he repeats, with new paragraphing for emphasis. "Somewhere cash registers ring" (p. 80).

Then there are the truly deprecating remarks, akin to the dropped portions of Vonnegut's writing conference essay. Clarke has been quoted concerning how other planets may be the cradle of biological discoveries about the beginnings of life; a few pages later these remarks are recalled as an eagerness "to found kindergartens on Jupiter" (p. 85). Carrying forward the notion of overdrinking leading to childish behavior, the author ties one on with a friend in the space program and notes him reducing it all to a vaudeville spectacle on the level of Harry Houdini, which prompts a cruel observation:

> It is the Houdini aspects of the space program which reward most Earthlings—the dumb ones, the dropouts, the elevator operators and stenogra-

phers and so on. They are too dense ever to care about the causes of craters on the moon. Tell them about the radio signals coming from Jupiter, and they forget right away. What they like are shows where people get killed.

Killed.

And they get them, too. (p. 82)

Cruel but true. The tone of Vonnegut's essay is that when it comes to contemplating the space program, one is better off drunk, or with at least a few stiff ones under the belt. The author's broadest view, near his essay's turn toward its conclusion, is taken from a jet high over Appalachia, where the region's terrible poverty is transformed into something looking from thirty thousand feet like the Garden of Eden, just as "Earth is such a pretty blue and pink and white pearl in the pictures NASA sent me. It looks so *clean*. You can't see all the hungry, angry Earthlings down there—and the smoke and the sewage and trash and sophisticated weaponry" (p. 83). Instead, all seems fine, as it does to Vonnegut on his flight. "I was a rich guy, way up in the sky," he notes, "munching dry-roasted peanuts and sipping gin" (p. 84).

At every point endorsements of the space program have been related to children's literature—and both kinds of literature to states of inebriation. At its best, space boosterism is effective advertising. At its worst, it leads people to imply that there is some divine purpose guiding such probes. "I prefer to think not, though," Vonnegut cautions, "for this simple-minded reason: Earthlings who have felt that the Creator clearly wanted this or that have almost always been pigheaded and cruel. You bet" (p. 87). Rather than finding God's purpose in space, he chooses to cite one text that is not childish or intoxicated at all, Guy Murchie's *Music of the Spheres*, which counsels space as a realm for imaginative exploration and nothing else, for the imagination is surely rich enough.

Vonnegut's mention of his riches marks a new development for him as an essayist and public spokesman. This piece has been his first conceived and written since *Slaughterhouse-Five* made him a famous and wealthy novelist—each a 180° turn in the conditions prompting him to write essays in the first place. In interviews of the time, Vonnegut would speak repeatedly of this change in conditions: of how money had motivated him for so long that now, in financial security, he would have to find new reasons to write. Not that everything previously was just hackwork to turn a dollar; those who knew Kurt Vonnegut before the onset of fame recall how even in his most penurious days he had a strong sense of saying something important in his work. But fame and money certainly change one's sense of audience; and for an author given to telling anecdotes about himself and his background as a way of interpreting the topic at hand, one's sense of self has to change as well.

A moral dimension had always been apparent in Vonnegut's work, but whereas in "Yes, We Have No Nirvanas" the references to divine ethics are lighthearted, the moon launch essay finds the author being considerably more caustic in his references to the way humankind misuses interpretations of Godly purpose. That the author is now a success gives him a certain authority: of having struggled through life's trials and come out well, not to speak of the Protestant (and very American) doctrine of success being a sign of election—not that Vonnegut would feel this way, but that how the culture he writes in is so influenced. Yet it is possible to take an even simpler view: that nothing argues so well as success, an empowerment that allows Vonnegut to speak with a somewhat greater assumption of authority, no matter how humble his own view of self may be.

That Kurt Vonnegut could emerge as a moral spokesman without losing his familiarity, generosity, and underlying sense of the comic is evident in his address to the American Physical Society. Published in essay form as "Physicist, Purge Thyself,"[9] it begins like the moon launch piece with a story about his brother Bernard, even more appropriate because Bernard, like those in Vonnegut's audience, is a physicist. The tale is one of brotherly bonding, at first with no direct relationship to Vonnegut's topic of physics and humanism. It involves the condition of Bernard's lab at General Electric, the messiness of which never ceased to terrify the plant's safety officer. Bernard's reply: "If you think this is a mess, you should see what it's like up here," pointing to his head. "I loved him for that" (p. 92), Vonnegut remarks, and finds in that mutual sympathy they share a way of explaining how the sciences and the humanities can share ideals.

If Bernard Vonnegut, eminent atmospheric physicist and inventor of the technique of cloud seeding with silver iodide, is the author's first example of a humanist, his second is even more surprising: his sheep dog Sandy, the occasion for another family anecdote. This one involves taking Sandy to the zoo to see his fellow carnivores. "I assumed he would be thrilled out of his wits," Vonnegut reports, but he learns the dog has no interest whatsoever even in bears just three inches away. "He was too busy watching people" (p. 94), his true interest, and a good definition of what a humanist is: someone who is mainly interested in people.

These two stories are important factors in Vonnegut's approach to his audience. Rather than a hostile visitor from a world of different values, the author is more like one of them, thanks not just to having a physicist in the family but one he can relate to as a loving brother. And what a loving family, dog and all, especially since it is Sandy the sheep dog who exemplifies what may have seemed an alien topic, humanism. Thus introduced, Vonnegut can move more deftly into the moral dimensions of his speech: that a virtuous physicist is a humanistic physicist, because humanism would never knowingly hurt people. A humanistic physicist is nothing other than what anyone in his audience would want himself or herself to be: one who "watches people, listens to them, thinks about them, wishes them and their planet well" (p. 96).

There are, of course, physicists who do not feel this way, but to avoid any harsh posturing Vonnegut chooses one of his own fictive creations as an example. Dr. Felix Hoenikker of *Cat's Cradle* fits the bill because, as an absentminded old man, he "doesn't give a damn about people" and in the abstract process of his work discovers a form of crystallography that destroys the world. The first hint that such attitudes might happen in real life comes from a writerly anecdote of how Vonnegut once tested the idea's feasibility on a real scientist, who simply retired to a half hour's expressionless calculations and returned with the one-word verdict "Nope" (p. 97). A second example, also anecdotal, is more telling, referring as it does to a presentation by David Lilienthal, who at the time had just resigned from the Atomic Energy Commission in order to speak freely. Yet even here Vonnegut cushions the blow by having it fall on a group of physicists rather than be initiated by them. Lilienthal's speech to the scientists at G.E. revelled in possibilities for atomic measurement and medicine, especially how a man dying of a huge throat tumor was treated with an atomic cocktail, causing the tumor to disappear completely in a matter of days. That the patient died anyway did not discourage Lilienthal in the least, but it did his listeners:

> I have never seen a more depressed audience leaving a theater. *The Diary of Anne Frank* was a lighthearted comedy when compared with Lilienthal's performance for that particular audience, on that particular night, in that particular city, where science was king. The young scientists and their young wives had learned something which most scientists now realize: that their bosses are not necessarily sensitive or moral or imaginative men. Ask Werner Von Braun. His boss had him firing rockets at London. (p. 99)

The allusive references do Vonnegut's dirty work here; no direct commentary on the Holocaust and Hitler would be so effective as seeing a group of scientists make their own implications about misused science in these terms. As for himself, he is just telling another story, one in which he sympathizes with the scientists in both audiences. It is when he speaks to students, Vonnegut admits, that he does moralize, but only as echoes of what they are telling themselves, for to get the point it must be self-generated.

To conclude, the author makes his most telling point by criticizing himself. It involves a self-styled moralistic speech he gave at the University of Michigan that included a complaint that when Harvard students demonstrated against Dow Chemical for its manufacture of chemicals Professor Louis Fieser, napalm's actual inventor, was present on campus but totally overlooked. To the physicists in his present audience Vonnegut cites a letter received in the aftermath of his speech at Ann Arbor, from a student who exculpates Dr. Fieser as "a very funny and lovable man in the lecture room" on whom the effects of a protest would be lost—"I don't imagine he would understand" (p. 101). Yet even from this comment the author can draw a salient point: that although "old fashioned scientists like him were and are as innocent as Adam and Eve," the uses to which such newly powerful weaponry can be put change the terms of a physicist's game. "Scientists will never be so innocent again" (p. 102).

From this point in *Wampeters, Foma & Granfalloons* Kurt Vonnegut's hand becomes more evident in his selection and arrangement of materials. Chronology is abandoned briefly in order to shift the position of an essay so that a commentary on student attitudes can appear in closer proximity to the physicists' address; as a further evidence of public spokesmanship, editorials now appear; and one of his few book reviews to be chosen for this volume makes a key appearance in the midst of these supposedly weightier statements. In each piece Vonnegut fashions a moral statement of sorts; what is interesting is to see how varied his occasions for such consistent statement can be.

The author's first two appearances on the Op-Ed pages of the *New York Times* are prompted by the Vietnam War and especially our country's techniques in conducting it. The first of them, coming on the heels of his address to the physics teachers, is appropriately transitioned with a reference to high school—not entirely accidental, for it would have been the first thing written after his address. Its focus is much the same as the uncollected "Times Change" introduction that was commissioned about the same time. The Indiana friend's comment about middle age being a condition of learning how one is now ruled by former classmates from high school is repeated and expanded upon; the fact that one of these classmates is now married to the administration's most hawkish war-wager, Secretary of Defense Melvin Laird, is used in delivering the main point rather than as a fortuitous aside. What amazes Kurt Vonnegut in this editorial essay is not just that his old high school friends are now conducting a murderous war, "calling for nothing less than the construction of a doomsday machine" (p. 104), but that they are doing it with the same cheerful smiles that were their trademarks back during those happy days at Shortridge High. But then he remembers how their teachers taught them to respect each other's opinions, all in a frame of cheerful open-mindedness. And he admits that were he to meet the Lairds today, he would, despite his deep-seated opposition to the war, be just as friendly and polite.

With this Vonnegut hits his turning point. In his interviews of the time, including the one with *Playboy* that concludes *Wampeters*, he was fond of fending off challenges to his 1960s radicalism by insisting that "everything I believe was taught in junior civics during the Great Depression—at School 43 in Indianapolis, with full approval of the school board" (p. 274). Now, however, he makes a crucial distinction between the conduct of students from his day and now. "Kids don't learn nice manners in high school anymore," he remarks while being thankful none of today's students would be watching how polite and deferential he would have to be to the secretary of defense. "If they met a person who was in favor of building a device which would cripple and finally kill all children everywhere, they wouldn't smile. They would bristle with hatred, which is rude" (p. 105). The same tradition of dissent that allowed pacificism to be seen as a public virtue in the 1930s becomes, in the 1960s, a vehicle by which that era's grown-up high schoolers tolerate too much evil. Surely an adjustment is necessary, which is just what Vonnegut sees the counterculture doing.

His second editorial, "Torture and Blubber," also begins with a reference to school days in the old days, specifically when the author and his childhood friends would read gory accounts of torture. Once again the comparative technique works well: today's Defense Department officials may not use actual thumbscrews on the North Vietnamese, but the term remains a common metaphor in government announcements and speeches. It is children who believe that pain is an effective way to control people, even though history—including the history of the present war—is abundant with examples of it failing. That warfaring minds continue to be deluded by such beliefs is clear from the administration's policy of "torture from the air" (p. 171), a notably devastating but fully ineffective way to break a country's resistance. It is a theme Vonnegut would repeat again almost twenty years later at the Smithsonian Air and Space Museum's lecture series on strategic bombing, when the Vietnam experience was almost as historically distant as was World War II at the time of this editorial. In each case, he could cite air force generals themselves to the effect that strategic bombing alone cannot cause a country to capitulate; yet as a technique it is never abandoned, thanks to the childish fascination with applying so much gross punishment that the adversary will be made to "blubber" (p. 169).

A key that student sentiments are of great interest to Vonnegut is his slight alteration of chronology to bring "Why They Read Hesse"[10] into closer proximity with both his "Address to the American Physical Society" and the first of his editorials, "Good Missiles, Good Manners, Good Night." Asked by *Horizon* to explain the wild popularity of this otherwise obsolescent German writer from the 1920s among the same students who were making Vonnegut himself so popular at the time, he goes back to his old anthropology thesis chalk talk about fluctuations between good and evil in simple tales to show how Hermann Hesse tells an apparently clear and true story. It is a story filled with wonder, offering hope and romance. Above all, it is a tale that expresses what Vonnegut finds to be a simple but compelling sentiment: that "I miss my Mommy and Daddy, and I always will—because they were so nice to me. Now and then, I would like to be a child again" (p. 113). The simplicity of this explanation is part of its virtue, but complicating it are the more subtle threads Vonnegut weaves through it: that Hesse was a man of Vonnegut's father's generation and was seeking refuge from the holocaust of war and from history that had destroyed the culture he loved. That readers the age of Vonnegut's children now respond to this same voice is ironic, because any refuge from World War III would have to be much farther away than Switzerland, much too far to sustain life.

Into this carefully timed selection of address, editorial, and essay Vonnegut drops one of just three book reviews (of a possible sixteen) chosen for this volume, a commentary on Dan Wakefield's *Going All the Way* titled "Oversexed in Indianapolis."[11] Much like his manner in beginning speeches, Vonnegut opens the review by breaking all the standard rules for such writing. He reveals that the author is a friend of his and that they share a common publisher. "He has boomed my books," we learn. "So I would praise his first novel, even if it were putrid" (p. 117). A few years later Wakefield would describe how Vonnegut was cozy enough with the book's launching to be in on deciding its title.[12] But beyond all these disclaimers is a core of interests consonant with the preceding selections: thoughts on life after high school, memories of growing up in Indianapolis, and a feeling for how the deepest laughter can only be summoned from deep unhappiness.

The special value of this review is how Vonnegut allows his thoughts to grow from the book's material. "*Going All the Way* is about what hell it is to be oversexed in Indianapolis," he offers, "and why so many oversexed people run away from there." There is much in the novel about "the narrowness and dimness of many lives out that way," but the locale also provides Vonnegut with an effective caution about just how successful with these materials the author has been. "I guarantee you this," he warns: "Wakefield himself, having written this book, can never go home again. From now on, he will have to watch the 500-mile Speedway race on television" (p. 118). And so in sharing this understanding of things back home the writer turns his radically disclaimed obstacles into good reviewing, sympathetic as he is to Wakefield's treatment. Even the fuss he has made about sex contributes to the review's theme, for "this wildly sexy novel isn't a sex novel. It is really about a society so drab that sex seems to the young to be the only adventure with any magic in it. When sex turns out to be merely sex, the young flee to more of the same elsewhere—and they play dangerous games with, among other things, automobiles and razor blades" (p. 119). Magic was a topic included in the Hesse essay too, as was the lack of any refuge for today's young. Incorporating those subjects here deepens Vonnegut's high school thematics and helps them carry the editorial weight asked for elsewhere.

The Wakefield review is itself shifted a bit from its strictly chronological position, bringing it into closer proximity with the address, editorial, and Hesse essay and allowing the next three major essays to stand together: "The Mysterious Madame Blavatsky,"[13] "Biafra: A People Betrayed,"[14] and "Address to Graduating Class at Bennington College, 1970."[15] These are Kurt Vonnegut's first extended commentaries written in full appreciation of his newly found prominence, products of the Spring of 1970 when *Slaughterhouse-Five* had spent a full year as one of the most popular and critically important books in America. The year

1970 would find him undertaking the most radical alterations in his life since quitting General Electric twenty years before. Celebrityhood was a large part of it, as the year saw him writing and helping stage a Broadway play and being elected by Harvard students as that university's annual Briggs-Copeland lecturer. There were personal changes as well, including an informal separation from his wife and a move from the family home in Cape Cod to bachelor quarters in New York City. There he would meet photographer Jill Krementz and begin a relationship that would lead to his second marriage—and also an involvement in the city's literary and social life, a radical change from his isolation up in West Barnstable, from which trips to New York had been undertaken in the spirit of his fictive salesman from North Crawford venturing south to the glamor of Hyannis Port. With his Blavatsky, Biafra, and Bennington essays Vonnegut finds himself enjoying two benefits of fame: better markets and more space. *McCall's* and *Vogue*, in which these pieces appeared, are still middle-class venues, but on the higher end of the scale from *Life* and the *Saturday Evening Post*; yet neither journal has the pretentiousness of, say, the *New Yorker*. In them the author could speak to a serious but unassuming suburban audience, an extension of his own community enjoyed for so many years on Cape Cod. And he could speak at twice the length he had previously enjoyed.

On the surface, the three topics seem remarkably diverse, and as such they indicate the range of the author's imagination during this initially disconcerting period of celebrityhood. Yet Kurt Vonnegut's personality is even here sufficiently distinct not only to place his imprint on the materials but, much more importantly, to structure them in an idiosyncratic manner—a manner that in its very approach does much toward clarifying each topic's otherwise opaque nature.

A curious spiritualist active a century ago whose influence extends to an active society today; a new African nation being killed in its infancy, not just metaphorically but in fact, as its children died from starvation; and the first college class to graduate from the turbulent American 1960s—what these topics have in common is their problematics. Each lies beyond conventional explanations; indeed, their challenge to conventions is what makes them topics in the first place. But as spokesman Vonnegut cannot assume his customary role of a humorously skeptical insider. "I was no longer the glib Philosopher of the Prairies it had once been so easy for me to be" (p. xvi), as he observes in the preface to *Wampeters*. Instead, he must now address his readership as one of the privileged few who has been allowed inside the great American dream of financial and (in terms of approbation) philosophical success. Yet he is still Kurt Vonnegut, and these essays measure the idiosyncracies that survive.

One might expect that a newly famous author would be a bit self-conscious in addressing a public that is suddenly evident in such great numbers. But just as Vonnegut used his anonymity as a device before, now he employs his superior position to comment on his essay as it unfolds. Laying out the basics on Madame

Blavatsky, he begins with curious details about her dress, manners, and sexual values, down to the point of friends calling her "Jack" and that she sometimes signed her letters that way. "This is *such* a pre-Freudian tale" (p. 122), the author observes, taking time and space for his comment in a one-line paragraph. Then, agreeing how she does indeed seem part and parcel with "our P. T. Barnum past" (p. 123) of oddities and delusions that color the American late nineteenth century, Vonnegut turns the tables by claiming that she was not a quack at all—that it was the public who insisted on receiving her as a spiritualist, even though she never made such a claim. Instead, a traveling vaudeville of outrageous mediums not only produces what would be the most amazing wonders, but convinces Madame Blavatsky that they are true.

To balance this carnival of what would have to be ridiculous delusions Vonnegut next introduces evidence much the contrary in effect: a long list of notables who have been members of the Theosophical Society founded to espouse Madame Blavatsky's beliefs, an impressive group ranging from Abner Doubleday and William Butler Yeats to Motilal Nehru and Piet Mondrian. Its headquarters are not, as one might expect, in California, but in that center of stolid, conservative values, Wheaton, Illinois. But to keep things off balance, he follows with a string of fully improbable anecdotes, fired off in single-line bursts. Like the author's earlier aside, each is given independently paragraphed emphasis. And to make his own presence clear, Vonnegut concludes the series with a one-line paragraph of his own: "And so on" (p. 128).

This tag line echoes the "So it goes" of *Slaughterhouse-Five* and anticipates the "And so on" in *Breakfast of Champions*. It is repeated in this essay and serves the same function as in the novels: as a way for the author to signify his presence without having to assume an attitude or make a judgment. That, in fact, becomes the key to Vonnegut's method in presenting Madame Blavatsky's case—he is nonjudgmental almost throughout, taking uncritical interest in the wonders associated with her life and not risking any qualifications that would serve to tarnish that wonder. This is just the strategy Vonnegut uses in his essay on Biafra and his address to the Bennington students, in each case a determination to avoid the intellectually appropriate but emotionally facile responses to an event that only serve to obscure the true nature of it.

"So it goes" had been the author's device for not letting the terror and grief of death obscure the ongoing problems of life. In "Biafra: A People Betrayed" the danger is sentimentalizing the suffering of all those starving children, an image burned into the world's consciousness as an image of this beleaguered nation but one that served to monopolize all attention to what was a much larger and more complicated matter. Vonnegut tries to correct this fault by undertaking his primary mode of public spokesmanship, that of witnessing the event and testifying to his experience. Along the way he sees the starving children—and most immediately, noting that whenever in their presence he finds a tiny child seeking solace by just holding onto one of his fingers. Yet he does not shed a tear until the essay's end, until he has returned home and taken full view of the situation. What withholding grief until then allows is the detailing of a marvelously complete picture, a mosaic of telling details that might otherwise be forgotten. One is the fact that the briefly lived country's national anthem was the melody of *Finlandia* by Sibelius, made even more exotic for being played on an ancient marimba, appropriately chosen "because the Finns won and kept their freedom in spite of ghastly odds" (p. 140). Another detail is that a wounded Biafran soldier would customarily greet visitors with an apology, "a form of politeness I had never encountered outside Biafra. Whenever I did something clumsy or unlucky, a Biafran was sure to say that: 'Sorry sah!' He would be genuinely sorry. He was on *my* side, and against a booby-trapped universe" (pp. 153–54).

It is a Biafran who puts the grief Americans express for the starved children into perspective and prompts Vonnegut to argue for the larger issue:

> "We are grateful," he replied, "but I wish they knew more than that. They think we're a dying nation. We aren't. We're an energetic, modern nation that is being born! We have doctors. We have hospitals. We have public-health programs. If we have so much sickness, it is because our enemies have designed every diplomatic and military move with one end in mind—that we starve to death." (pp. 143–44)

Vonnegut then proceeds to tell how much Americans do not know: that Biafrans are village, not jungle people, who perish when forced back into the bush; and that in the former Nigerian nation of which they had been a part they were the best educated and most successful, and that "They were hated for that—perfectly naturally" (p. 148). But now a true spokesman's role is not to "move readers to voluptuous tears" (p. 142), for as Vonnegut explains to the Bennington students about responding to their own country's problems, "To weep is to make less the depth of grief" (p. 162), a quote from Shakespeare that encourages Vonnegut to find better and more clarifying uses for what his eminence brings to a topic.

The privileged graduating class at Bennington College is more than a world away from the tragedy of Biafra, but Kurt Vonnegut still finds methods and sentiments from that essay appropriate to his address here. His introductory material is also familiar, the customary breaking of rules for public speakers, in this case violating the traditions of commencement addresses by disclaiming his own lack of success among the educated classes and taking a pessimistic rather than conventionally optimistic approach. His first suggestions are equally confounding: though a pacifist, he insists that the college should have an active ROTC unit established, and that the students should make room in their otherwise educated intelligences for superstition.

Each violation in fact helps advance the speaker's thesis. His message has been rejected by the establishment because it too effectively undermines its purposes—purposes such as warfare and pollution to which the Bennington students, as part of the decade's protesters, would be opposed as well. As far as pessimism, it is a far more appropriate response to the world's present problems than what would have to be a baseless optimism. And having the military on campus is important for learning about how the military works. "The only man who ever beat a tank was John Wayne," Vonnegut advises. "And he was in another tank" (p. 160). Most important is having a belief in superstition. Scientific truth alone will not save the world; at age twenty-two, as young as the graduates he now addresses, he saw scientific truth dropped on Dresden. Scientific truth also degrades humanity's position in the overall importance of things, and so one must turn to superstition in order to place it back at the universe's center.

"The arts put man at the center of the universe, whether he belongs there or not," the students are told. "Military science, on the other hand, treats man as garbage—and his children and his cities, too. Military science is probably right about the contemptibility of man in the vastness of the universe. Still—I deny that contemptibility, and I beg you to deny it, through the creation and appreciation of art" (p. 165). To emphasize how that is possible on a simple scale, the speaker breaks another rule for graduation addresses, the most important one of all: instead of urging the class to go out and change the world, he warns them that they are in fact powerless to change anything. Instead, they can improve things by refusing to believe in the "great swindle" (p. 167) of feeling responsible for righting all the world's wrongs. It is far better for them to ease off and enjoy themselves, building reserves of superstition and art so that when, much older, they do have the power to change things, they make the right choices.

Stay open to wonder, Vonnegut counsels these graduates, which is the same uncritical approach he took to Madame Blavatsky's story. Note how his approach allows the subject to work its true magic, not in the hocus-pocus of spiritualist tricks but in simple marvels of perception and appreciation:

Colonel Olcott often kept Madame Blavatsky company while she wrote at night. And he tells us that she chain-smoked as she wrote, and rolled cigarettes with one hand. Meanwhile, large balls of light crept over the furniture or jumped from point to point, "while the most beautiful liquid bell sounds now and again burst out from the air of the room."
I find that I believe this. (p. 135)

With his Bennington address Vonnegut reaches the apex of his public spokesmanship, at least as far as the organization of *Wampeters, Foma & Granfalloons* can take him. From here he continues in the public mode, but to more scattered effect, coursing through social and political topics that for cumulative power would need the more carefully planned organization of his subsequent collections, *Palm Sunday* (subtitled "An Autobiographical Collage" and arranged with the author's life in mind) and *Fates Worse than Death*, "An Autobiographical Collage of the 1980s" that takes its structural cue from events of that decade. Given the almost strictly chronological format of *Wampeters*, the most dramatic story is Kurt Vonnegut's rise to fame and dedication to public spokesmanship; once there, which happens at midbook, that spokesmanship assumes a more even level.

At his best the author continues to make salient points, interesting in themselves but more remarkable for the conclusion he draws from them. Even when working on a philosophical or theoretical level, Vonnegut feels most secure (and makes his most telling observations) when drawing on anecdotes from his personal past. In "Address to the National Institute of Arts and Letters, 1971"[16] he talks about some course work during his master's program in anthropology at the University of Chicago. There at the time his favorite professor, Dr. Robert Redfield, was developing his hypothesis of the ideal folk society, a group sufficiently small yet variously balanced so that all its individual needs could be fulfilled. From this Vonnegut draws two conclusions: not just that conditions of modern civilization make the folk society impossible, but that with its functions otherwise unperformed marriage is expected to do the job—which it can not, of course, as the author's own *Mother Night* propounds. That the principle of folk societies can still be adapted is subject matter that must wait for Vonnegut's novel *Slapstick* to be published in 1976. Covering the 1972 Republican National Convention for *Harper's*,[17] he once again frames the problem anthropologically: the two parties in contest are not so much the Republicans and the Democrats as the winners and the losers, designations that shift from party to party across the decades but in either case describe consistent behavior. For the members of the National Institute of Arts and Letters, Vonnegut's diagnosis was clear: that "we are full of chemicals which require us to belong to folk societies, or failing that, to feel lousy all the time. We are chemically engineered to live in folk societies, just as fish are chemically engineered to live in clean water—and there are not any folk societies for us anymore" (p. 178). Regarding the contenders for the presidency, he identifies Richard Nixon as a child of hardscrabble times in the Depression who, having succeeded in life, detests failure in any form and thus has only scorn for losers. "As for the Nixon versus McGovern thing," Vonnegut sees the contrast as instrumental to relative failure and success:

Everybody was sure that Nixon would win. McGovern, I gathered, though nobody said so out loud, was the butt of a rather elegant practical joke. He was a Winner who had been encouraged by other Winners to identify himself with Losers, to bury himself up to his neck in the horseshit of Populism, so to speak.

Losers hate to vote for Losers. They know what Losers are.
So Nixon would win. (p. 189)

In each case Vonnegut not only makes an original point but carries it one step further into uniqueness: beyond folk societies to the impossible burdens placed on husbands and wives to be entire societies to each other, and beyond the arrogance of winners to the way that some winners are turned into losers.

But these are just opinions, echoing the volume's subtitle and reflecting the terms by which Kurt Vonnegut titles his book. Wampeters, foma, and granfalloons are the intentionally comic sounding names he invented in *Cat's Cradle* for the doctrinal notions of Bokononism, the religion that effectively deconstructs the unstated assumptions of most other established faiths. There is, however, no organized approach in *Wampeters* as a collection—no Bokononism, in other words, just an assemblage of wampeters, foma, and granfalloons captured as they happen. That an organizing principle as evident as religion's would benefit Kurt Vonnegut's public spokesmanship emerges in his next decade's activities, where many of his speeches would be delivered from church pulpits and called sermons, and where his next collection would reflect this orientation in its title, *Palm Sunday*.

Chapter Five

PALM SUNDAY

If *Wampeters, Foma & Granfalloons* follows the progress of public spokesmanship in the making, *Palm Sunday*[1] displays the presentational talents of a
spokesmanship fully formed. Nearly half the materials of the earlier book were
written in virtual anonymity, certainly with no thought of their ultimate collection in book form. "I keep no records of my work," Kurt Vonnegut had noted in
that volume's preface, "and had been delighted to forget a lot of it" (p. xviii);
retrieved by other hands, those essays, addresses, and reviews were arranged by
the expedience of chronology and published in the same wave as other Vonnegut
miscellanies—a play, a television special, a book of critical essays on the author
and his works—by Seymour Lawrence in the wake of *Slaughterhouse-Five*'s
great popular success. The contents of *Palm Sunday*, however, fall entirely within
the period of their author's greatest fame and most consistent production as a
writer. Therefore Vonnegut takes special care in fashioning the volume, adding
an extra step to bring it in line with his more considered books:

> It began with my wish to collect in one volume most of the reviews and
> speeches and essays I had written since the publication of a similar collec-
> tion, *Wampeters, Foma & Granfalloons*, in 1974. But as I arranged those
> fragments in this order and then that one, I saw that they formed a sort of
> autobiography, especially if I felt free to include some pieces not written
> by me. To give life to such a golem, however, I would have to write much
> new connective tissue. This I have done. (p. xvii)

That Vonnegut is serious about producing not just a random collection but a
"collage," as he puts it in the volume's subtitle, is evident from the way he starts
his preface. One recalls his manner in opening his speeches and prefacing his
collection of short stories, that of systematically breaking every rule involved as
a way of not just getting attention but redirecting it from an audience's presuppo-
sitions to his more exceptional designs. In *Palm Sunday*'s opening comments
Vonnegut forsakes the customary authorial humility to claim that "This is a very
great book by an American genius" involving years of hard work and great per-

sonal suffering. "I have walked through every hotel lobby in New York," he rues, "thinking about this book and weeping, and driving my fist into the guts of grandfather clocks" (p. xv). All this effort, he advises, has been in pursuit of a new literary form—a form that turns out to be the autobiographical collage described two pages later. In truth, collage demands just such effort, for two unlikes must be forced together in order to form a radical yet integral new, third entity—yet one that retains the clear identities of the composite two. The work of successful collagists such as Max Ernst and Joseph Cornell speaks for an energetically physical artistic manner as images are wrestled from their customary context and hauled bodily into another where they meet to form a strikingly new entity.

Palm Sunday's collage is one built on several levels: of mixing public issues with personal autobiography, nonfictive writing with fictive visions, and one's own material with contributions by others. The author's own experience is formed by many things, not just national events but also country and western tunes, all of it equally quotable in this collage form. As in *Wampeters*, there's an interview; but appropriately to his new method here, Vonnegut interviews himself, a technique he had used as the centerpiece of his 1977 speech at the University of Northern Iowa. Throughout this new volume the author's hand is evident everywhere, not just in the individual selections but with how they are arranged, introduced, and in several cases interpolated; in sum, it reflects the more broadly reaching autobiographical approach he was taking to his fiction in the aftermath of *Slaughterhouse-Five*.

With almost a full decade's material to draw on, Kurt Vonnegut can start his book just about anywhere he pleases. Thus it is significant that he draws on an editorial for the *New York Times*, a speech to the American Civil Liberties Union at Sands Point, Long Island, and personal letters to individuals in North Dakota and the Soviet Union, all of it introduced, knit together, and concluded with new commentary directed to *Palm Sunday*'s readers.

The reprinted materials concern censorship, a problem that dogged *Slaughterhouse-Five* not for the announced reasons of obscenity but because of its satirically effective rewriting of Christian liturgy, including the crucifixion story. Vonnegut's concern, however, is larger than the specific issue of having one of his books banned. Instead, as he argues in the original pieces and explains in the new writing that puts them together, it is a matter of one very real individual, himself, having his rights of expression abrogated by a process in which abstraction, error, and ignorance seem to reign. That is why he for the most part avoids the customary arguments against censorship, that peoples' rights as a class are being infringed when their reading materials are prohibitively screened in advance of their own decisions. Arguing in such a manner would not be characteristic of Kurt Vonnegut's strengths as a public spokesman. Rather, his success has always come in being able to translate general issues into particulars—personal particulars, in fact, drawn from his own experience and presented anecdotally in a way that makes his listeners feel they are sharing some life-tested wisdom.

That is why he begins the overall seventeen-page essay with a story not about censorship but about his own generation of novelists, a generation he feels may be the last to be recognized as such—not because of inhibitions of censorship but thanks to changes in the industry that produces novels. As a young writer undertaking his first efforts in the late 1940s and early 1950, his "was an era of romantic anarchy in publishing which gave us money and mentors, willy-nilly, when we were young—while we learned our craft" (p. 1). Now, however, accountants and M.B.A.s run the trade, and their methods prohibit the enfranchising of entire generations of new writers. "Novelists will come one by one from now on," Vonnegut believes, "not in seeming families, and will perhaps write only one or two novels, and let it go at that. Many will have inherited or married money" (p. 2).

Having not just defined his generation but identified it as somewhat of an economically endangered species, Vonnegut then tells his readership what its most remarkable contribution was: "that we were allowed to say absolutely anything without fear of punishment." Future Americans may marvel, as foreigners do now, "that a nation would want to enforce a law which sounds more like a dream": the First Amendment to the Constitution, which he quotes in full (p. 3). Because the law is impossibly ideal, Vonnegut suspects it may be repealed, and he has already learned that on lower judicial levels it is not enforced. This brings him to the topic of censorship, but only after he has established his own vulnerability on much higher grounds. The result is that he need not defend his work at the point of censorship, but only cite censorship as a threat to something already argued for and accepted as uniquely valuable and endangered quite on its own terms.

Yet even his arguments with the censors are emphatically personal. "I am writing this letter," he tells the chairperson of the Drake, North Dakota, school board, "to let you know how real I am" (p. 5). Having protested here and again on the editorial pages of the *New York Times*, Vonnegut suggests dealing individually with each banning member, advising them to "Have somebody read the First Amendment to the United States Constitution to you, you God damned fool!" (p. 9). Even his speech to the ACLU on Long Island, where another district had banned his book, is framed with individuality in mind; his argument there is that people do wrong when they cite divine or natural law as an endorsement of what are in fact just their personal beliefs. This orientation persists through his letter to Felix Kuznetsov, an officially sponsored Russian writer to whom Vonnegut protested the censorship of some forbidden countrymen. Kuznetsov replies with the implication that Kurt Vonnegut is speaking as a representative of "American authors" (p. 14); no he isn't, Vonnegut insists, reminding his Russian friend that the issue itself is individuality of expression. As far as spokesmanship,

Vonnegut is consistently, on all fronts, speaking for his unique personhood as a writer. It is a theme he will return to when asked to counsel young writers on how to express themselves with style, and in the portrait he draws of himself as a writer for a self-interview with the *Paris Review*. If the separate essays and reviews collected in *Wampeters, Foma & Granfalloons* employed idiosyncracy as a technique, in *Palm Sunday* it is developed and exploited as a theme.

Yet for effective argumentation, idiosyncracies must have a pattern and purpose, drawn as they are from an individual personality and not a random assemblage of unrelated traits. That the author is intrigued by his own family background is evident from his inclusion of "An Account of the Ancestry of Kurt Vonnegut, Jr." as not just the longest excerpt from another's work but the largest section by far in *Palm Sunday*. The work of his relative John G. Rauch, it describes in fine detail not just the historical figures but also the personalities who in emigrating from Germany to Indianapolis formed Kurt Vonnegut's immediate ancestry. Following the book's initial section on the sacred freedom of writing and preceding further examples of more candidly autobiographical materials, this part of *Palm Sunday*'s collage serves not only as a report but as a text on which Vonnegut can comment as it proceeds. He interrupts its historical narrative a dozen times, highlighting certain features and adding his own family lore to the saga. The piece itself is framed by Vonnegut's comments and is heavily edited from the original version as published in 1971.[2] Throughout the pages of this section of *Palm Sunday* Kurt Vonnegut's hand is evident in foregrounding the elements he believes have contributed to his own stock of idiosyncracies as a writer.

Given the size and importance of his family in Indianapolis, their wealth and their attention paid to offspring (a communal support system including traditional family schools and a thriving family business with summer jobs for all), it is not surprising that Kurt would draw on their influence. And what a rich and varied influence it was. German culture ruled it for three generations, but for Kurt's era had to be almost abolished because of animosities bred by the virulent anti-Germanism of World War I. Though originally Catholic, the family cultivated a style of Free Thought leading to a discreet agnosticism by Kurt's day. Artistically gifted, earlier family members gravitated toward European educations and cultural sojourns, easily financed by fortunes earned at home; but by the century's turn, hometown business values discouraged any prolonged involvement in the modern arts, particularly when that included living in New York City. Very wealthy thanks to this first generation's hard work, members of the second generation would skim its profits while the third generation survived by depleting its capital; thanks to the coup de grace of the Great Depression, the fourth generation—Kurt's—found itself back to shirtsleeves and being cautioned that culture and the arts were poor hopes indeed. This prompted Kurt's education in the sciences, something he always explains as making him a writer of new works rather than an admiring reflector of the classics on which he would otherwise have been educated. As far as the vernacular American style and middle-class values that form the basis of Kurt Vonnegut's style of expression, those are accidents of his need for public (and not private) schooling in the 1930s and represent, at least in terms of intention, a failure of his forebearers' plans. With both culture and riches erased in one clean sweep, the field is clear for Vonnegut's work, which often seems as purely American and totally postmodern as can be.

Yet there are traces of influence in the family, and the author's commentary on this genealogical manuscript says much about the values that help form his platform as a public spokesperson. The past itself is less pertinent than one's interaction with it, and the collage form of this "Roots" chapter underscores just that, first as John Rauch (a distant relative by marriage) selects from his vast trove of genealogical lore to create a family history highlighting Kurt's antecedents, and then as Kurt himself interpolates his own comments on what has been provided.

The anti-Germanism of World War I is the initial feature singled out for comment and something Vonnegut sees as a complex rather than simple phenomenon. His was not just the case of having his ancestors' culture challenged. Instead, he reprints sections of the commentary that highlight the tremendous wealth of German culture brought over by Kurt's great-grandparents and the impact and continuing influence they had as cultural and social leaders in Indianapolis. Then, in the propaganda campaign rallied from the top by President Woodrow Wilson, that entire culture was discredited, leaving the Vonnegut family denuded of its aesthetic past. That left business, each branch of which fell to historical circumstance, including the brewery (to Prohibition), architecture (the Depression), and hardware (postwar discounting).

Yet for a slate supposedly swept clean, family history leaves plenty for Vonnegut to treasure beyond a lost culture and riches, each of which would have proven foreign to his American egalitarianism as it developed. There is the cultivated eccentricity of his great-grandfather Clemens Vonnegut, an advocate of Free Thought; the fairy tale marriage of his parents in a style of splendor in the waning days of Edwardian indulgence, an image much more effective in memory than in reality; and the sad story of his grandfather Bernard, whose artistic career in New York City was aborted by demands that he return to Indianapolis and take his place in the ongoing local family history. "He should have moved into the very house I live in now," Vonnegut remarks. "This house was standing back then" (p. 43), a structure built on speculation by a German-American home builder. Saying so is an effective way for the author to keep in close proximity to this family history, much of which now takes shape as an imaginative journey—just as it is so fabulous to recall (and difficult to grasp) that among his mother's other suitors in those grand Edwardian days of European residencies were the heir to the Royal Doulton Works and a lieutenant in one of the kaiser's most glamorous regiments, "a dashing figure in his colorful dress uniform with shako and 'Merry Widow' accoutrements" (p. 49).

Equal in detail to these more distant stories is the tale of Kurt Vonnegut Sr.'s demise. For the author's mother, loss was a matter of fortune and status. But for Kurt's father, decline took shape more mortally as the disappointments of a declining profession and advancing age took their toll on the man's spirit. Elsewhere there is abundant evidence of how this decline affected the writer-son, who was twice blocked by emotional confrontations with his father's image: in 1957 and 1958, when for most of a year he was unable to write following Kurt Sr.'s death; and in 1971 and 1972, when *Breakfast of Champions* was stalled just short of its ending, an ending Vonnegut would satisfactorily write only once he recast his character Kilgore Trout in the person of his father and then released him from imaginative servitude. The decline of Kurt's father was a lesson in mortality for his son, one that shows directly in the writing and figures as the point to which John Rauch's family history impends.

In concluding this collage section of *Palm Sunday*, Vonnegut emphasizes that his relative's story stops with Kurt Sr.; words from Goethe are all that refer to the son, who will be allowed to "tell his own story" (p. 60). "And my story seems to be this to me," Kurt Vonnegut begins in the transition that announces his volume's third part, "When I Lost My Innocence": "I left Indianapolis, where my ancestors had prepared so many comforts and privileges for me, because those comforts and privileges were finally based on money, and the money was gone" (p. 61). This makes the author's tale an expression, inversion, and then redemption of the American Dream—gaining a fortune, losing it, and then achieving wealth, respectability, and influence all over again from scratch. Only Kurt's progress is in distinction to his parents and those before them. Unlike his older siblings, he is given a public rather than private education; unlike his father and grandparents, he is denied training in the arts and urged to study science instead; yet unlike his grandfather Bernard, he leaves Indianapolis for the East Coast and a career in the arts and stays there, finding himself at age sixty living in a house his grandfather might well have moved to instead of forsaking his genius for a familial role back home. Kurt Vonnegut's history, genealogical ties and all, is therefore emblematic, a pilgrim's progress toward artistic expression through four generations of American history struggling with just such issues.

Telling his own story, the story that begins with his leaving home, comprises five pieces filling three collage segments of *Palm Sunday*. Following most immediately from the family history are a talk given at his alma mater, Cornell University; an essay on how not so much Dresden as Hiroshima cost him his innocence at age twenty-two; and some brief words spoken at an antinuclear rally during the height of his fame in 1979. At Cornell, Vonnegut addresses the current staff of the student paper he helped edit during his own college days, the Cornell *Daily*

Sun. Delighted to be back, Vonnegut toys with the images of youth to create a melange of adolescence and barely beckoning maturity:

When I was a freshman here, I didn't know or care where the life of Ginger Rogers ended and the life of General Douglas MacArthur began. The senior senator from California was Mickey Mouse, who would serve with great distinction as a bombardier in the Pacific during the Second World War. Commander Mouse dropped a bomb right down the smokestack of a Japanese battleship. The captain of the battleship was Charlie Chan. Boy, was he mad. (p. 64)

The author was indeed young when he was managing editor of the *Sun*; he recalls once spelling Ethel Barrymore's name E-T-H-Y-L—in a headline, no less. Nor as a Cornellian did he know that school's famous writers, Vladimir Nabokov and Thomas Pynchon (well after his time, anyway). Who did he know? He knew Miller Harris, his editor in chief that freshman year, who has since gone on to be president of Eagle Shirtmakers, a different style of power indeed. This leads Vonnegut to a self-appraisal of his happiness and also his sense of importance during those years. Though widely professed as an enemy of loneliness, his happiest moments at Cornell were when he was alone, walking up the hill after having put to bed that morning's edition of the paper:

All the other university people, teachers and students alike, were asleep. They had been playing games all day long with what was known about real life. They had been repeating famous arguments and experiments, and asking one another the sorts of hard questions real life would be asking by and by.

We on the *Sun* were already in the midst of real life. By God, if we weren't! We had just designed and written and caused to be manufactured yet another morning newspaper for a highly intelligent American community of respectable size—yes, and not during the Harding administration, either, but during 1940, '41, and '42, with the Great Depression ending, and with World War Two well begun. (pp. 66–67)

Note how the cartoonish references to immaturity now yield to pride in coming to terms with those same issues of the day, and how the "By God!" prepares the ground for the author's otherwise sentimental conclusion to this episode. "I am an agnostic as some of you may have gleaned from my writings," he reminds his listeners. "But I have to tell you that, as I trudged up the hill so late at night and all alone, I knew that God Almighty approved of me" (p. 67).

In this instance innocence is not so much lost as tempered by the experience of a maturing job. Vonnegut's loss of innocence itself is matter for a Swedish newspaper that had polled him on the subject. Otherwise just the most occasional piece of writing that might drop from the typewriter of a famous and busy author, his two-page response assumes importance from its new role in *Palm Sunday*'s autobiographical collage. In describing how innocence could be maintained, he looks back to his book's section of family history to recall how one branch owned the largest hardware store in Indianapolis, where he worked many a summer job in the happy surroundings of simple tools and supplies. "When I feel most lost in this world," he confides, "I comfort myself by visiting a hardware store. I meditate there" (p. 69). This is why, as he shows in a roundabout but effective manner, the atomic detonation at Hiroshima so disturbed him. The technology that created the Dresden firestorm was understandable, manageable, and therefore capable of being redirected to humankind's benefit. "There was nothing in the bombs or the airplanes, after all, which could not, essentially, be bought at a small hardware store" (p. 69). But the technology of Hiroshima was beyond such common and simple understanding; it demanded trust, and that trust was rewarded with a demonstration of how diseased the human mind can be. This brings Vonnegut to his antinuclear rally topic, of how publicity for such research and its applications has been a matter of deception and outright lies.

Speaking truthfully is, for Kurt Vonnegut, often a matter of talking plainly. It is the style he pursues for the student journalists at Cornell, for the readers of his comments in Sweden, and for the listeners assembled at the Washington, D.C., rally. It is at this point in *Palm Sunday*'s development that he dedicates an entire section to the framing and presentation of a short essay, actually copy for an advertisement, that he did for the International Paper Company titled "How to Write with Style." His point in the ad itself was that "I myself find that I trust my own writing most, and others seem to trust it most, too, when I sound like a person from Indianapolis, which is what I am" (p. 79). But there is also a recapitulation of *Palm Sunday*'s own thematics, as a comment on the First Amendment brings back into focus the concerns of the volume's initial section. It is the free choice of subject matter, Vonnegut believes, and not ornate self-indulgence that is the key to good personal style, and under the Constitution that right is protected.

Framing the essay are more autobiographical comments—not ones that would aid the student audience of "How to Write with Style," but helpful to readers who have shared the author's ideas as collaged together throughout this larger volume. The section's focus is education, and the light it casts is by no means winsome. Titled "Triage," it speaks of the system of attrition that separates off the lower third of a class as unpromising and therefore undeserving of the instructor's careful attention. This was where Kurt Vonnegut found himself categorized as a graduate student in anthropology at the University of Chicago, assigned to a dead-end adviser who would himself commit suicide before being published. He admits to using the same technique in apportioning attention to his own classes at Iowa, Harvard, and the City University of New York. That the term originates in medical response to trauma cases, where those without hope of surviving must be neglected in favor of working on cases who can be saved, only makes the imagery more grisly, especially when Vonnegut has to admit that "One third of every class was corpses as far as I was concerned" (p. 76) and that being triaged out at Chicago was infinitely better than being handled so by a combat hospital. His distinction, however, is that in his "How to Write with Style" essay he is addressing not the higher third, who are born to be brilliant writers anyway, but the middle group who may well benefit from his advice. As readers of *Palm Sunday* will know, it is the way Kurt Vonnegut himself became a successful writer.

Such is the story told in the book's next section, a long one reprinting the author's "Self-Interview" from the Spring 1977 (No. 69) issue of *Paris Review*. For this the most distinguished series of literary interviews ever undertaken (and restricted to a conservative judgment of the modern and contemporary period's leading figures, commencing with the likes of E. M. Forster, Graham Greene, William Faulkner, and Ernest Hemingway) Vonnegut uses his collagist's method to draw the best materials from four unsuccessful attempts and arrange them as an interview with himself. First presented months before at the University of Northern Iowa, it is a clearly dramatic affair, with the "interviewer" not just asking questions but being drawn into a running dialogue with the answers, some of which Vonnegut presented in a comically altered voice. Therefore, as opposed to the conventions of literary interviews—conventions that are discredited within the author's prefatory remarks—this rendition of an artist commenting on himself and his craft is arranged as a piece of public spokesmanship. Vonnegut does not comment to an interviewer but testifies to an audience his "self-interviewing" implies. Again like a speaker, he works that audience with devices both aesthetic and vaudevillian, much in the manner of his actual public speaking. And like the best of his essays, the piece accomplishes the goal of making its author seem believable, its audience feel comforted, and its readership in general persuaded that in their own wisdom a formerly vexing problem is now something not so threatening after all.

The self-interview begins, like other more formal interviews, with an inquiry about the author's experience in World War II. But this time the effect of its mention is comic, with Vonnegut insisting in great solemnity that not only is he a veteran but one who expects a full military funeral when he dies—bugler, firing squad, and all. Which is surprising, because nowhere else has he ever addressed the issue of his soldiery in this way. Why, he asks himself. Because "It will be a way of achieving what I've always wanted more than anything—something I could have had, if only I'd managed to get myself killed in the war." This prompts an even more curious query, to which he replies, "The unqualified approval of my community" (p. 84).

Thus what turns out to be the story of Dresden and the root motivation for

Kurt Vonnegut's public spokesmanship is introduced on a comic level, one sustained by the imagery of his military narrative. How was he trained? On the 240-millimeter howitzer, a weapon so huge it not only had to be assembled for each use but practically invented; its breech-block was equally monstrous, "like the door on the vault of a savings and loan association in Peru, Indiana, say." Its explosives, tossed in bags, were equally improbable—"They were damp dog biscuits, I think." The ignition process was so slow and cumbersome that it seemed like cooking a turkey—"In utter safety, I think, we could have opened the breechblock from time to time, and basted the shell" (p. 85). As for muzzle velocity, the projectile would eventually come floating out "like the Goodyear blimp. If we had a stepladder, we could have painted 'Fuck Hitler' on the shell as it left the gun" (p. 86).

Thus prepared, the reader is not surprised that Vonnegut's own combat experience was as comically unfortuitous as Billy Pilgrim's in *Slaughterhouse-Five*. Even as the narrative proceeds along more familiar lines, comic images intrude to keep the mood self-effacingly light, such as describing what Vonnegut elsewhere calls "corpse-mining" as "a terribly elaborate Easter Egg Hunt" (p. 90) for the bodies of 130,000 Dresdeners who had been asphyxiated in the rubble of their shelters underground. But there is other "hokum" with more serious consequences, much of it related to burdens of guilt: "The hokum about the Norden bombsight," for example, fed to American newsreel audiences as a weapon so precise and of such strategic importance that it had to be guarded by M.P.s with drawn weapons at all times—"and hell, all they were doing was just flying over cities, hundreds of airplanes, and dropping everything" (p. 91). As for the Dresden raid itself, Vonnegut can counter the hokum of how much good all its destruction did. It did not shorten the war by half a second, did not save one Russian or American life, and saved no one from a concentration camp. "Only one person benefitted," and that was Kurt Vonnegut himself—"I got three dollars for each person killed. Imagine that" (p. 94).

These grisly profits from *Slaughterhouse-Five* bring the self-interview to literary matters, including professional and personal influences. Even here the turn of Vonnegut's remarks is self-deprecating, including how his mother failed as a short story writer because she lacked the necessary vulgarity, something her son was loaded with and so found it easy to market materials to *Collier's* and the *Saturday Evening Post*. Whenever the topic threatens to get technical, he returns to the comic past for a reference, even to his fate as a captured soldier. Did the bad reviews of *Slapstick* hurt? "I never felt worse in my life," Vonnegut confides; "I felt as though I were sleeping standing up in a boxcar in Germany again" (p. 104). As for collegiality in the writing world, he reminds himself that he has spent more time (and enjoying it) talking with scientists than with writers—and with plumbers, carpenters, and automobile mechanics too, all of whom rate well ahead of literary figures in terms of natural congeniality. And in affinity as well, for Vonnegut emphasizes that his own style of narrative is less of a precious art than an applied trade: "Carpenters build houses. Storytellers use a reader's leisure time in such a way that the reader will not feel that his time has been wasted. Mechanics fix automobiles" (p. 111).

The literary nature of his self-interview's conclusion leads naturally to a section of *Palm Sunday* devoted to literary matters. But in each case the material is both framed and presented in terms of friendship, the more unprofessional the better. Vonnegut's review of Joseph Heller's *Something Happened* is shaped in personal terms, reflecting on the two authors' generation of war veterans; following it is a discussion of how the happenstance of a summer rental led to their friendship just when the review was being written (Heller was anxious over the matter, and so Vonnegut dropped hints that the *Times* had assigned it to Robert Penn Warren, probably the next on their alphabetical list). Two addresses—one at a birthday party, another at a funeral—attest to writers whose obvious influence on Kurt Vonnegut as a very young man takes second place to the friendship he developed with them in later years, complete with charmingly personal notes—such as how Irwin Shaw reminds the author of central casting's image of a New York City cab driver, and of how James T. Farrell showed that it was "perfectly all right, perhaps even useful and beautiful, to say what life really looked like, what was really said and felt and done—what really went on. Until I read him, I wished only to be well received in polite company" (p. 143). *Palm Sunday*'s interpolated comments do all they can to demystify friendship, particularly literary friendships at the top—following a short essay on William F. Buckley Jr., Vonnegut remarks that theirs is a "New York friendship" (p. 121), meaning they have met thrice for a grand total of sixty seconds. There follows a five-page list of other such friends, drawn from the inventory of his photographer-wife Jill Krementz.

The literary friendships Kurt Vonnegut treasures are those that have enriched his life anecdotally—not because they provide interesting chatter, but because something in their nature has generated a story that memorializes a certain truth or telling moment in the author's own life. One of the warmest (and funniest) such remarks comes as an interpolation between the Buckley and Heller reviews, and concerns Vonnegut's days at the University of Iowa Writers' Workshop. It features two colleagues, Nelson Algren and José Donoso, but is motivated less by their eminence than by their common presence as neophytes at the university, uninitiated newcomers who do not yet know that visiting writers need not attend the humdrum meetings of the English department. But attend the meeting they do, which, as the first one, has involved introductions:

> So Algren and Donoso and I were going down a staircase afterward. Algren had come late, and so had sat separate from Donoso and me. He and Donoso had never met before, so I introduced them on the staircase,

explaining to Algren that Donoso was from Chile, but a graduate of Princeton University.

Algren shook Donoso's hand, but said nothing to him until we reached the bottom. He at last thought of something to say to a Chilean novelist: "It must be nice," he said, "to come from a country that long and narrow." (p. 127)

Here is Kurt Vonnegut dealing with literary friendship in a way that reflects his public speaking manner: telling a story because it fleshes out a point he wants to make, a point that his listeners will understand if it is freed from abstraction and formed instead in substance of personal testimony. Positioned as it is as interpolated material in the "literary friends" section of *Palm Sunday*, it indicates that such friendships are only going to mean something if they have occurred as part of one of the author's own passages in life—such as learning from James T. Farrell that polite manners need not circumscribe one's rendition of reality, and from Irwin Shaw that sometimes the greatest eloquence can be prompted from an otherwise silent cab driver.

The method carries over into "Playmates," a complementary section of *Palm Sunday* given over to Vonnegut's old friends. Asked to speak at the funeral of an old General Electric coworker's wife, he comes across with great sentiment—much more, in fact, than one would expect from a writer so darkly comic elsewhere. But he has a soft spot for persons from those days; "it may have genetic roots of some sort," he confides when introducing the piece, a matter of having "been born with some sort of clock in me which required me to love those working alongside me so much at that time. We were just getting our footing as adult citizens" (p. 148), and he notes that others have shared this idea. In Vonnegut's own work its most common manifestation is an allegiance to old war buddies, something that becomes part of his fiction when at the start of *Slaughterhouse-Five* he travels to Philadelphia for a visit with his colleague from the Battle of the Bulge and Dresden, Bernard O'Hare; and recall how his talk at the Smithsonian on strategic bombing was recast in impromptu fashion by the unanticipated presence of another fellow prisoner-of-war, Tom Jones. In both interviews and literary commentaries Vonnegut will forever maintain solidarity with his associates at Iowa City: Algren, Donoso, and especially Richard Yates, who became a friend for life and in rough periods found refuge on the author's couch. The war, General Electric, and the Writers' Workshop found Kurt Vonnegut in similar circumstances, that of being a newcomer to strange surroundings; the fact that others were there to share the experience was a comfort then and continues as a repository of values today, to the extent that he collages in the full text of a country-western song, "The Class of '57," as an anthem to such sentiments.

Influences themselves are something Vonnegut habitually shrugs off, deflecting such questions by giving what he feels are inappropriate answers: not eminent writers but radio comedians, slapstick film stars, and even the dogs he played with as a child. But one influence merits special treatment in *Palm Sunday*, in a section bracketed by the "Playmates" segment and another, "Funnier on Paper Than Most People," consisting of his own speech on how jokes work. The subject is Mark Twain, a writer whose own popularity almost one hundred years before took the same shape as Vonnegut's, including the substance and methods of great public spokesmanship and entertainment. "Mark Twain" is delivered in Hartford to celebrate the one-hundredth anniversary of Twain's lavish Connecticut home—an invitation prompted, Vonnegut believes, because he is "simultaneously a humorist and a serious novelist" (p. 166).

That humor is essential to Twain's art becomes evident from the structure of his best-known statements. They are, according to Vonnegut, constructed like jokes, "with a disarmingly pedestrian beginning and an unexpectedly provoking conclusion" (p. 167), a procedure also followed in the Christian statements of the Beatitudes. It is ironic, of course, to ally Twainian humor with the sentiments of Christianity, but that is the novelty of Vonnegut's approach. "Mark Twain is saying what Christ says in so many ways," the speaker insists: "that he could not help loving anyone in the midst of life" (p. 167). It recalls Vonnegut's understanding of the radio comedians Bob and Ray, who instead of showing characters tormented by bad luck and evil portray them as threatening "to wreck themselves and their surroundings with their own stupidity." Such a call is not judgmental but indicative of "a refreshing and beautiful innocence." Man is not evil, these comedians say. "He is simply too hilariously stupid to survive" (p. 142). This same comic sympathy informs Twain's humor and Vonnegut's as well, especially the joke he sees Twain and other agnostics like himself playing on the Almighty: "Live so that you can say to God on Judgment Day, 'I was a very good person, even though I did not believe in you'" (p. 168).

To demonstrate his own affinity with both Twain and Twain's methods, Vonnegut reprints a speech given a year earlier, this time to the graduating class at Fredonia College. Its subject is how humor functions, and the address is prefaced by two jokes improvised at the harmless expense of the class spokesperson and college president preceding him. The formal opening consists of a string of Kin Hubbard jokes, the last of them pointed at the humor implicit in a graduation ceremony—how after attending one the old Indiana humorist said he thought it might be better if all the really important stuff was spread out over four years rather than being saved up for the very end. Therefore Vonnegut limits his advice to simple rubrics, such as suggesting joke telling as a good way to start speeches and then explaining how a joke works. As with his analysis of Mark Twain's humor, it is a question of perceiving the two-part nature of such devices. Taking as his example the simplest joke, which asks a question and then gives a comic answer, he runs his audience through one, tells a story of its inception (which is itself hilarious), and then deconstructs the process as it has just worked.

The joke itself is absurdly simple. Does the audience know why cream costs so much more than milk? As prompted by the speaker, his audience answers No. "It is because," he tells them, "the cows hate to squat on those little bottles" (p. 176). Then the story about it follows:

> That is the best joke I know. One time when I worked for the General Electric Company over in Schenectady, I had to write speeches for company officers. I put that joke about the cows and the little bottles in a speech for a vice-president. He was reading along, and he had never heard the joke before. He couldn't stop laughing, and he had to be led away from the podium with a nosebleed. I was fired the next day. (p. 176)

This seeming digression is an important part of both Vonnegut's platform manner and method of structuring an essay. For one thing, it makes fun of the joke, which by itself is not really that funny. But by holding it before the audience's attention for so much longer, and especially for making it part of a genuinely funny story, it takes on added importance. And the humor of it all is self-effacing, because the punch line is that Vonnegut himself is fired—fired for being too effective at his job.

Thus apprenticed to the making of humor, Vonnegut's listeners are now ready for their initiation into the secret of how such jokes work. The first part of the joke just told, and of any others cited in shorthand fashion, consists of a question, a challenge to think. "We are such earnest animals," the author explains. "When I asked you about cream, you could not help yourselves. You really tried to think of a sensible answer. Why does a chicken cross a road? Why does a fireman wear red suspenders? Why did they bury George Washington on the side of a hill?" (p. 176). The joke's second part announces that thinking is really not necessary, not expected. This is a relief, and the listener laughs for joy.

Though Vonnegut's speech promises no more jokes, it does offer comforting relief: the six-seasons theory that he continued to use throughout the next decade, advice on what older people expect from those younger, and how the pains of maturation are in fact the distress at living in a culture that lacks sufficient puberty ceremonies (which does prompt one more joke, that if receiving a driver's license is indeed a puberty ceremony, then ours is the first culture to have a corresponding rite for the revocation of puberty).

Subsequent speeches in *Palm Sunday* will be rich with content, especially those grouped within the section titled "Religion." But before presenting that material Vonnegut pauses for something that happens only one other place in his book: he includes an entire subdivision, "Embarrassment," that reprints nothing at all. Instead, he spends seven pages speaking firsthand to the reader, offering an important element in his autobiographical collage for which no previous speech, essay, or introduction exists—only a comment from *Indianapolis Magazine* that makes an oblique but apparently hurtful comment on how some hometown family members are put off by the language in Vonnegut's novels. As will happen later in *Palm Sunday*, when the author reprints nothing of his own but rather a Statler Brothers song as an occasion for reflecting on its topic, Vonnegut uses the magazine quote as a way of discussing his own reaction and preparing his readership for moments in subsequent commentaries when the issue of good manners is raised.

Here the focus is less on the bad manners of vulgar language, which *Indianapolis Magazine* has raised, than the even more locally unspeakable action of divorce. It allows Vonnegut to suggest some reasons for his marriage's breakup, reasons that become issues in the next speech he reprints, albeit in a distinct section and introduced with something different in mind. *Palm Sunday*'s method is not discourse but rather collage; the author will be making his points not simply by direct commentary but by letting them stand in juxtaposition to reflect on one another, a mutual reflection that most pointedly allows them to remain themselves. "The shock of having our children no longer need us happened somewhere in there," he observes. "We were both going to have to find other sorts of seemingly important work to do and other compelling reasons for working and worrying so" (p. 189). Later on, the fragility of just such marriages is ascribed to the lack of extended families as structures that would otherwise help bear the weight and supply the needs of a husband and wife. Now, however, the focus remains on how Vonnegut's divorce causes a fissure in his own extended family, or what is left of it, back home in Indianapolis.

"Toward the end of our marriage," Vonnegut begins his next section, the one titled "Religion," "it was mainly religion in a broad sense that Jane and I fought about" (p. 192). It is why, he explains, he has chosen an epigraph from his great-grandfather Clemens Vonnegut's booklet on Free Thought to begin this autobiographical collage: *Whoever entertains liberal views and chooses a consort that is captured by superstition risks his liberty and his happiness.* Linking his spouse to "superstitious" aspects of religion, to needs for alliance with the supernatural for strength and understanding, is an important tactic in framing his speeches that follow, for in them Vonnegut will propose that it is a new religion that is needed to keep marriages happy and people strong. Addressing the graduates at Hobart and William Smith Colleges, he notes that "Our most dismaying failure is in the use of our knowledge of what human beings need in the way of bodily and spiritual nourishment. And I suspect that some of the guesses made by our ancestors are partly responsible for the starved bodies and spirits we see everywhere" (p. 197). Note the collagist at work: readers of *Palm Sunday* are being told this in the context of learning about the author's divorce and of how he attributes it in part to his wife's traditional view of religion and in part to the unfair burdens their marriage had to bear. Thus what follows in terms of a new religion sharing these burdens carries greater impact and serves not just as opinion but as autobiography, personal statement in the most emphatic sense of the term.

By suggesting an effective religion, Vonnegut speaks much as he does in *Cat's Cradle*, where Bokononism was proposed as an ideal scheme for employing folks full-time as actors in a play they could understand, transforming life from something chaotic into a work of art. "An effective religion allows people to imagine from moment to moment what is going on and how they should behave" (p. 199). Drawing on what he learned when training as an anthropologist, he gives his analysis of current malaise: that the communal and familial structures needed to support people are no longer there—none except marriage, which is forced to bear the full burden alone. In terms of his own vision, it is a matter of needed diversity:

> Let's talk about incompatibility between parents and children, which happens often merely because of genetic rotten luck. In a nuclear family, children and parents can be locked in hellish close combat for twenty-one years and more. In an extended family, a child has scores of other homes to go in search of love and understanding. He need not stay home and torture his parents, and he need not starve for love.
>
> In an extended family, anybody can bug out of his own house for months, and still be among relatives. Nobody has to go on a hopeless quest for friendly strangers, which is what most Americans have to do.
>
> Massage parlors come to mind—and bus stations and bars. (p. 207)

Thus are the themes of two otherwise distant novels, *Cat's Cradle* and *Slapstick*, bridged, given how religion and social practice are combined in an expression of art.

Vonnegut employs that art effectively as well, not just outlining better religions but actually rewriting doctrines presently in hand so that they function more usefully. Speaking on the two-hundredth anniversary of William Ellery Channing's birth, he reflects that congregations were immensely more homogeneous in those days, that Channing's listeners would have constituted a closely knit folk society that became impossible even thirty years later (with the great flood of European immigrants to the United States). But there are ways to adapt, and to show how Vonnegut rewrites once more (as he did in *Slaughterhouse-Five*) the crucifixion liturgy, where mourners at the cross disavow any divine connections for the person they wish to comfort: "If he were the Son of our God, he would not need us. It is because he is a common human being exactly like us that we are here—doing, as common people must, what little we can" (p. 218).

With religion established along with free speech, family history, influences, and the nature of his comic writing as key elements in his autobiographical collage, Vonnegut amplifies the structure of his interpolations by cross-referencing these topics. "Obscenity," first dealt with in the curious little section titled "Embarrassment," is given further treatment, again in terms of family history. Back then good manners counseled that certain things not be mentioned—too many things, the author felt at the time. To make his point he tells a story of how his parents were bilked of funds during the Depression by a well-mannered, rich-looking couple whose apparent wealth and good breeding prompted the senior Vonneguts to invest money in what turned out to be a fraudulent scheme, one engineered for the sole purpose of robbing them. Young Kurt, disciplined already for asking the cost of things, could only sit and watch his folks be taken for a ride: "Good manners had made them defenseless against predatory members of their own class" (p. 224), for their vocabularies were allowed to hold no language for such behavior. Later on he tells of a family friend who lived in Nazi Germany during the war and returned afterward to report that Hitler really had not been that bad at all—understandable, since her proper, upper-class education had made it impossible for her to think coherently about any such upsetting things, be they unmentionable parts of the anatomy or places like Auschwitz. And near the end of *Palm Sunday*, in a chapter dealing with the viciously vulgar Louis-Ferdinand Céline, Vonnegut still has this orientation on his mind when he credits this author for having discovered "a higher and more awful order of literary truth by ignoring the crippled vocabularies of ladies and gentlemen and by using, instead, the more comprehensive language of shrewd and tormented guttersnipes" (p. 293).

One's language is a matter of training, and so are moral values. To an audience of mental health workers Vonnegut tells a story he has concocted for their edification, about a concentration camp officer who finds himself unable to perform his duties and seeks help from the SS psychiatrist. He is given therapy and also praise for having "recognized nature's little danger signals early and put himself into the hands of modern medicine"—otherwise "he might have tried to shoot Adolf Hitler by and by. That is how sick he was" (p. 243).

Amid the thematic cross-referencings to language, morals, and other such concerns emerges one of Kurt Vonnegut's primary interests: the work of writers who have been great public spokesmen. Mark Twain was the first he considered; now, as his volume concludes, he adds two more, each from a vastly different culture and circumstance—Jonathan Swift and Louis-Ferdinand Céline. Here *Palm Sunday*'s collagist rather than chronological method is especially justified, for although these pieces predate the Twain address they incorporate attitudes toward speech and manners that were not among the concerns when discussing Twain's humor but which have been introduced and developed in subsequent sections of the book.

What draws Swift and Céline together is their employment of disgust as both a theme and technique in their fiction. Having spoken so pointedly on his own need for the occasionally vulgar, Vonnegut quite naturally shows affinities for these writers. But he also makes subtle identifications with them, remarking that *Gulliver's Travels* was undertaken by Swift when he was Vonnegut's own age, that Swift was considered bitterly funny but was also recognized for his "highly responsible sermons" (p. 256), that Céline suffered from splitting headaches, and that Vonnegut himself suffers them only when thinking about Céline. As for disgust, it surely has its dangers, such as damaging our reason and common sense, prompting action against our best interests or even making us insane. But in *Gulliver's Travels* the dosage is measured carefully so as not to infect but to immunize. Céline's fiction, in turn, results from its author's not having "the damping apparatus which most of us have, which keeps us from being swamped by the unbelievability of life as it really is" (p. 297).

Other cross-references are more subtle. In the section devoted to his children, Vonnegut speaks in great detail about his natural and adopted sons but for the most part leaves his daughters out of the discussion—for the sake of their privacy, he demurs. Those who follow such things know his daughter Edith's privacy needs safekeeping, thanks to a hideously unhappy marriage to Geraldo Rivera (and detailed by the man in his notorious autobiography, *Geraldo*). Yet a bit later, when Vonnegut prints the script of his modern-day musical adaptation of *Dr. Jekyll and Mr. Hyde*, he names one of its nitwit characters "Jerry Rivers"—which is, of course, Geraldo Rivera's real name. When he does focus attention on his younger daughter, Nanette, it is by means of her own writing, a letter she drafted to a dissatisfied patron whose complaint led to the firing of a desperate coworker; in it the daughter is seen espousing the same moral principles her father has been arguing throughout *Palm Sunday*. Even the inclusion of his own short story "The Big Space Fuck" bears less importance by itself than for the light it sheds on his comments about language elsewhere in the volume.

"Perhaps half of all experience, the animal half, [has] been concealed by good manners" (p. 293), Kurt Vonnegut observes. And so a certain amount of impoliteness will be necessary to make writing adequately expressive. Yet care must be exercised to make sure language does not smother the truth with insensitivity either. Here is where the author's understanding of both joke structures and language use rallies *Palm Sunday* to its most telling statement, in the "Palm Sunday" sermon itself that concludes the book. Its focus is Jesus' response to Judas, who had chided him for enjoying the pleasure of a soothing but expensive lotion while the poor still want. "The poor you always have with you," Jesus says, "but you do not always have me."

This reminds Vonnegut of something back in Indianapolis, a frequent refrain in *Palm Sunday*. "Whenever anybody out that way began to worry a lot about the poor people when I was young, some eminently respectable Hoosier, possibly an uncle or an aunt, would say that Jesus himself had given up on doing much about the poor" (p. 327), and would cite the verse in question.

What his relatives missed, and what most other readers of the verse misunderstand as well, is that Jesus is making a joke. To prove it, Vonnegut translates Christ's statement into a more familiar vernacular, "about what Mark Twain or Abraham Lincoln would have said under similar circumstances"—when tired, foreseeing great pain, and exasperated by the phoniness of someone like Judas. In the words of their and Vonnegut's own great public spokesmanship, Jesus would say, "Judas, don't worry about it. There will still be plenty of poor people left long after I'm gone." As Vonnegut explains: "If Jesus did in fact say that, it is a divine black joke, well suited to the occasion. It says everything about hypocrisy and nothing about the poor. It is a Christian joke, which allows Jesus to remain civil to Judas, but to chide him about the hypocrisy all the same" (p. 329). It is, in fact, the very method Kurt Vonnegut has been using in this book.

Chapter Six

FATES WORSE THAN DEATH

Kurt Vonnegut's third collection of nonfiction prose[1] is called an autobiographical collage as well, but it takes a further step toward seamlessness by forsaking the subject headings that distinguished *Palm Sunday*. There, most notably in the volume's table of contents, each essay, review, or address retained its original title. Now the author no sooner lists a table of contents than he would for a novel, for his materials are blended into an almost continuous narrative. Nor is it simply an autobiographical collage, but "An Autobiographical Collage of the 1980s." Not that the book is peppered with commentaries on famous events of that decade. Instead, the focus, both in the reprinted matter and in Vonnegut's original writing, is on the author's own life during those years, much of which involves thinking back on his personal experiences of earlier times. That perhaps is why there are no table of contents and no titles for the essays themselves; even more than in *Palm Sunday*, the emphasis is on Kurt Vonnegut's ongoing story.

Fates Worse than Death: the title comes from a little fifty-pence pamphlet done for the Bertrand Russell Peace Foundation[2] in 1982, a tractlike booklet reprinting Vonnegut's cover letter plus his sermon at the Cathedral of Saint John the Divine in New York City that same year. The sermon is reprinted just past halfway through the larger volume, where it appears in the context not of public issue-taking but of Vonnegut's thoughts on his own style of speech-making. Thus *Fates Worse than Death: An Autobiographical Collage of the 1980s* makes a narrative of Kurt Vonnegut's judgments about himself as a public spokesman, even as his pronouncements have appeared in a "Spokesman Pamphlet Series" endowed by one of history's great spokespersons.

Less an example of public spokesmanship than a consideration of the art of it, Vonnegut's third collection concerns itself with who the speaker is. Literary activity is rarely a part of it. To make the point, Vonnegut prefaces the volume with a photograph of himself and Heinrich Böll and a description of its occasion. Yes, the two famous writers are being honored for their work, in this case at a P.E.N. festivity in Stockholm. And they are indeed enjoying each other's company. But what prompts their friendship is not that they are writers but that they were both infantrymen in World War II, in armies that opposed each other. Their smiles, Vonnegut reports, are due to a comic point in their discussion of how malingerers shot themselves (in the foot or elsewhere) to avoid service; Böll has just revealed that the correct way to do it was "through a loaf of bread, in order to avoid powder burns" (p. 13). They laugh as participants and as survivors, and probably as public spokespersons too—for what unites them in their humor is not that they are writers but that they have been public witnesses to their personal experiences in the war.

Befitting *Fates Worse than Death*'s autobiographical function, the volume's first essay deals with the author's memories of his father, actually a tribute to the man who is honored by the book's dedication. Vonnegut's framing material, however, is a bit longer than the essay itself, a change in proportion since *Palm Sunday* and a refocusing from subject to speaker that lets the audience of readers appreciate the personhood informing these attitudes.

At first the frame seems rambling to no real purpose, talking about unicorns, which in turn prompts some comments on Dr. Seuss's invention of similarly mythical animals. Dr. Seuss himself, when known by his real name of Theodor Geisel, once visited a friend at what would later become Kurt Vonnegut's own fraternity house at Cornell, and there left some drawings on the lounge walls. After comments on his own college days and the practical jokes he then performed, Vonnegut mentions the family tradition of going away to school and then returning home to work in Indianapolis, a tradition of which his father was the last bearer. And thus, with the person of a joking college boy in mind, we listen to Kurt's tribute to his father, a person so unlike the era's typical fathers that he might well have been a unicorn.

A unicorn, or Sleeping Beauty, for in detailing his father's career Vonnegut remarks on its vulnerability, of how "All architects I have known, in good times or bad, have seemed to be waiting forever for a generous, loving client who will let them become the elated artists they were born to be" (p. 24). Elsewhere, the author has regretted that he was not allowed to study architecture, to become a third-generation Indianapolis architect and his father's partner. Those concerns are absent from this piece, for here the emphasis is on a college boy's perception of his father, a wonderful and wondrous man who admired chess sets without knowing how to play the game and anything from moths to clarinets for their beauty of design. It is the man's purity that distinguishes this memory. But framing it is another aspect of Kurt Vonnegut himself, worked into the surrounding narrative as an example of how his father would preserve memories, in this case by mounting and varnishing a letter from his son. Beginning "Dear Pop" and dated October 28, 1949, it describes young Kurt's first sale of a short story, his first step as a public writer. "I think I'm on my way," he tells his father. "I've deposited my first check in a savings account and, if I sell more, will continue to do so until I have the equivalent of one year's pay at GE. . . . I will then quit this goddamn nightmare job, and never take another one so long as I live, so help me God." Appended to this letter is the father's own response, a quote from Shakespeare's *The Merchant of Venice*: "An oath, I have an oath in Heaven: Shall I lay perjury on my soul?" (p. 26). Thus, in the context of *Fates Worse than Death*, Vonnegut's essay on his father's work as an architect becomes a comment on his own as much freer artist.

The subject of his family and the arts continues with an address to the American Psychiatric Association in Philadelphia, but again the new writing that makes this book a narrative contains essential thought on Vonnegut as a spokesman in the making. Although he mentions his mother's mental illness to the psychiatrists, it is just the clinical details; readers are given a much fuller picture, one that begins not with his mother but with his father. Once more the image is of a unicorn, this time how to catch one—"If a maiden sits on the ground in a clearing in a forest where a unicorn lives, they say, the unicorn will come to her and put its head in her lap" (p. 27). The maiden becomes Kurt's sister Alice, whom his father treasures as an antidote to the hostility he suffers from his wife, the details of which are especially lurid in contrast to the charming unicorn tale. Then, after the American Psychiatric Association address, Vonnegut begins a new chapter by continuing his mother's story, this time with the opening focus on her. No stories of unicorns here, for the picture is a disturbing one. "When my mother went off her rocker late at night," he explains, "the hatred and contempt she sprayed on my father, as gentle and innocent a man as ever lived, was without limit and pure, untainted by ideas or information" (p. 36). The account once more serves a bridging purpose, linking the author's thoughts on artistry and madness with an essay that follows on Jackson Pollock, whose own combination of depression and alcoholism recalls Kurt's mother's condition. In the process another family story is told, this time how his father's flattery of Alice's art spoiled her talent and made her lazy. Vonnegut's method is now clearly accumulative, less a collage than a narrative whose recurring elements roll along together, picking up a new item at each turn—but always in relation to something existing previously as an apparent aside, then featured as a principal subject, and finally used to snare something new.

In the midst of his most devastating comments on his mother's madness Vonnegut will make an aside to jokes at Cornell, something he had mentioned more prominently in the chapter before; and as he writes about his second wife, Jill Krementz, well toward the middle of his book, he cannot let a remark about his adopted daughter Lily pass without mentioning that she, too, will be a lazy artist just like his sister Alice, thanks to his own overindulgence. "My work is done" is a comment the author ascribes to everyone from Ernest Hemingway and George Eastman to the programmers of Voyager 2. Most such references are noticed; but others are not, serving to unify *Fates Worse than Death* in the same subliminal manner that offhand but repeated references to color and event unify *Slaughter-*

house-Five. And behind it all stands an accumulative portrait of Kurt Vonnegut, here drawing together the bits and pieces of his spokesmanship's art.

Where his method is not accumulative, it is associative—not quite the collage of *Palm Sunday*, but rather a progressive affair of linkages. From the Jackson Pollock essay, which had been introduced with references to both madness (his mother's) and art (his father's and his sister's), the author proceeds to a reminiscence on his parents' summer cottage on Lake Maxincuckee. The ostensible link is psychological, how there in his childhood (and today near any large body of water) Vonnegut can achieve the balance and orientation needed for probing the meditative depths just described in Pollock's work. But the implications reach farther, back across the Pollock essay to another framing comment on how his father's paintings were spoiled by being worked on too long. The method is a complex one, yet in delivery seemingly as natural as Vonnegut's mode of public speaking, free-associating as he does from one topic to another until the pattern of autobiographical reference and personally won wisdom is clear. Lake Maxincuckee offers the serenity from which to make all such judgments, plus it ties into another of *Fates Worse than Death*'s developing themes as well, that of a once happy and stable extended family's breakdown and dispersal (together with another bit of family history that updates things to the author's adulthood):

> If I were ever to write a novel or a play about Maxincuckee, it would be Chekhovian, since what I saw were the consequences of several siblings' inheriting and trying to share a single beloved property, and with their own children, once grown, moving to other parts of the world, never to return, and on and on. Our cottage, owned jointly and often acrimoniously by my father and his brother and his sister, was sold to a stranger at the end of World War II. The buyer put off taking possession for a week in order that I, just married after being discharged from the Army, might take my bride there for a honeymoon. He was Concert Master of the Indianapolis Symphony Orchestra, and so must have been a romantic man. My bride, whose name was Jane Cox and who was of English ancestry, confided in me that one of her own relatives had asked her, "Do you really want to get mixed up with all those Germans?" (p. 51)

This paragraph pulls several strands together, including references to the Germanic character of the lake community's owners and the romanticism associated with such a place, especially the serenity Kurt Vonnegut had drawn from it and the imprint he still carries today when seeking similar peace. (The essay is packed with other incidental references as well, such as the lakeside military academy firing its cannon at sunset as happens in *Hocus Pocus* and the mention of a real Coggin's Pond, which is the retirement home of the OSS spymaster at the very end of *Mother Night*.)

Whatever topic comes up in the essays and speeches collected in *Fates Worse than Death*, the author turns them in an accumulative manner toward comments on his art. Pondering the architects' careers of his father and grandfather, he finds kinship with Donald Barthelme as another son of an architect and decides this is why "we were aggressively unconventional storytellers," because as sons of architects "Barthelme and I tried hard to make every architect's dream come true, which is a dwelling such as no one has ever seen before, but which proves to be eminently inhabitable" (p. 55). Both the phrase and its sentiment recall Vonnegut's statement from *Palm Sunday* regarding his mother's futile attempts at short story writing, that sons are often destined to remedy their mother's greatest disappointments by fulfilling their impossible dreams. *Fates Worse than Death* alludes to it when the author finds his own lost hopes of continuing the Vonnegut line of architects salvaged somewhat in the career of his nephew Scott, and his aborted career in the sciences (and specifically his curiosity over how chemicals in one's blood influence behavior as he trained in biochemistry) resurrected in the person of his son Mark. But the associations always come first as necessary stimuli; habitually, he introduces himself to an audience of Hemingway scholars by noting that the two of them were both reporters, middlewesterners, sons of fathers who were gun nuts, and admirers of Mark Twain (p. 61). All of this is a buildup for an appreciation of Hemingway's powerfully simple style—something that prompts a similar note in the framing material that concludes the essay's presentation here, that another powerfully plain speaker, Tennessee Williams, grew up in Saint Louis, the same city as did T. S. Eliot; "but Williams admitted it. He didn't all of a sudden start talking like the Archbishop of Canterbury" (p. 68).

The effectively plain speech that Vonnegut so admires (recall his "How to Write with Style" from *Palm Sunday*) is given full treatment in a chapter describing how his requiem, "The Hocus Pocus Laundromat," corrects the language problem in the traditional requiem, based as the old one is on threats and condemnations from the Council of Trent. The singers at Andrew Lloyd Webber's production, Vonnegut notes, "were behaving as though God were a wonderful person who had prepared all sorts of goodies which we could enjoy after we were dead." But turning from Latin to the English translation, as Vonnegut does in his program, reveals that "They were in fact, if only they had known what they were saying, promising a Paradise indistinguishable from the Spanish Inquisition" (p. 71). Note the accumulative direction of the author's argument: that their Latin, sung indecipherably by English speakers to English-language listeners, yields the same alienation as an American such as T. S. Eliot speaking in High Church Anglican. He then carries forth his argument in a chapter about the attorney general's Commission on Pornography, wishing to address the body with language so "obscene" as to shock it from its very foundations, which is a reading of the First Amendment to the Constitution. In good public spokesmanship sometimes rewriting is necessary, as the author does in the happier text to his own requiem; but more often that not, simply reading the text in a clear, uncluttered voice serves as the most effective deconstruction of pretense and false assumption. In subsequent speeches Vonnegut works the same technique against the right-to-bear-arms advocates by forcing them to acknowledge not just the last half but also the first words of the Fourth Amendment (that such rights pertain to a well-regulated state militia), and against those who too smugly consider America the birthplace or cradle of liberty, reminding them that one hundred years' tardiness in abolishing slavery and an even longer delay in granting civil and women's rights make us more properly just a country where liberty was conceived, "a motel of liberty, so to speak" (p. 84).

Throughout the addresses which form the bulk of *Fates Worse than Death*, Kurt Vonnegut delights in pointing out not just contradictions (which by now everyone knows) but subtler facts that all the more thoroughly undermine unwarranted assumptions. Widely acknowledged is the irony that Thomas Jefferson, that great architect of human liberty, owned slaves; much more ironic (and more indicting of the concept of slavery) is that he could not free them even if he wished, because they were mortgaged. He finds himself unable to give uncritical respect to works by great thinkers of the past, not because their specific ideas are obsolete or incorrect but "because they almost all accepted as natural and ordinary the belief that females and minority races and the poor were on earth to be uncomplaining, hardworking, respectful, and loyal servants of white males, who did the important thinking and exercised leadership" (p. 114). Even in current times he is startled to discover blatant irrationalities, such as when he tries to dissuade the students at MIT from working on President Reagan's "Star Wars" antiballistic missile program. "They didn't think there was any way it could be made to operate," he rues, "but they all wanted to work on it anyway" (p. 121).

Fates Worse than Death's accumulative force, however, is in the direction of even greater readjustment. In the title sermon of *Palm Sunday* Vonnegut had retranslated one of Jesus' comments into more effective language by fashioning it as a joke; in one of this new volume's concluding sermons he makes a similar retranslation, changing the imperative of "to love one another" to an instruction "to *respect* one another." Incorporating phrases and ideas from much earlier commentaries on the First Amendment (p. 75) and the American Academy of Arts and Letters (p. 68), he clarifies the difference:

> "Ye shall respect one another." Now there is something almost anybody in reasonable mental health can do day after day, year in and year out, come one, come all, to everyone's clear benefit. "Respect" does not imply a spectrum of alternatives, some of them very dangerous. Respect is like a light switch. It is either on or off. And if we are no longer able to respect

someone, we don't feel like killing that person. Our response is restrained. We simply want to make him or her feel like something the cat drug in.

Compare making somebody feel like something the cat drug in with Armageddon or World War III. (p. 160)

As for jokes, consider Vonnegut's coda to his essay on Mozambique, where bandit-style right wing revolution had made the people's life almost unlivable. His essay for *Parade* magazine can give little more than the facts; in his framing material, which in this case is interpolated as asides within the essay, Vonnegut's comments are even more hopeless, though tinged with humor—a neoconservative defense of the rightist bandits is compared to Dean Martin's introduction of Frank Sinatra, that Sinatra was going to speak about all the *good* things the Mafia was doing. Yet what most disturbs the writer is that after seeing emaciated prisoners in World War II and then starving Biafran children during Nigeria's civil war he can no longer feel shock or horror at the sight of similar suffering in Mozambique. But these are not his final comments. Instead, he looks back to the photograph beginning this chapter and reproduced from the *Parade* magazine story itself, in which the author, dressed in a safari outfit, talks with some natives on-site. Here, Vonnegut says, he is seen "in action in Mozambique, demonstrating muscular Christianity in an outfit that might have been designed by Ralph Lauren. The aborigines didn't know whether to shit or go blind until I showed up. And then I fixed everything" (p. 175). As the last of Vonnegut's parenthetical asides, it is both the funniest and most cynical joke. But it is cynical at one's own prospects, which shows the depth of Vonnegut's sorrow: joking, we recall from his Biafra essay in *Wampeters, Foma & Granfalloons*, is his response to misery he cannot do anything about, and what he has witnessed in Mozambique grants him no prospect of being able to help things one bit.

Kurt Vonnegut's concluding emphasis in this volume is a profound one. Among its closing pieces, suicide is the most common topic: William Styron's hint at such in *Darkness Visible*, Hemingway's, even Hamlet's. Other comments are directed to figures recently lost to death, such as his Italian translator Roberta Rambelli, his war buddy Bernard V. O'Hare, and the much-admired Abbie Hoffman. Kurt's own father's last years are dealt with in some detail, most pathetically as the old man loses his memory (even for ten-minute intervals). But most unsettling is the author's revelation, for the first time ever, of his own suicide attempt in 1984. "I wanted *out* of here" (p. 181), he observes, echoing the comment used here and in *Palm Sunday* to describe his grandfather Bernard's welcoming of an early death.

Underscoring the seriousness of these comments is another admission, that in 1989 the author found himself losing his effectiveness and appeal as a public speaker—but not as a writer, for he felt his jocular approach could continue within the confines of print. "But jokesters are all through when they find them-

selves talking about challenges so real and immediate and appalling to their listeners that no amount of laughter can make the listeners feel safe and perfectly
well again" (p. 185), which is the necessary third part to any joke's structure.
And so he cancels the rest of his talks and takes himself off the circuit.

Yet in 1991 and 1992 Kurt Vonnegut returned to speak, and he continues
doing so as this study is written. *Fates Worse than Death* ends on a positive note,
its accumulated references to suicide and death actually phrased in ways that
emphasize survival. Kurt Vonnegut, after all, survived his suicide attempt, and
in his framing commentary he marvels at how the materials he introduces in its
wake would not have been created had he died in 1984. He takes the suicide of
Ernest Hemingway, to whom he has earlier compared himself, and reshapes it
into a positive image, citing Ray Bradbury's story in which the broken old man,
on his way to shoot himself, is offered the more enhancing death in a plane
crash atop Mount Kilimanjaro instead. In Bradbury's story Hemingway takes the
option; and thoughtful readers will recall that in *Fates Worse than Death*'s preface, on the volume's third page, in fact, Vonnegut answers a reporter's question
as to how he would like to die by saying "In an airplane crash on the peak of
Mount Kilimanjaro," a response that assumes full weight only after nearly two
hundred pages of autobiographical collage.

Then there are the jokes about death: how a prisoner being strapped into the
electric chair in Cook County Jail observed that this would certainly teach him a
lesson; how a scientist at General Electric offered the advice that buying life
insurance was ridiculous because after one's death one would not be worrying
about a wife and children or anything, that one would be completely unaware,
dead.

But more compelling are the references to life. Life goes on in Vonnegut's
essays, most notably in the ones published after his suicide attempt. And though
Bernard O'Hare is gone, the author can sustain his presence by recounting memories and reprinting (in the volume's appendix) O'Hare's contribution to Kurt's
sixtieth birthday Festschrift. As a public spokesman, Vonnegut concludes with
the same thoughts (and words) as his great-grandfther Clemens used to close his
booklet on Free Thought, a translation from Goethe that notes how only mankind
can "make the moment last" (p. 202), which is just what the author has been
doing. The last twenty pages of *Fates Worse than Death* do it self-consciously,
but even in the appendix that follows there is a more graphic depiction of survival's advantage. There on the book's last page appears a photograph from 1945,
one not brought to the author's attention until 1990 when fellow prisoner-of-war
Tom Jones brought it to his friend's speech at the Smithsonian.

There, in the auditorium of the Air and Space Museum, Kurt Vonnegut spoke
as a survivor of strategic bombing. As noted in this study's first chapter, he
happily modified his speech about that past event in order to accommodate this
wonderful surprise from the present, not so much that Tom Jones was there but

that he was "still alive," Vonnegut's first words of recognition. But Jones's gift of the photograph, showing him and Kurt and several other POWs in the countryside just after the German surrender, speaks for the future as well: a future after 1945 that might well not have existed for Kurt Vonnegut, had the firestorm raid been totally effective and killed everyone in Dresden (instead of almost everyone).

Vonnegut, of course, has survived. But *Fates Worse than Death* is structured to make a public statement of that survival. As a collection, it serves as witness to what the author has done during those past forty-five years—and in the twenty-three that proceeded them, inasmuch as those activities contributed to what he would write and say afterward. Making moments last has been a large part of it, something he sees as central to his art. It is one of the lessons he draws from the example of another survivor, Louis-Ferdinand Céline, who fascinates the Vonnegut of chapter 1 in *Slaughterhouse-Five* as a writer who rages against the passage of time and the disappearance of people and the world before him, struggling to freeze everything so it does not all disappear. That motive helps create Kurt Vonnegut's first publicly successful novel, the vehicle which did the most to establish his credibility and provide a forum for his spokesmanship. As *Fates Worse than Death* ends, in its commentary with the poem from Goethe and in its appendix with the photograph from Tom Jones, that motivation's product in terms of being one of America's great public writers is apparent as well.

Chapter Seven

A Public Preface
for Personal Fiction

Between 1966, when the hardcover edition of his paperback original *Mother Night* was issued, and 1985, when his eleventh novel, *Galápagos*, was published, Kurt Vonnegut would begin each of his books with comments indicating his own involvement with the text. In the cases of *Happy Birthday, Wanda June* and *Between Time and Timbuktu*, there would be nothing usual about such a beginning, for in each his thoughts are directed to working in a new medium, stage and television respectively. Nor should the business of prefacing his story collection *Welcome to the Monkey House* be especially significant, other than that the author did not do it for his first gathering of stories seven years earlier in *Canary in a Cat House*. And the introductory remarks to his three books of essays, reviews, and addresses fit the tradition for retrospective collections of nonfiction prose. But including autobiographical comments on a novel and even going so far as to introduce them into the text is thoroughly unconventional, violating the aesthetic distance that critics assume must exist between reality and the fictive. Yet Vonnegut does it not just in *Mother Night* but for six novels in a row thereafter; and not just gratuitously, for the essence of *Mother Night* is changed by his decision, just as the subsequent novels would be shaped by this decision.

Why did Vonnegut suddenly choose to go with prefaces? The notion of putting himself in his fiction had occurred as early as the drafting of *Cat's Cradle*, when he toyed with the idea of having his narrator find the name "Vonnegut" on an old tombstone; because that would be the narrator's own family name, editors talked Vonnegut out of the idea as being too radical. By 1966, when he was writing the new introduction to *Mother Night* from his post as an instructor at the University of Iowa Writers' Workshop, innovation was more of an option, surrounded as he was by novelists much more radical in their pursuit of new techniques. But *Mother Night* itself offered more evident reasons; its text was already enfolded in commentaries by its fictively presumed author (Howard Campbell) and editor (Kurt Vonnegut), and the book's subject matter—Nazi Germany—coincided with that of the novel he was now struggling to write,

Slaughterhouse-Five. The key to that struggle was clarifying his own role in "the Nazi monkey business" and presence at Dresden when it was firebombed, which is just what he does in this new introduction to the earlier book.

Iowa City and the key to writing *Slaughterhouse-Five* may be the reasons for his first two prefaces, but Vonnegut would continue writing them consistently through the 1970s and in his first two novels of the 1980s. At that point his fame, if not outright notoriety, might have been a reason to do so. But *Mother Night* and *Slaughterhouse-Five*, where the practice starts, are works written in obscurity. What was happening in 1966, before the fame and even before the enabling structure for his Dresden novel is discovered, is Vonnegut's emergence as a personal essayist. His pieces on science fiction, *The Random House Dictionary*, and cruising the inland waterway date from this period, as do the entertaining book reviews that after 1965 had to generate the income previously earned from writing short fiction. By the time of *Slaughterhouse-Five* three years later the author had reported on the Maharishi and writers' conferences (and was preparing to cover the Apollo XI moon launch), getting the job done by placing himself within the materials and describing his own involvement. That, as will be seen, is what he does to get *Slaughterhouse-Five* rolling—and also to sustain its momentum and provide a meaningful conclusion. Something quite different than a shifting from metaphor to discourse, this practice involves not so much public spokesmanship as taking the devices for such speech and applying them to fiction. Because Kurt Vonnegut's own person stands at the center of his public discourse, it is not surprising that when employing such techniques in personal fictions his autobiographical involvement similarly stands out.

Mother Night is an excellent example of how the introduction of Kurt Vonnegut's presence changes a reader's response to the narrative itself. The novel's initial presentation, in fact, was in a format that prompted the most naive response of all: as a cheaply produced paperback original, packaged in the subgenre of espionage thrillers and operatives' confessions that were then so popular, and formatted in a way to let readers think the fictive account was a true one. Vonnegut encourages this reading in the way he writes his book. Each of his five novels published before *Slaughterhouse-Five* depends upon a subgenre or set of popular conventions in order to tell its story: *Player Piano* as wry dystopia, *The Sirens of Titan* as hokey space opera, *Mother Night* as espionage confession, *Cat's Cradle* as an apocalyptic novel, and *God Bless You, Mr. Rosewater* as a combination of the prince-and-the-pauper tale and stories of sudden, unexpected riches. Self-taught as he was, it is almost as if the author needs excuses to write and for his readers to read; given that adding a new introduction to *Mother Night* in 1966 would help him move into autobiographically generated and ascribed fiction after that, it would be 1987 and the publication of *Bluebeard* before he would write a simple, flat-out novel.

Of his five involvements with subgenre, *Mother Night* is the one that comes closest to posing as fact. Picking up the 1962 Fawcett paperback original, readers would find the term *novel* nowhere in evidence. All the cover mentions beyond the title and Vonnegut's name is the description promising "An American traitor's astonishing confession—mournful, macabre, diabolically funny—written with unnatural candor in a foreign death cell." Nor does the title page itself indicate that what follows is fiction. Instead, Vonnegut conspires toward just the opposite when he begins the book with an editor's note discussing his preparation of this, the American edition of the confessions of Howard Campbell—a device reinforced a few pages later by running a new title page saying just that.

Much of Vonnegut's commentary as "editor" suits this supposed function. But it also allows him to be somewhat of a spokesman for his own fiction, pointing out the dangers of letting the demands of art justify one's lies while still admitting that lies told for the sake of artistic effect can be the most beguiling forms of truth. He also throws some comments by his character, Howard Campbell, into higher relief by reflecting on them as if they are statements actually made in this real world. It also takes Campbell himself outside the narrative, letting him look back in from outside, so to speak, in order to make the same kind of judgments Kurt Vonnegut is making; indeed, it is Vonnegut's "editorial" device that foregrounds these comments that Campbell, as "author," would have otherwise dropped.

But note how everything changes when the author begins speaking as the novel's creator in 1966.[1] "This is the only story of mine whose moral I know," he begins, explaining what the reader would otherwise have to digest Campbell's full confessions in order to know: that "We are what we pretend to be, so we must be careful about what we pretend to be" (p. v). But then, when he begins detailing his own part in the Nazi monkey business, as he calls it, it is with a joke, the story of how during the 1930s an aunt, having moved to Hitler's Germany and planning to marry, writes back home for proof that she has no Jewish blood—to which the mayor of Indianapolis replies with a hoked-up document sealed and beribboned like an eighteenth-century peace treaty. When it comes to noting his presence in Dresden, it is similarly offhand; the war has come, Vonnegut was in it and was captured, and he got to see a little of Germany and was sent to work as a prisoner in Dresden, where he saw more of the German people. *And so on*, his language and structure seem to imply. The first story Vonnegut tells is about working in a factory that made a vitamin-enriched malt syrup for pregnant women, the first detail being that "It tasted like thin honey laced with hickory smoke. It was good. I wish I had some right now" (p. vi).

With this comment the author makes use of senses, his and ours, to actualize the narrative: by tasting the syrup, he is there. But something else happens as well, something that anticipates the technical manner of *Slaughterhouse-Five*, for with his comment that he wishes he had some right now he is equally here, sitting in Iowa City twenty-one years later recalling that taste. When immediately after that he goes into the story of the firebombing that destroyed the malt syrup factory and everything else in Dresden, the author remains implicated in his narrative both ways, in its happening and in its telling. The Dresden experience itself will wait until *Slaughterhouse-Five*, but Howard Campbell's eminently domestic story of living inside Germany during the Nazi years has become Vonnegut's as well, given the careful way he has introduced his participation.

Campbell, of course, will seem amoral at times in his detachment. But so is Vonnegut in this introduction. "If I'd been born in Germany," he admits, "I suppose I would have *been* a Nazi, bopping Jews and gypsies and Poles around, leaving boots sticking out of snowbanks, warming myself with my secretly virtuous insides. So it goes" (p. vii). Note how the single expression of morality is reserved for what would be the Nazi point of view; and note the author's first usage of the phrase that would be incanted one hundred times in his Dresden novel as an index to how the prevalence and inevitability of death make moral statement a hollow issue.

This new introduction to *Mother Night*, then, makes the novel much more obviously Vonnegut's own, but not as much as is *Slaughterhouse-Five*,[2] the personalized comments for which are not even sectioned off in a preface or introduction but rather incorporated directly into the novel's structure as chapter 1. Here an emphatically real Kurt Vonnegut describes the trouble he had setting out to write the book; then, after eight chapters of narrative action, he will conclude with an equally personal chapter 10, ending his novel simultaneously on a shady street in the suburbs of Dresden (where his fictive characters experience the coming of V-E day, May 8, 1945) and in his study in West Barnstable, Massachusetts, where he is just finishing up the book on an equally notable historical day: June 5, 1968, the day Americans woke up to learn that presidential candidate Robert Kennedy had been shot late the night before.

Vonnegut's strategy occurs in an interesting context, not just that of the technically self-conscious Iowa Workshop but in the wake of a half-decade's innovation by writers such as Ronald Sukenick, Robert Coover, and Steve Katz, all of whom put themselves in their narratives and made the writing of a novel just as much the action as what that novel would describe. For Katz and Sukenick the issue involved the breaking down of all suspensions of disbelief, while Coover's interest would be in exploiting the fabulative tension between a story's telling and its unfolding narrative. Vonnegut, however, incorporates chapters 1 and 10 within his novel in order to justify its form—to make the reader appreciate just why the book has to be "so short and jumbled and jangled" (p. 17), why it lacks the customary heroic roles for actors like "Frank Sinatra or John Wayne" (p. 13), and even why it merits public spokesmanship as an antiwar book (the greatly unpopular Vietnam War was then at its height) when making such a statement is about as effective as writing "an anti-*glacier* book instead" (p. 3).

Indeed, much of chapter 1's business is given to the impossibility of writing a traditional book about Dresden and the author's experience there. Conventional forms distort the nature of his experience, turning it into something else; hence wars continue as inevitably as glaciers. Time itself is the enemy, as events fade into memories and memories perform the necessary function of filtering out the bad while preserving the good. The author must therefore find a way to stop time, or at least to make its elements so omnipresent that he can move among them at will. He gets the inspiration to do this from the example of Louis-Ferdinand Céline, and the technical example in the science fiction device of time travel. He must use, in fact, a different mode of public spokesmanship, for "there is nothing intelligent to say about a massacre" (p. 17). Thus the massacre never takes place but is just enfolded within the attempts of a very real writer to find a fictive format. As a device, it resembles that of the several apparatuses surrounding the central narrative of *Mother Night*, only here with the author becoming part of the action rather than just having points in common with it.

Imaginative challenges make for the strength of this work. Having to speak about the unspeakable is hard enough, but death—referred to precisely one hundred times during the novel and highlighted by the repeated phrase "so it goes"—is an even more difficult subject. Of all things to write about, it is the one unverifiable experience, and thus in personal terms remains work for the imagination rather than for any empirical faculties. The Dresden firebombing is death in both its largest and most particular senses—yet, because Kurt Vonnegut survived where by all rational measures he should have died, it remains for him a matter beyond conventional strategies of writing. Earlier in the 1960s Philip Roth had despaired of fiction capturing the absurdities of his age and was joined by a legion of critics proclaiming "the death of the novel." Simply posing a protagonist such as Billy Pilgrim among his multiform, fragmented adventures was by itself not an answer. Indeed, one of Billy's activities is to be an uninvited participant in a death-of-the-novel symposium. Instead, something would have to be done to integrate Kurt Vonnegut's writerly struggles with his character's readerly plight. This is done by adopting a style of public spokesmanship that can be incorporated within the book itself, as its first and last chapters supplemented by three reminders of Kurt Vonnegut's presence in the fictive narrative itself.

Much of what Vonnegut does in chapter 1 involves what the reader will be doing in the chapters that follow: handling texts. In the course of nineteen pages he deals with more than a dozen, including a story he wrote twenty-two years ago for Chicago's City News Bureau, several military histories and strategy works on aerial bombardment, a poetry collection, a literary biography, a postcard, a circular limerick, a friend's wife's narrative, and any number of telephone books. In their context he is able to jump about in time and space, much as Billy Pilgrim will begin doing in chapter 2. All of this activity is prompted by the absence of a central text, the United States Air Force historical document on the Dresden raid, which after so many years still remains secret. That in itself is inexplicable, reflecting the speechlessness Vonnegut feels in the face of the raid's atrocity. Yet just as he unifies these diverse texts by his own act of reading, a new meaning emerges: that of production itself.

Here Billy Pilgrim's and the reader's problems are solved in much the same manner as the author's. Whereas meaning as a prize seems ungraspable, the production of meaning can be plotted as a simple human activity—simple, once it is clarified as a process rather than an end. Billy strives to fill the blank that Dresden's bombing is for him, just as the reader seeks to explicate the problem. Billy handles texts just like Kurt Vonnegut does, in his case everything from letters to the editor and lyrics of barbershop quartet songs to the novels of Kilgore Trout. As for the reader's activity, meaning is achieved by sorting through the same texts as the author does, accumulating their sense not in an orderly, step-by-step process but rather by appreciating their sum held in juxtaposed suspension. In chapter 1 Kurt Vonnegut has been a public spokesman for these activities, a historical person standing both before and within his novel much like the figure at Ohio State University in 1967 chatting about the ironies of himself making a speech even as he gives it.

His next novel, *Breakfast of Champions*,[3] was written in much different circumstances. Whereas at Ohio State and during the struggle with *Slaughterhouse-Five* Vonnegut could exploit the fact of being a self-acknowledged failure, from 1970 onward he was a widely acclaimed success. In a year he had gone from anonymity to celebrityhood, from an annual income at the lower end of middle-class earnings at best (averaging between $8,000 and $25,000 per year to support a family of eight) to the windfall of bestsellerdom, paperback rights, and the fairy-tale sums paid out by Hollywood for film properties. Scheduled for 1971 or 1972 publication, *Breakfast of Champions* did not appear until May 1973, having been called back by its author as he worked through a writer's block with its form—a block most likely caused by the prospect of having to write fiction for the first time as a wildly popular figure whose words were awaited as if religious truth.

Perhaps this is why he begins his preface with a story about a woman he worked for as a teenager back in Indianapolis: Phoebe Hurty, who "was rich" but "had gone to work every weekday of her adult life" (p. 1). She wrote humor for the daily newspaper during times that needed it, as reflected in the book's dedication, "In memory of Phoebe Hurty, who comforted me in Indianapolis— during the Great Depression" (a similar dedication, to the film comedians Laurel and Hardy, would grace *Slapstick* three years later; these figures were also thanked in the preface to *Between Time and Timbuktu* for helping him through the Great Depression and all the lesser depressions afterward). For this new novel, Phoebe Hurty does more than comfort Vonnegut, for the reminder of her sustaining humor and lack of reverence for sacred cows reorients him for writing as a successful author, albeit one in the midst of great personal malaise.

As always, that orientation involves a joke. The one of Phoebe Hurty's that Kurt Vonnegut recalls involved an ad for straw hats on sale—"For prices like these, you can run them through your horse and put them on your roses" (p. 2). The tenor of this joke tells what the author learned from her: that it was all right to be impolite about sacred or unspeakable matters, all the way from sex to national legends and heroes. This is what he now does in his preface, mocking himself and the stuffier aspects of his culture before undertaking *Breakfast of Champions* itself, where the narrative voice will do much the same. Not until near the end will Vonnegut identify that voice as his own, at least as far as being integrated with the plot. At that point he introduces himself as author in order to play some mechanical tricks on characters such as making a phone ring to distract them. At first this seems mere trickery—as indeed it was in the draft Kurt Vonnegut sent to his publisher. But readerly dissatisfaction, in the person of the messenger carrying these pages from the author's home to Delacorte Press's offices just two blocks away, prompted Vonnegut to revise his ending into something more substantial. Thus what transpires from this evasive funny business with the phone shows the writer closing more effectively with his material, ending the novel in a way more appropriate to the issues raised in its preface.

The essence of that preface is Vonnegut's appraisal of himself at midlife and in midcareer. A time of change and renewal, it involves, as he says, a great deal of throwing away, clearing out junk that is no longer wanted. But in doing so the author also must face his new responsibility, and for that he must not simply discard things but in doing so recognize how his relationship to them has changed. In this manner he comes to terms with himself, most notably in his dealings with one of the main characters in *Breakfast of Champions*, Kilgore Trout.

By appearing in *God Bless You, Mr. Rosewater, Slaughterhouse-Five,* and *Breakfast of Champions* this figure of a beleaguered science fiction writer coincides with Kurt Vonnegut's own transition from anonymity to fame, from failure to success, and, most importantly, from ineffectiveness to great influence. The first novel was published in 1965, surely the financial low point of Vonnegut's career. His short story markets had dried up, the novels he had turned to for replacement income were not selling, and the matter of Dresden was still an unwritable affair. In his own sense of shambling failure Kilgore Trout is an image of what Vonnegut feared he himself might be: an unheeded crackpot, someone so piteously ruined as to look like an aging and frightened Jesus whose crucifixion had been remitted to a life sentence in solitary confinement. *God Bless You, Mr. Rosewater* thus features him as an author's spokesman and more, appearing near the end to explain and pose a solution for the novel's problems. In *Slaughterhouse-Five* that same role becomes interactive, as summaries of texts by Trout are included as ways of letting readers consider implications of Vonnegut's own themes. But while in these first two novels Trout, like Vonnegut, writes

117

from a posture of neglect, *Breakfast of Champions* portrays him being recognized as a genius—being given a Nobel Prize, no less, in medicine rather than in literature for the healing power of his ideas. The very plot of this novel tracks his progress in traveling to an arts festival where for the first time he will be recognized and honored. Here something else will happen that has never occurred before, meeting a reader and witnessing the impact of his writing. What happens to Kilgore Trout in *Breakfast of Champions*, then, is much like what has transpired in Kurt Vonnegut's own professional life during the years of its composition.

This novel's growth from its preface involves coming to terms with such change. At first the author just spends time enjoying his power, metafictionally giving characters histories and fortunes and making things happen like their puppetmaster that he is. But metafictive puppetry can become as boring to a writer as it is to readers, and so it is not long before Vonnegut vows to set his characters free. At similar times in their lives, he notes, Thomas Jefferson freed his slaves and Count Tolstoy freed his serfs. Yet as in their cases, such freeing involves coming to terms with his investment, and for dealing with a character such as Kilgore Trout that means recognizing all he has invested in this figure. Such recognition constitutes the novel's resolution in an epilogue that along with the preface frames *Breakfast of Champions* much as the autobiographical chapters 1 and 10 frame *Slaughterhouse-Five*.

Who is Kilgore Trout? As a character, he is Kurt Vonnegut's literary creation. But in dealing with this fact the author goes on to consider all he has put into him. Much of that is an image of Vonnegut himself, including judgments, fears, and aspirations. For the aesthetics of such an operation Vonnegut enlists the aid of another character, the painter Rabo Karakebian, who explains the motive of his own abstract expressionist style of art, which in the manner of Barnett Newman projects a thin line in each color field as the self-awareness constituting the essence of life. Invested as he is with so much of the author's own self-awareness, Trout is the only character Vonnegut has created who might suspect he is a figure in someone else's imagination.

Throughout the novel Vonnegut has shown characters being animated only by another's notice, and losing that sense of animation when they are not noticed. Such animation and its source are what distinguish people from being mere machines. In considering the case of Kilgore Trout the author turns his insight around to consider what it implies for the giver of such attention and not just for the recipient. Trout, after all, has been the enfiguration of Kurt Vonnegut's own presumed failure. Now that his works are read and acted upon, that relationship must be rethought. The self-deprecating spokesman is now being heard, and this new condition has changed the conditions under which he writes.

Thus in the epilogue to *Breakfast of Champions* a modified Kilgore Trout appears. During the years of Vonnegut's own neglect Trout had been an image of the failed writer. Now, with his creator a success, he reemerges as a depiction of the author's father in old age: failing not in terms of worldly success but in health and spirit, crying out *"Make me young, make me young, make me young!"* (p. 295). Like his mother's question in *Slaughterhouse-Five* that Billy Pilgrim cannot answer ("How did I get so old?"), this is something that Vonnegut himself cannot do. There are limits to even metafictive puppetry; having invested so much of one's self-awareness in a character, the author shares a responsibility for that character even as it takes on a life of its own. And having projected onto that character a vision of one's own father's physical decline, it is no easier to undo this process in the character than in the original. It is in this new awareness, the awareness of a successful and widely heeded and thus necessarily responsible writer, that Kurt Vonnegut will continue to work.

This spokesmanlike sense of responsibility is evident from the very start of *Slapstick*,[4] where in a substantial prologue the author explains the autobiographical element that informs the novel itself. "This is the closest I will ever come to writing an autobiography," he announces, and titles it *Slapstick* "because it is grotesque, situational poetry—like the slapstick film comedies, especially those of Laurel and Hardy, of long ago" (p. 1). It is, in fact, shortly after this novel that Kurt Vonnegut's fictive and nonfictive writings most closely coincide, specifically with the "autobiographical collage" that structures *Palm Sunday*. Which work, then, is closest to a real autobiography? Perhaps the latter, because there the author grades *Slapstick* as his weakest novel by far, almost a total failure. Critics on the whole have agreed with him. But with Vonnegut's new style of personal incorporation in mind, two points must be considered: that *Slapstick*'s nineteen-page prologue is itself one of his best-written and most important essays, and that every one of its components and its overall style are replicated in novel form by what follows. From this introductory, confessional material—the same length and of equal importance as the remarkable first chapter of *Slaughterhouse-Five*—one sees Vonnegut choosing the themes and laying the structure not just for the fictive narrative that subsequently unfolds but for his public spokesmanship as it is shaped for *Palm Sunday*.

Why Laurel and Hardy, and why slapstick as a structural device? Because this is what life *"feels* like" to the author. "There are all these tests of my limited agility and intelligence," he explains. "They go on and on." In *Slapstick* those tests are contrived for Wilbur Swain, a man who will eventually become president of a largely dismantled United States; in *Palm Sunday*, as in Kurt Vonnegut's personal life, those tests are presented by everything from the government's conduct to the ecology's endangered future. What distinguishes the author's response in those latter tests are the same qualities he admires in Laurel and Hardy and in his protagonists of this and other novels. "The fundamental joke with Laurel and Hardy, it seems to me, was that they did their best with every test," never failing "to bargain in good faith with their destinies." And what is the benefit of that? The same as for Kurt Vonnegut in *Palm Sunday*, readers would suppose: that doing so allows one to be "screamingly adorable and funny on that account."

Specifically, Vonnegut spends much of his prologue detailing his own life experiences that set the philosophy practiced in the novel to follow. As points advocated by public spokesmanship, they seem directed much more toward policy than aesthetics. But as elements in a narrative, they make for an excellent autobiographical anecdote, one of the most interesting and substantial personal essays the author has written. Within the novel Wilbur Swain conducts his presidential campaign on the issue that governmental structures are less able to care for people than family ones, leading to the proposal for large, artificially extended families. Vonnegut's prologue finds him discussing just how he learned of these values from his own family's experience and now finds himself implementing them in his own adult life.

Take love, for instance—please, *take* it, as a slapstick comedian might exclaim. As a basis for the nuclear family, its unfair demands too often prompt a degeneration into hatred and meanness. Why not "common decency" instead, a less trying obligation that works well for Kurt Vonnegut in his own life. In *Slapstick* it will become a fiction for public policy; here it is a matter of simple advice, much as the author would give in his speeches on campuses and elsewhere. He offers stories from his family history as well, especially how their great numbers and success in Indianapolis made them into a true extended family, one that maintained itself by a devotion to one's relatives. Elsewhere Vonnegut would talk about Professor Robert Redfield's notion of the folk society and how modern conditions make such groupings impossible; here in his prologue the author reminds his readers that it was the anti-German sentiment of World War I that first began fracturing this family unity, a dissolution abetted by financial failures in the Depression and following World War II:

> So—by the time the Great Depression and Second World War were over, it was easy for my brother and my sister and me to wander away from Indianapolis.
>
> And, of all the relatives we left behind, not one could think of a reason why we should come home again.
>
> We didn't belong anywhere in particular any more. We were interchangeable parts in the American machine.
>
> Yes, and Indianapolis, which had once had a way of speaking English all its own, and jokes and legends and poets and villains and heroes all its own, and galleries for its own artists, had itself become an interchangeable part in the American machine. (p. 7)

A sad situation—but family history provides an antidote as well, one that *Slapstick* will employ as part of its social preachment. The prologue's story involves

Kurt's Uncle Alex, who though not an alcoholic founded the Indianapolis chapter of Alcoholics Anonymous to combat the loneliness caused by the decline of his once richly supportive extended family. It is Kurt Vonnegut's own return home for Uncle Alex's funeral that prompts the fiction of *Slapstick*, for the occasion is one of further loss: in memory, as the empty airplane seat between Kurt and his brother reminds them of their dead sister, Alice; and in present reality because with Uncle Alex's death they no longer have an immediate family relative left in town.

Alice Vonnegut Adams's death in 1958 had led to Kurt Vonnegut's own device of an extended family, as he and his wife at once adopted her three orphaned sons. But losing Alice, the ideal reader and projected audience for his work, had deprived Kurt of part of his genius as well—another theme *Slapstick* will develop in the person of siblings who by themselves are unexceptional but when together are geniuses (or rather form a single genius). Together with his own extended family (through adoption) and his Uncle Alex's even more artificially contrived but no less supportive group, this notion of not artistic isolation but cooperation speaks the message of Vonnegut's novel to follow.

Readers of *Wampeters, Foma & Granfalloons*, *Palm Sunday*, and *Fates Worse than Death* will recognize these themes as common to Kurt Vonnegut's public spokesmanship. By repeating them here in the prologue to *Slapstick*, he brings them into play for readers who may not know those works. But even more intentionally, these thoughts set the structural pattern for the novel, locating the author's fictive strategies within an American life he and his readers share. On the second to last page of the prologue that story begins and blends almost seamlessly into the novel that follows. It is an action that carries Kurt Vonnegut as author directly into the narrative, for on the prologue's last two pages he describes how on the flight back to New York, while his brother Bernard toyed with his own imaginative specialty (detecting electrical charges in clouds far away), he himself daydreamed the plot of *Slapstick*, a plot that begins just now: not in the first chapter that gets under way on page 21 but right here on pages 18 and 19 while the airliner wings its way east. Having said that this book is the closest he will ever come to writing an autobiography, Vonnegut proposes the image of an old man sitting in a desolated New York City and doing just that, beginning with the words Kurt's Uncle Alex told him a religious skeptic must always use as a prelude to prayer: "To whom it may concern." Those words both end the prologue and begin chapter 1, making the transition smoothly transformative.

Slapstick proceeds to tell two stories of two distinct time frames in two separate modes. On the one hand, Wilbur Swain weaves a narrative beginning with his own childhood and climaxing with his administration as president of the United States. With this past tense, however, he alternates a scene from the present: not just conditions from the novel's "present" day, which is well into a putative future, but comments on his act of writing. Here he is an old man, much older (at age one hundred) than Vonnegut but reflecting the author's awareness of old manhood as emerging from *Breakfast of Champions*. Looking forward to the theme of *Galápagos* is the notion of deevolution, of a weakened civilization's ability to do less damage to the environment and to itself. But the greater parts by far of *Slapstick* play out notions that are not only introduced by the prologue but made eminently personal sense in that piece of writing, writing with which the reader can readily identify. There the author has remarked how his midtown New York neighborhood is named Turtle Bay despite a total absence of turtles; now, in altered ecological conditions, the turtles have returned. On a more serious level love and its symbiotic twin hate are rehearsed in narrative terms that make sense in the wake of anecdotes from the novel's prologue, just as any number of otherwise exotic and futuristic touches seem familiar from the author's most credible introductory essay. The correlations make this narrative seem less distant, while its structure follows a route to resolution that readers will already know and trust. Thus is *Slapstick* spokesmanship and fictive writing combined.

Kurt Vonnegut's next novel, *Jailbird*,[5] uses the term "Prologue" as well, this time for material running twenty-nine pages, almost half again as long as the ample material standing before the fictive action of *Slaughterhouse-Five* and *Slapstick*. Like both of those novels, *Jailbird*'s prologue functions to place the author in his work and determine a structural approach to theme. Of all Kurt Vonnegut's novels, this one is the most emphatically socially activist. Its protagonist, Walter F. Starbuck, is styled as a Nixon administration official who is jailed in the wake of Watergate. What enriches his tale are references to his idealistic past as a social reformer during his collegiate days in the 1930s; indeed, his story is told as the failure of New Deal and socialistic principles in the postmodern world of widespread political corruption, corruption not so much of material elements as ideological ones.

The technical achievement of *Jailbird* proper is the integration of these two time frames in Walter Starbuck's life that the narrative must express as one. Vonnegut's prologue sets the structure for that, recalling how his own view of current times has been colored by memories of the past, specifically by the example of an old family friend, Powers Hapgood, who distinguished himself as a union organizer and socialist spokesperson during the same era as Walter Starbuck's fictive young manhood. What Vonnegut admired about Hapgood was his life of social action, long after Kurt's own father was "in full retreat from life" and his mother "had already surrendered and vanished" (p. xiii). Hapgood thus offered a model for living, especially to the young private just back from World War II and Dresden and in need of ideals for rebuilding his world.

Powers, born to wealth and making more through his own industry, is nevertheless an outstanding advocate of the working person's welfare. His factory is a model of its kind, with the business it generates tailored to benefit its employees as much as its owner. Appearing in court on labor's behalf just hours before he is to meet the young Kurt Vonnegut, Hapgood is asked why a man of his standing and accomplishments devotes himself to such issues. His answer is, "Because of the Sermon on the Mount, sir" (p. xix). In the novel's epilogue, in which instead of returning as autobiographical author Vonnegut wraps up Walter Starbuck's own story, Starbuck himself is given this same line to answer a congressional committee probing his own failed idealism.

This is only one, and by no means the least complicated, of the integrations Vonnegut weaves between fact and fiction. As an index to Walter Starbuck's failure, he as a 1930s student leftist and New Deal administrator is fated not only to suffer the McCarthyism of the 1950s but to be innocently dragged down among the Watergate conspirators in the 1970s, none of whom have such liberal roots. Yet Starbuck winds up in the same prison as they do—perhaps shamed more deeply even though he is fully innocent of their crimes. In similar manner an old lover's economic idealism is intermixed with the fortunes of some very real and imposing companies, all of which are fictively acquired in the hope of rededicating their wealth to the people. There is even a technical device introduced to interweave fact with invention: a full index, unique for a novel but effective in both materializing characters' names and integrating autobiographical appearances from real life in the prologue with fictive references within the novel. Completing the sense of seamlessness are the details of something just the opposite, a story that for Kurt Vonnegut as author is an artistic fabrication but for his character Walter Starbuck becomes a mainstay of truth. This is "a violent confrontation between strikers and police and soldiers called the Cuyahoga Massacre. It is an invention, a mosaic composed of bits taken from tales of many such riots in not such olden times" (p. xxi). The story, we are told, is a legend in Walter Starbuck's mind, one of the narratives that has shaped his life. As Vonnegut's composition from various sources, it encapsulates the points Powers Hapgood has been discussing, including the role of unions, employers, and the state in establishing the true public interest. But its product is a fictively surprising one: Walter Starbuck himself, who as a child is set upon his impossibly idealistic course by a curious result of the massacre that Vonnegut describes. In the novel itself, this situation is invented; but in the prologue, the author does all he can to make it real. By integrating the two, Vonnegut shows how experience generates a personal sense of meaning—in other words, a myth.

Furthering *Jailbird*'s mythmaking potency is the return of Kilgore Trout. At the end of *Breakfast of Champions* the author had sought to set him free, yet his image returned as an encapsulation of something else Vonnegut had not yet put to rest: the image of his father's decline in old age as a premonition of his own. Now, in *Jailbird*, the first words of Vonnegut's prologue advise that Kilgore Trout is back again, but not as a firsthand creation of the author. Rather, Trout becomes a pseudonym for Dr. Robert Fender, one of Kurt Vonnegut's many idealists come to ruin, in his case serving a life sentence for treason when his only fault has been having too much humanitarian kindness. From the prison where Starbuck is serving a two-year term (and where he is about to return again at the novel's end) Fender writes science fiction stories that yield another Borgesian imaginary library, this time at a second remove. Before Kilgore Trout was a character whose plots could summarize all the fictions Vonnegut might wish to write but need not; here in *Jailbird* Trout is not just his own creation but a figment in the imagination of another character, a character whose own stories thus assume new complexities of meaning and effect. For a novel in which great public themes are a major issue, this technique allows Vonnegut further benefit of spokesmanship while maintaining his essential guise as a fictive writer.

With *Deadeye Dick*[6] Kurt Vonnegut begins stepping back from his autobiographically implicative role. The front matter is no longer a prologue and is certainly nothing like the fully incorporated first chapter of *Slaughterhouse-Five*; instead, it is just five pages long, is called a preface, and actually functions most conventionally in that mode, offering directly explanatory comments on certain curiosities that merit clarification. Readers are told what a "deadeye dick" is, for instance, and where (but not why) the author has found the recipes that will appear now and then in the novel. Next, as if to parody his own previous prologues with their autobiographical linkages, he runs down the "main symbols in this book" (p. xii), giving the personal coordinates for each. The empty arts center in this novel is the author's own head, as he sees it, nearly depleted of fresh ideas by age sixty; the neutron bomb that depopulates Midland City conforms to the absence of the author's friends and extended family in Indianapolis; and Haiti, where some of the book's action takes place, is Vonnegut's home in New York City. "The neutered pharmacist who tells the tale is my declining sexuality," he confides. "The crime he committed in childhood is all the bad things I have done" (p. xiii).

As clues to the novel, Vonnegut's prefatory comments are accurate, but they are needed only if the reader knows nothing of his public spokesmanship. Everything he says reflects prominent themes in *Wampeters, Foma & Granfalloons*, *Palm Sunday*, and *Fates Worse than Death*; the central image, of a lost Indianapolis after a childhood that started wonderfully but economically deconstructed beneath him, is one of the most familiar echoes in all his work, and is sufficiently accessible for most Americans even beyond a specific readership of what Kurt Vonnegut has written. But for those who have followed the issues raised by his essays, prologues, and prefaces, *Deadeye Dick* presents a compendium of personal attitudes and experiences now turned to their most public effectiveness yet.

The bulk of those attitudes and experiences relate to art, an issue central to the author's publicly expressed attitudes since *Breakfast of Champions*. One of Vonnegut's most persistent stories had been how his grandfather and father were artists, supporting themselves in the only slightly less risky profession of architecture; how the failure of this profession during the Great Depression prompted

Vonnegut's father to forbid him to follow in the business, or study any kind of arts for that matter, but to advocate instead learning something materially useful—which in the author's case turned out to be biochemistry. On the home front, Kurt would remember an artistically gifted father disappointed by life and seeming to float free of it, and a mother whose economic and cultural disappointments drove her to instability and eventual suicide.

In *Deadeye Dick* the narrator's father is a more extreme example, that of a person who only dabbled in the arts, found he had little or no talent, but continued to live as an empty, artless counterfeit instead of doing anything useful. The mother remains somewhat distantly indifferent, existing weightlessly in a past where her only tether is to an image everyone else knows is false. The son, who tells their and his stories, would seem to be the least drawn from life, as he is a colorless, inexpressive "neuter" who after a happenstance experiment as a dramatist stays at home to live hardly any kind of life at all. Indeed, he withdraws so fully from the imaginative properties of existence as neither to touch or be touched by anything—just the opposite of a very public Kurt Vonnegut who has engaged himself with the major issues of his times.

Yet why he wishes to remain beyond touch is the most direct autobiographical correspondence of all. The incident that puts him at such a remove from both art and life is an irresponsible accident that happens to him at age twelve. Having been given charge of his father's gun collection at far too young an age, he fires a .30-.06 shell out the window into seeming space, only to strike and kill a pregnant mother some distance away. By doing so he ruins what remains of his family's fortunes and condemns himself to shame so deep he is unable to relate socially; it also makes him suspect of the arts, suspect of the very things that have motivated the author's public statements and fictive achievements. But one detail corresponds to Kurt Vonnegut's life: the shooting takes place on Mother's Day, 1944, the day Vonnegut's mother took her own life with an overdose of sleeping pills.

Had *Deadeye Dick* been provided with a prologue as full as those in the novels that preceded it, Kurt Vonnegut might well have retold the story of his mother's death. Yet the candor with which it had already been told elsewhere makes it one of the most commonly known public facts about the author; it is understandable that here he wishes to maintain more tacit distance between autobiography and fictive event. Yet other devices make the point more than adequately, including those of the recipes (from a protagonist who ardently wishes to give physical nourishment to compensate for the emotional bonds he is unwilling to form) and of the Shangri-la-ish adventure tales (from a narrator who yearns for distance and death). Significantly it is the protagonist's misinformed and misdirected mother, now suffering from radiation-induced brain tumors, who undertakes an effective campaign against nonrepresentational art, specifically the same Rabo Karabekian painting that motivates Vonnegut's understanding of art's efficacy at the end of *Breakfast of Champions*. Thus it is the mother's ultimate emptiness, of both maternal emotion and of artistic depth, that turns Midland City's art center into a vacant hulk and may have (by alienating philanthropist and military industrialist Fred Barry) led to the city's depopulation by a neutron bomb.

Galápagos[7] is an understated work of art even more so, letting its author draw implications for the novel's theme from just a single-page dedication to a childhood mentor who introduced young Kurt and his friends to nature, and who actually prompted a dialogue of sorts with the wild that now yields a most unusual narrative. As an antievolution story *Galápagos* can proceed without the author needing to interpolate items from his autobiography, once this autobiographical dedication has launched it. But there is another, even larger informing text for what happens, and that is Charles Darwin's account of his own visit to the Galápagos Islands that generated his thesis of evolution. That Vonnegut wishes now to invert the thesis, to show humankind devolving into the kind of creature no longer a danger to itself and its world, reflects much more universally than any references to Indianapolis, General Electric, or the like might be expected to convey. As public spokesmanship, it finally allows the author to speak by means of and within his narrative, without having to build a platform for it.

Elements from earlier autobiographical prologues and epilogues now function as integral parts of Vonnegut's fiction, examples of how public spokesmanship assumes a new level of literary art. The devices for doing so are minimal. One premise is biological, as foolproof as Darwin's own thesis: that by process of natural selection attributes that work against rather than for human survival are slowly bred out, until after one million years people have reduced their oversized brains and removed their emotional volatility in favor of more harmonious means of life. By this device the author is able to address any number of current social and political issues. Rather than stridently corrective, this spokesmanship can now be warmly congratulatory, reflecting in positive terms on how, from a perspective one million years into the future, humankind has done so well to evolve beyond its problematic state of the late twentieth century. The other premise is structural, in a narrative sense: that such a story can be told because one person from the old days has survived as a contemporaneous self, dying in 1986 but declining to enter the afterlife in favor of remaining on earth as a ghost. As such, he observes and comments not just on current problems but on how the next million years of evolution solved them. It is a role custom-made for a science fiction writer. And that is, in a way, what Kurt Vonnegut makes him: specifically, the son of a science fiction writer, a man named Leon Trout.

Throughout his career Vonnegut has used Leon's father, Kilgore Trout, as more than just a character. On the one hand, Trout serves as an image of everything Vonnegut feared he himself might be: a subgeneric distraction, an unheeded spokesman, a financial and artistic failure, and most of all a lonely, embittered old man. On the other hand, from *God Bless You, Mr. Rosewater* through *Jailbird* (with a furlough from service only in *Slapstick*) Trout as the author's creation could "write" hundreds of novels and short stories, dozens of which are "citable" in the larger narrative itself—thus allowing Vonnegut an imaginary library to quote from, a universe of volumes he could have written but need not thanks to Trout's presence as their "author." Fearful of becoming a science fiction hack and occasionally branded so by malicious critics, Vonnegut thus insures that he himself is not one of the benighted SF crowd. The person guiltily deserving of such status is Kilgore Trout, who is nevertheless allowed to contribute what good ideas a science fiction writer might have.

In *Galápagos*, much as in *Jailbird*, Kilgore Trout appears at second remove. In *Jailbird* he was a pseudonymous creation of another character, Robert Fender; here he appears briefly as another character's father. Being a son, Leon Trout can comment on the old man's oddness but also appreciate the struggle of his work. As an author himself, he can redeem his father's work by rewriting it a million years hence, turning what was once a negative stance into a positive one and transforming lamentation, irony, and satire into celebration and praise.

Yet one element of artistic discrimination remains. In looking back at one million years of human history, Leon Trout is able to brand what passes for "intelligence" as really being little other than "opinion." Darwin's thesis, after all, is nothing more than that: not proof positive of the real thing, but rather an interpretation of what it may be. But by virtue of that interpretation's popularity any number of judgments are made:

> If Charles Darwin had not declared the Galápagos Islands marvelously instructive, Guayaquil would have been just one more hot and filthy seaport, and the islands would have been worth no more to Ecuador than the slag heaps of Staffordshire.
>
> Darwin did not change the islands, but only people's opinion of them. That was how important mere opinion used to be back in the era of great big brains.
>
> Mere opinions, in fact, were as likely to govern people's actions as hard evidence, and were subject to sudden reversals as hard evidence never could be. So the Galápagos Islands could be hell in one moment and heaven in the next, and Julius Caesar could be a statesman in one moment and a butcher in the next, and Ecuadorian paper money could be traded for food, shelter, and clothing in one moment and line the bottom of a birdcage the next, and the universe could be created by God Almighty in one moment and by a big explosion in the next—and on and on. (pp. 16–17)

This same manner of thinking lets Vonnegut solve a major problem in his spokesmanship, that of the planet's slender chances of surviving, at least as things appear to current eyes such as his own. Mere doomsday preaching has its limits. But having Leon Trout speak from a million years hence yields a unique benefit. The end is not necessarily near. True, there are economic crises as well as ecological ones, but the key lies in discerning just where the crisis is located:

This financial crisis, which could never happen today, was simply the latest in a series of murderous twentieth century catastrophes which had originated entirely in human brains. From the violence people were doing to themselves and to each other, and to all other living things, for that matter, a visitor from another planet might have assumed that the environment had gone haywire, and that people were in such a frenzy because Nature was about to kill them all.

But the planet a million years ago was as moist and nourishing as it is today—and unique, in that respect, in the entire Milky Way. All that had changed was people's opinion of the place. (p. 25)

Galápagos begins a stretch of novels that would run to much greater length than the customary Vonnegut fiction: three hundred pages instead of the two hundred readers had come to expect. And these novels would do much more to speak for themselves. *Bluebeard*[8] is given the minimal courtesy of an author's note, one that disclaims any intention of the book representing a valid history of abstract expressionism; what the author does have in mind is something quite apart from the painters and their paintings, which is how the egregiously large sums now paid for artworks distract from their playfulness and impose a style of seriousness never intended. But that is not a major theme in *Bluebeard*, and it is to be emphasized that with this work Vonnegut no longer stands in front to suggest what his novel is but rather wishes to clarify what it is not.

Sentiments against the fortunes spent for abstract expressionist art, like the sums themselves, postdate the paintings themselves. It was the movement known as conceptual art, prominent more than half a generation later, that sought to produce work immune to appropriation by the financial marketplace. Although his author's note reflects this sentiment, Vonnegut's novel is concerned with a more innocently nascent stage in the style's development: when, during the immediate postwar years, painters such as Pollock and de Kooning struggled in poverty and obscurity to create paintings that meant nothing beyond themselves—and only then, after having repaid small debts to the narrator by giving him supposedly worthless canvases, how the painters saw their works become worth millions.

That latter process makes the narrator, Rabo Karabekian, a wealthy man. But, more importantly, the ideals and achievements of abstract expressionism empower him as a momentarily successful painter himself. And it is this success that becomes the subject of Kurt Vonnegut's spokesmanship.

The argument here is reminiscent of Karabekian's role in *Breakfast of Cham-*

pions, where in response to claims for representational art he explains how the Barnett Newman–like lines in his otherwise stable color fields suggest the self-awareness that is a living being. In *Bluebeard* Karabekian is challenged on broader grounds by a visitor named Circe Berman, author of young adult novels in the manner of Judy Blume, who disparages the abstract art in Karabekian's collection and urges him to move beyond his own nonreferential style in order to depict meaningful moments from his own autobiography.

Coming to terms with his life story is the challenge that generates this narrative. The charges against Karabekian are similar to claims Kurt Vonnegut's own innovative fiction has had to answer, and the author turns his plot on several similarities between his own career as a writer and Karabekian's as a painter. When Circe Berman asks her host to paint pictures with recognizable, referable subjects, she is not asking him to do the impossible. Indeed, his first talent had been for realistic depiction, and much of the autobiography she prompts him to write involves his apprenticeship to a master illustrator. Yet, as accurate as such illustrations are, they lack life's fluid quality. As frozen moments rather than living time, they enshrine death; and it is no accident, from Karabekian's point of view, that this illustrator goes on to serve the purposes of fascism, extolling the praises of Mussolini and eventually dying in his army. The death of one era and its style clears the way for the birth of the new, in this case abstract expressionism and its role in recentering the art world from Europe to New York. Here is the perfect scene for Karabekian's spokesmanship, for as he argues with Circe Berman about the purposes of art, his own autobiography develops on the page with memories of what great talkers the abstract expressionists were. Thus, while Karabekian continues in present-day Springs, Long Island, Jackson Pollock and the others make their claims for art in the Cedar Tavern during the late 1940s, the two scenes (and modes of narrative) reinforcing each other.

From another character Vonnegut introduces his theory of revolution: that any great renovation, whether in the arts or in politics, must be the work of not just one but three persons. A radical genius alone is not enough; his or her efforts must be recognized and commended by a recognized authority and then in turn disseminated by a third person with the talents for simple, clear explanation. Such stages are retold in the history of how the work of Jackson Pollock was recognized for its energy and elucidated as a style of action painting, how the canvas became not a surface upon which to represent but an arena within which to act. In telling this story Rabo Karabekian justifies his own art. Yet in having to write an autobiography for Circe Berman he discovers a way of returning to his past for subject matter without sacrificing abstract expressionism's ideals. The work he paints sums up his own heritage and experience in a grand scene from the end of World War II. Though its close-hand depictions are accurate, their immense numbers, mammoth scope, and the canvas's gargantuan size prevent any static reading. So large that it cannot be viewed all at one time, his rendition of an after-the-battle scene with tens of thousands of soldiers, prisoners, and refugees of all armies and nations and peoples becomes an action painting as fluid as the most energetic Pollock masterpiece.

This sense of history not as product but as process informs *Hocus Pocus*,[9] in which Vonnegut finds a way to be both spokesmanlike and fictive at the same time. His solution is to assume neither as a prefatory role but rather to resume the pose used thirty years before in *Mother Night*. Once again he presents himself neither as a novelist nor as a speaker preparing readers for a public statement, but as a simple functionary of the text, as the "editor" (for this "Editor's Note") who must comment on the supposed author's conditions of storytelling. Yet for all it shares in form with *Mother Night*, this new novel does even more to incorporate public spokesmanship with personal fictions. In *Bluebeard*, Circe Berman had urged Rabo Karabekian to paint his mother's survivorship of a massacre, depicting her finding glittering jewels falling from the mouth of a corpse. Instead, he paints a larger scene whose immensity makes the figures themselves sparkle in a manner representative not of their historical roles but of jewels. *Hocus Pocus* accomplishes a similar broadening of intent and effect, empowering a narrator, Eugene Debs Hartke, quite naturally to assume a spokesman's responsibility as he tells the story of his life, a fictive construct (of course) which reflects the issues Vonnegut himself had been addressing in *Wampeters*, *Palm Sunday*, and the essays being rewoven into *Fates Worse than Death*.

In 1969 Kurt Vonnegut, speaking as a World War II veteran, told a story about his war in terms understandable to the current Vietnam War times. Biographically, his first step in that series of events dated from 1940 when his father disallowed any study of the arts and instructed him to study something useful, in Kurt's case biochemistry at Cornell. In updating his fictive spokesmanship for *Hocus Pocus* in 1990, Vonnegut lets his protagonist and narrator be born in 1940 and to have his first future-determining step be made when the father again redirects the son, this time away from the study of journalism at the University of Michigan in favor of an appointment to West Point. This makes Gene Hartke prime officer material for Vietnam, where he serves with distinction—and also prime spokesmanship material as after the war he turns to college teaching at a private school for learning-impaired children of the rich and powerful. As *Slaughterhouse-Five* sought to grasp the unspeakable nature of the Dresden bombing, *Hocus Pocus* struggles with the legacy of Vietnam. That legacy includes not just the war itself but any number of other issues Vonnegut has addressed in his essays and speeches, including the geopolitical role of nations and the changing status of non-ruling-class people in the American economy, all of which is couched in an awareness of the planet's deteriorating ecology. Yet Hartke is no simple *raisonneur* for the author. Rather, by piecing together his own life story in a fluid manner from more than a dozen distinct time frames that comprise America in the 1950s, 1960s, 1970s, 1980s, 1990s, and into a future of the year 2001 (when he writes), this narrator is allowed to construct a valid work of art that relies less on exposition than on an imaginative construct much like Rabo Karabekian's end-of-the-war masterpiece.

That is the function of Kurt Vonnegut's "Editor's Note": to explain how Hartke wrote his story on small scraps of paper, the size of each suggesting that with the filling of this space he was saying all that could be said on the matter. Sectioned off in the narrative, these scraps facilitate the constant movements in time, backward and forward, from 1940 through 2001. Simultaneously several major narrative lines are developed, including a childhood in the 1950s, an education at the U.S. Military Academy, service in Vietnam, a failing marriage and much philandering afterward, the career in college teaching which ends in disgrace, work as a teacher in prison, and the narrator's own imprisonment. All these narratives develop in each other's company, throwing light not just on one another but on the larger issues of geopolitics and economics. Thus does Vietnam anticipate economic crises a generation later, while crumbling infrastructures and piracy of assets are explained by developments dating from the end of World War II. It is an experience too vast to be comprehended all at once. Yet neither does a close-hand examination of any one part serve a purpose beyond confirming minute authenticity. Instead, like Karabekian's painting, Hartke's narrative is experienced with the movement of an action painting, the notion of "all over" replacing any privileging of hierarchy.

Along the way Gene Hartke quite naturally becomes a spokesman. As the last American soldier to leave Vietnam (in the devastating scene of helicopters lifting off the embassy rooftop and then being unloaded and pushed into the sea from waiting ships), he bears a certain responsibility for regaining self-respect, both for himself and for his country. But he has been a spokesman twice before, at the war's beginning to motivate troops and near the end to make losses look like victories. He is widely known in the service by his legendary nickname, "The Preacher." But he has earned it for the manner of his spokesmanship as well, a manner that eschews all profanity and vulgarity for one simple reason: because such usages "entitle people who don't want unpleasant information to close their ears and eyes to you" (p. 16). In the all-embracing presence of his narrative, he can speak to major issues of five decades with the sense of bringing it all together in himself. It is, in fact, the method of New Journalism Kurt Vonnegut admires in Dan Wakefield (there is a mentor named General Wakefield in this novel) and Hunter S. Thompson: that of taking part in an otherwise incomprehensible story and reporting on what one can safely know, which is oneself.

As a spokesman, Gene Hartke finds it helpful to cite texts. These include the Bible, John Gay's *The Atheist's Bible*, and *Bartlett's Familiar Quotations*. These are excerpts, of course, rather than narratives. The only narrative other than his own is a Kilgore Trout story that motivates him much as another Trout fiction gives Dwayne Hoover an explanation and reason to act in *Breakfast of Cham-*

pions. Here Trout's tale involves the manipulation of human history as a device for culturing strong germs capable of spreading life through the universe. In Trout's fictive scheme, such culturing explains the human and ecological disasters civilizations have created. For Hartke, as for spokesman Leon Trout in *Galápagos*, it suggests the mischief that results when people take their intelligence and dexterity too vainly. Both types of sources, excerpts from the world's wisdom and abstracts of Trout's story, let Hartke proceed much as Kurt Vonnegut does in public performance, flipping through textual materials as a way of both contextualizing and advancing his argument.

That argument is, in the end, a simple one: that increasingly over the past fifty years ruling classes have transformed their riches from ownership of managed assets to assets that can be management free. Such a process begins with industrial automation and ends with the selling off of everything in favor of one last generation's self-privilege. Yet this bare-bones structure is fleshed out with colorful, interesting, and ultimately compelling stories, not the least of which is Hartke's own on the roller coaster of success and failure, failure and success. Along the way he makes reference to what readers will recognize as familiar Kurt Vonnegut essays: "Teaching the Unteachable" (p. 112), "Brief Encounters on the Inland Waterway" (p. 205), "Yes, We Have No Nirvanas" (p. 246, with a reference to "scuba diving in lukewarm bouillon"), the address on strategic bombing at the Smithsonian's Air and Space Museum (p. 253, with such bombings today serving as acts of "show-biz"), and most centrally the piece on Lake Maxincuckee with its location of one type of institution on the south shore and another on the north. For Kurt Vonnegut, these materials have been expository; in Hartke's narrative they become wonderfully fictive, the most colorful parts of his engaging story. But in each case the issues are advanced.

It is because Hartke's story is so rich that Kurt Vonnegut as author wishes him to speak for himself. "To virtually all of his idiosyncracies I, after much thought, have applied what another author once told me was the most sacred word in a great editor's vocabulary," Vonnegut says in his note at the beginning. "That word is 'stet' " (p. 8).

With this acknowledgment Kurt Vonnegut lets his protagonist, Eugene Debs Hartke, step forward to tell his own story, one whose concerns with national policy make it Vonnegut's most committed fictive work of social and political argument. He makes those arguments through a fictive character because, beginning with the Vietnam War and following through the internationalization of American business and industry during the 1990s, they are not exclusively of Kurt Vonnegut's self or generation. For once, his autobiography is not at issue; rather, just as a general knowledge of Darwinian science carries the reader into *Galápagos* and even a rudimentary knowledge of American art history does the same in *Bluebeard*, a character speaking for a span of history Kurt Vonnegut has himself addressed as a spokesperson must bear the fictive burden.

As a writer, Gene Hartke's motivation is one that Vonnegut shares. Each feels the need to speak: Hartke to the issues, Vonnegut to the potency of those issues in motivating the literary creation that Eugene Debs Hartke is. In *Bluebeard*, Kurt Vonnegut had engaged in a little bit of raisonneuring, when Rabo Karabekian and his friend the novelist Paul Slazinger debate the roles of writers in closed and free societies. Slazinger bemoans the fate of authors silenced by their Iron Curtain governments. Karabekian counters with the question, "Who is more to be pitied, a writer bound and gagged by policemen or one living in perfect freedom who has nothing more to say?" (p. 176). Throughout his career Vonnegut has had much to say, and his genius lies in the ways he has devised to say it. That his narrator/protagonists achieve their fullest characterizations as spokespersons bears out the committed nature of his art.

From 1990 through 1996 no Vonnegut novel appeared—by far the largest gap in the author's canon since his career as a short story writer had ended following the 1950s. Yet he was at work all that time on a novel called *Timequake*,[10] completing several drafts but being pleased by none of them. Finally, in the closing months of 1996, he disassembled the typescript in order to produce something new and quite different. His preface to the work as published explains what has been done, taking the best of his prototypical novel, explaining why the worst parts did not fit, recounting how he had struggled so long with these recalcitrant materials, and stringing together an account of this whole process structured by his "thoughts and experiences during the past seven months or so" (p. xii). As such, the author provides not a piece of autobiographical fiction but rather something new: the autobiography of a novel.

The central thematic device of Vonnegut's novel per se is as clear-cut as the Ice-9 of *Cat's Cradle* and the deevolution of *Galápagos*: that for a period of time the universe ceases expanding, considers reversing course toward implosion, but after a ten-year regress halts this retraction and begins expanding again. For human life, this means that everyone's existence suddenly skips back a decade, then repeats itself in an inexorable déjà vu until time once again catches up with itself. Just as with the modifications of gravity's power in *Slapstick*, the idea—however implausible—is nevertheless consistent with physical behavior. Much more interesting, though, are the ramifications of this event, telling readers much about the quality of late-twentieth-century existence. That a timequake has forced people simply to go through the motions for ten years as if they could care less explains much contemporary malaise; it also suggests why folks seem unable to learn from their mistakes, apathy overcoming everything except the urge to buy a one-in-a-million lottery ticket. There are also analogs Vonnegut can cite from his own experience, such as when at the end of World War II he meets a dying SS officer who confesses, "I have just wasted the past ten years of my life."

There are positive analogs to timequakes as well. People do invent them as necessary, such as playwrights scripting the behavior of actors; as a joke, Vonnegut's spokesperson Kilgore Trout quips that John Wilkes Booth's assassination of Abraham Lincoln "was the sort of thing which is bound to happen whenever an actor creates his own material" (p. 197). More winsomely, the author himself can tell an audience at Butler University that if he had to do it all over again, he would choose to be born and grow up in Indianapolis, just as he had done. Later on Vonnegut says the same for his experiences in the Great Depression and in World War II. Even within the timequake device there is a moral of sorts: that all the real trouble starts when the ten-year repeat ends and "free will kicks in again," a phrase repeated in this novel in the manner of *Slaughterhouse-Five*'s "so it goes." Like much of the author's work, the narrative device explains the unexplainable; as Kilgore Trout writes in one of his many quoted stories, "Listen, if it isn't a timequake dragging us through knothole after knothole, it's something else just as mean and powerful" (p. 46).

Such explanations, fictive as they are, serve more as palliatives than rational solutions. Yet in a more general way Kurt Vonnegut's autobiography of a novel provides hope where pessimism might seem a more likely attitude. His own feeling of exhaustion is understandable; he had to undertake the hard work of writing a novel ten years past retirement age in a world apparently deteriorated from the ideals and promise of his youth and young manhood. An increasingly Darwinian view of existence had become thematic in his recent work, and much of that is repeated here. Yet there is also an antidote provided in Kilgore Trout's advice for recovering after the timequake: people have been sick but they are better again, and there is work to be done. Vonnegut himself has done that work in salvaging the ten-year project of *Timequake* and redoing it in the form now published. As such, it is rich in the best of his methods, from incorporating Kilgore Trout's lifework as a vast imaginary library to bonding his otherwise loose story line together by repeating key phrases in otherwise different circumstances. Throughout, the author relates the autobiography of this novel to his own life's story, remarking how in both the key is simple human awareness, an awareness that the forces of life too often conspire to crush.

One such correlation lets Kurt Vonnegut speak directly to the purposes of art. It comes in a letter to his brother Bernard, a scientist who late in life experiments with abstract expressionist painting. Is it art?, Bernard asks. Here is the younger brother's answer:

> People capable of liking some paintings or prints or whatever can rarely do so without knowing something about the artist. Again, the situation is social rather than scientific. Any work of art is half of a conversation between two human beings, and it helps a lot to know who is talking at you. Does he or she have a reputation for seriousness, for religiosity, for suffering, for concupiscence, for rebellion, for sincerity, for jokes?

There are virtually no respected paintings made by persons about whom we know zilch. We can even surmise a lot about the lives of whomever did the paintings in the caverns underneath Lascaux, France.

I dare to suggest that no picture can attract serious attention without a particular sort of human being attached to it in the viewer's mind. If you are unwilling to claim credit for your pictures, and to say why you hoped others might find them worth examining, there goes the ballgame.

Pictures are famous for their human-ness, and not for their picture-ness. (pp. 144–45)

The paintings talked about above are not representational but rather are fully abstract. Yet Vonnegut, having described the eminently personal manners of Jackson Pollock and Willem de Kooning previously, emphasizes that his brother's work will have merit only to the extent that it expresses and shares the truth of his life. *Timequake* follows the same strategy, taking a scientific experiment, an intellectual exercise worthy of the best German physicists, and working it out not abstractly but in the most completely human dimensions the author can manage. As the autobiography of a novel, it takes public spokesmanship and directs it not just to social issues, politics, or morals, but to the essence of Kurt Vonnegut's activity as a fiction writer, a business he has always thought of as a vitally communicative affair.

NOTES

CHAPTER ONE: EMERGING FROM ANONYMITY

1. Granville Hicks, "Literary Horizons," *Saturday Review* 52 (Mar. 29, 1969): 25.
2. Robert Scholes, *"Slaughterhouse-Five," New York Times Book Review*, Apr. 6, 1969, pp. 1, 23.
3. C. D. B. Bryan, "Kurt Vonnegut, Head Bokononist," *New York Times Book Review*, Apr. 6, 1969, pp. 2, 25.
4. Kurt Vonnegut, "The Latest Word," *New York Times Book Review*, Oct. 30, 1966, pp. 1, 56; collected as "New Dictionary" in *Welcome to the Monkey House* (New York: Delacorte Press/Seymour Lawrence, 1968), pp. 106–11.
5. Kurt Vonnegut, "How To Write with Style," International Paper Company Publicity Handout, May 1980, also featured as a national advertisement in many magazines as part of the company's "Power of the Printed Word" promotion; collected in *Palm Sunday* (New York: Delacorte Press/Seymour Lawrence, 1981), pp. 76–81.
6. Kurt Vonnegut, "Science Fiction," *New York Times Book Review*, Sept. 5, 1965, p. 2; reprinted in *Page Two*, ed. Francis Brown (New York: Holt, Rinehart & Winston, 1969), pp. 117–20; collected in *Wampeters, Foma & Granfalloons* (New York: Delacorte Press/Seymour Lawrence, 1974), pp. 1–5.
7. Seymour Lawrence, "A Publisher's Dream," *Summary* 1, no. 2 (1971): 73–75.
8. "Vonnegut's Gospel," *Time* 95 (June 29, 1970): 8; Vonnegut's speech was published as "Up Is Better than Down," *Vogue* 156 (Aug. 1970): 54, 144–45; and collected as "Address to the Graduating Class at Bennington College, 1970," in *Wampeters, Foma & Granfalloons*, pp. 159–68.
9. A program for the event was published by the Ohio State University Libraries; a privately made tape recording of Vonnegut's remarks is in the author's personal collection.
10. Jane Vonnegut Yarmolinsky, *Angels without Wings* (Boston: Houghton Mifflin, 1987).
11. "Kurt Vonnegut: A Self-Interview," National Public Radio Options Series audio cassette OP-770726.001, 01-C (1981), a partial transcription of Vonnegut's lecture of the same title at the University of Northern Iowa, Cedar Falls, Iowa, on Mar. 31, 1977; a full transcription was made for private use by the university's broadcasting services, KUNI-FM.
12. "Kurt Vonnegut: The Art of Fiction LXIV," *Paris Review* no. 69 (Spring 1977): 56–103; collected as "Self-Interview" in *Palm Sunday*, pp. 82–117.
13. Kurt Vonnegut, "Requiem: The Hocus Pocus Laundromat," *North American Review* 271 (Dec. 1986): 29–35; collected as "Mass Promulgated by Me in 1985" in *Fates Worse than Death* (New York: Putnam, 1991), pp. 227–34.
14. Kurt Vonnegut, "Tough Question, Tough Answer," *Smart*, June 1990, pp. 73–79; collected in *Fates Worse than Death*, pp. 98–105, accompanied by Vonnegut's

commentary; a videotape of Vonnegut's appearance, including a concluding question-and-answer session, was supplied by Robert Weide.

15. Letter from Kurt Vonnegut to Jerome Klinkowitz, Jan. 3, 1990.

CHAPTER TWO: SHORT-STORY SALESMANSHIP

1. Kurt Vonnegut, "Report on the Barnhouse Effect," *Collier's* 125 (Feb. 11, 1950): 18–19, 63–65; collected in *Welcome to the Monkey House*, pp. 156–70, from which subsequent quotations are taken and identified in text parenthetically.

2. Kurt Vonnegut, "The Euphio Question," *Collier's* 127 (May 12, 1951): 22–23, 52–54, 56; collected in *Welcome to the Monkey House*, pp. 171–86, from which subsequent quotations are taken and identified in text parenthetically.

3. Kurt Vonnegut, "The Hyannis Port Story," collected in *Welcome to the Monkey House*, pp. 133–45, from which subsequent quotes are taken and identified in text parenthetically; in a letter to Jerome Klinkowitz dated Jan. 17, 1971, Jane C. Vonnegut (Kurt's wife) indicates that the story was accepted for publication by the *Saturday Evening Post* but canceled in galleys when President John F. Kennedy was assassinated on Nov. 22, 1963.

4. Kurt Vonnegut, *Canary in a Cat House* (Greenwich, Conn.: Fawcett, 1961).

5. Kurt Vonnegut, "You've Never Been to Barnstable?," *Venture—Traveler's World* 1 (Oct. 1964): 145, 147–49; collected as "Where I Live" in *Welcome to the Monkey House*, pp. 1–6, from which subsequent quotations are taken and identified in text parenthetically.

6. Kurt Vonnegut, "EPICAC," *Collier's* 126 (Nov. 25, 1950): 36–37; collected in *Welcome to the Monkey House*, pp. 268–75, from which subsequent quotations are taken and identified in text parenthetically.

7. Kurt Vonnegut, "The Manned Missiles," *Cosmopolitan* 145 (July 1958): 83–88; collected in *Welcome to the Monkey House*, pp. 256–67.

8. Kurt Vonnegut, "The Foster Portfolio," *Collier's* 128 (Sept. 8, 1951): 18–19, 72–73; collected in *Welcome to the Monkey House*, pp. 53–66, from which subsequent quotations are taken and identified in text parenthetically.

9. Kurt Vonnegut, "Custom-Made Bride," *Saturday Evening Post* 226 (Mar. 27, 1954): 30, 81–82, 86–87.

10. Kurt Vonnegut, "Unpaid Consultant," *Cosmopolitan* 138 (Mar. 1955): 52–57.

11. Kurt Vonnegut, "Poor Little Rich Town," *Collier's* 130 (Oct. 25, 1952): 90–95.

12. Kurt Vonnegut, "Hal Irwin's Magic Lamp," *Cosmopolitan* 142 (June 1957): 92–95; this is the only story collected in *Canary in a Cat House* that was dropped from *Welcome to the Monkey House.*

13. Kurt Vonnegut, "My Name Is Everyone," *Saturday Evening Post* 234 (Dec. 16, 1961): 20–21, 62, 64, 66–67; collected as "Who Am I This Time?" in *Welcome to the Monkey House*, pp. 14–26.

14. Kurt Vonnegut, "Go Back to Your Precious Wife and Son," *Ladies' Home Journal* 79 (July 1962): 54–55, 108, 110; collected in *Welcome to the Monkey House*, pp. 187–200, from which subsequent quotations are taken and identified in text parenthetically.

15. Kurt Vonnegut, "Lovers Anonymous," *Redbook* 121 (Oct. 1963): 70–71, 146–48.

16. Kurt Vonnegut, "Any Reasonable Offer," *Collier's* 129 (Jan. 19, 1952): 32, 46–47.
17. Kurt Vonnegut, "More Stately Mansions," *Collier's* 128 (Dec. 22, 1951): 24–25, 62–63; collected in *Welcome to the Monkey House*, pp. 121–32.
18. Kurt Vonnegut, "Unready to Wear," *Galaxy Science Fiction* 6 (Apr. 1953): 98–111; collected in *Welcome to the Monkey House*, pp. 229–43.
19. Karla Kuskin, Kurt Vonnegut, and others, "HOLE BEAUTIFUL: Prospectus for a Magazine of Shelteredness," *Monocle* 5, no. 1 (1962): 45–51.

CHAPTER THREE: THE ROAD TO *WAMPETERS*

1. Kurt Vonnegut, "Headshrinker's Hoyle on Games We Play," *Life* 58 (1962): 15, 17, from which subsequent quotations are taken and identified in text parenthetically.
2. Kurt Vonnegut, "Infarcted! Tabescent!," *New York Times Book Review*, June 27, 1965, pp. 4, 38, from which subsequent quotations are taken and identified in text parenthetically.
3. Kurt Vonnegut, "Second Thoughts on Teacher's Scrapbook," *Life* 59 (Sept. 3, 1965): 9–10, from which subsequent quotations are taken and identified in text parenthetically.
4. Kurt Vonnegut, "Hello, Star Vega, Do You Read Our Gomer Pyle?," *Life* 61 (Dec. 9, 1965): R3, from which subsequent quotations are taken; collected in *Wampeters, Foma & Granfalloons*, pp. 21–24.
5. Kurt Vonnegut, "The Scientific Goblins Are Gonna Git Us," *Life* 65 (July 26, 1968): 8, from which subsequent quotations are taken.
6. Kurt Vonnegut, "Topics: Good Missiles, Good Manners, Good Night," *New York Times*, Sept. 13, 1969, p. 26, and "Torture and Blubber," *New York Times*, June 30, 1971, p. 41; both guest editorials are reprinted in *Wampeters, Foma & Granfalloons*, pp. 103–5 and pp. 169–71.
7. Kurt Vonnegut, "Closed Season on the Kids," *Life* 70 (Apr. 9, 1971): 14, from which subsequent quotations are taken.
8. Kurt Vonnegut, "Everything Goes Like Clockwork," *New York Times Book Review*, June 13, 1965, p. 4, from which subsequent quotations are taken.
9. Kurt Vonnegut, "The Unsaid Says Much," *New York Times Book Review*, Sept. 12, 1965, pp. 4, 54, from which subsequent quotes are taken and identified in text parenthetically.
10. Kurt Vonnegut, "Don't Take It Too Seriously," *New York Times Book Review*, Mar. 20, 1966, pp. 1, 39.
11. Kurt Vonnegut, "The Fall of a Climber," *New York Times Book Review*, Sept. 25, 1966, pp. 5, 42.
12. Kurt Vonnegut, "Money Talks to the New Man," *New York Times Book Review*, Oct. 2, 1966, p. 4, from which subsequent quotations are taken.
13. Kurt Vonnegut, "War as a Series of Collisions," *Life* 69 (Oct. 2, 1970): 10, from which subsequent quotations are taken.
14. Kurt Vonnegut, "Der Arme Dolmetscher," *Atlantic Monthly* 196 (July 1955): 86–88, from which subsequent quotations are taken and identified in text parenthetically.
15. Kurt Vonnegut, "Let the Killing Stop," *Register* (Yarmouth Port, Mass.), Oct. 23, 1969, p. 3, from which subsequent quotations are taken.

16. Kurt Vonnegut, "Times Change," *Esquire* 74 (Feb. 1970): 60, from which subsequent quotations are taken; adapted with one minor change (a reference to the book in question) from Vonnegut's introduction to *Our Time is Now: Notes from the High School Underground*, edited by John Birmingham (New York: Praeger, 1970), pp. vii–x.

17. Kurt Vonnegut, "Nixon's the One," in *Earth Day—The Beginning*, edited by the National Staff of Environmental Action (New York: Bantam, 1970), p. 64, from which subsequent quotations are taken.

18. Kurt Vonnegut, "Foreword," in Anne Sexton, *Transformations* (Boston: Houghton Mifflin, 1971), pp. vii–x, from which subsequent quotations are taken and identified in text parenthetically.

19. Kurt Vonnegut, "Reading Your Own," *New York Times Book Review*, June 4, 1967, p. 6, from which subsequent quotations are taken.

20. Kurt Vonnegut, "The High Cost of Fame," *Playboy* 18 (Jan. 1971): 124, from which subsequent quotations are taken.

CHAPTER FOUR: *WAMPETERS, FOMA & GRANFALLOONS*

1. "Der Arme Dolmetscher" is in fact Vonnegut's first personal essay, but one that predates by almost a decade his first sustained work in nonfiction. Listed incorrectly (by its working title) in the credits for *Welcome to the Monkey House*, it was dropped before that volume's publication and was rejected a second time when the materials for *Wampeters, Foma & Granfalloons* were reviewed by Kurt Vonnegut. The author's second essay (and second piece of nonfiction), "You've Never Been to Barnstable?" begins his steady stream of essays and reviews in late 1964 and was included in *Welcome to the Monkey House*. "Science Fiction" followed four uncollected reviews in 1965 and is thus chosen by Kurt Vonnegut as the first of his previously uncollected nonfiction pieces that he wishes to save. Originally published on page 2 of the *New York Times Book Review* for Sept. 5, 1965, it is reprinted on pp. 1–5 of *Wampeters*, from which subsequent quotations are taken and identified in text parenthetically.

2. Kurt Vonnegut, "Brief Encounters on the Inland Waterway," *Venture—Traveler's World* 3 (Oct./Nov. 1966): 135–38, 140, 142; collected in *Wampeters*, pp. 7–19, from which subsequent quotations are taken and identified in text parenthetically.

3. Kurt Vonnegut, "Teaching the Unteachable," *New York Times Book Review*, June 6, 1967, pp. 1, 20, from which the closing quotation is taken; collected in revised form in *Wampeters*, pp. 25–30, from which subsequent quotations are taken and identified in text parenthetically.

4. Kurt Vonnegut, "Yes, We Have No Nirvanas," *Esquire* 69 (June 1968): 78–79, 176, 178–79, 182; collected in *Wampeters*, pp. 31–41; from which subsequent quotations are taken and identified in text parenthetically.

5. Kurt Vonnegut, "Fortitude," *Playboy* 15 (Sept. 1968): 99–100, 102, 106, 217–18; collected in *Wampeters*, pp. 43–64.

6. Kurt Vonnegut, " 'There's a Maniac Loose Out There,' " *Life* 67 (July 25, 1969): 53–56.

7. Kurt Vonnegut, "Excelsior! We're Going to the Moon! Excelsior!," *New York Times*

Magazine, July 13, 1969, pp. 9–11; collected in *Wampeters*, pp. 77–89, from which subsequent quotations are taken and identified in text parenthetically.

8. Kurt Vonnegut, "Man on the Moon: The Epic Journey of Apollo XI," *CBS News Transcript* (excerpt), July 20, 1969 [broadcast 1:16 P.M., Eastern Daylight Time], p. 4.

9. Kurt Vonnegut, "Physicist, Purge Thyself," *Chicago Tribune Magazine*, June 22, 1969, pp. 44, 48–50, 52, 56; collected as "Address to American Physical Society" in *Wampeters*, pp. 91–102, from which subsequent quotations are taken and identified in text parenthetically.

10. Kurt Vonnegut, "Why They Read Hesse," *Horizon* 12 (Spring 1970): 28–31; collected in *Wampeters*, pp. 107–15, from which subsequent quotations are taken and identified in text parenthetically.

11. Kurt Vonnegut, "Oversexed in Indianapolis," *Life* 69 (July 17, 1970): 10; collected in *Wampeters*, pp. 117–19, from which subsequent quotations are taken and identified in text parenthetically.

12. Dan Wakefield, "In Vonnegut's *Karass*," in *The Vonnegut Statement*, edited by Jerome Klinkowitz and John Somer (New York: Delacorte Press/Seymour Lawrence, 1973), pp. 55–70; Vonnegut's suggestion for a title was "Getting Laid in Indianapolis."

13. Kurt Vonnegut, "The Mysterious Madame Blavatsky," *McCall's* 97 (Mar. 1970): 66–67, 142–44; collected in *Wampeters*, pp. 121–37, from which subsequent quotations are taken and identified in text parenthetically.

14. Kurt Vonnegut, "Biafra: A People Betrayed," *McCall's* 97 (Apr. 1970): 68–69, 134–38; collected in *Wampeters*, pp. 139–58, from which subsequent quotations are taken and identified in text parenthetically.

15. Kurt Vonnegut, "Up Is Better than Down," *Vogue* 156 (Aug. 1970): 54, 144–45; collected as "Address to Graduating Class at Bennington College, 1970" in *Wampeters*, pp. 159–71, from which subsequent quotations are taken and identified in text parenthetically.

16. Kurt Vonnegut, "What Women Really Want Is . . . ," *Vogue* 160 (Aug. 15, 1971): 56–57, 93; delivered as a speech entitled "The Happiest Day in the Life of My Father" and collected in *Wampeters* as "Address to the National Institute of Arts and Letters, 1971," pp. 173–84, from which subsequent quotations are taken and identified in text parenthetically.

17. Kurt Vonnegut, "In a Manner That Must Shame God Himself," *Harper's* 245 (Nov. 1972): 60–63, 65–66, 68; collected in *Wampeters*, pp. 185–206, from which subsequent quotations are taken and identified in text parenthetically.

CHAPTER FIVE: *PALM SUNDAY*

1. Kurt Vonnegut, *Palm Sunday* (New York: Delacorte Press/Seymour Lawrence, 1981), from which subsequent quotations are taken and identified in text parenthetically.

2. "An Account of the Ancestry of Kurt Vonnegut, Jr., by an Ancient Friend of the Family," *Summary* 1, 2 (1971): 76–118. The bound page proofs of *Palm Sunday* distributed to reviewers in advance of publication include a longer version of the

"Account" than finally included, indicating that the author's editing continued through the book's production.

CHAPTER SIX: *FATES WORSE THAN DEATH*

1. Kurt Vonnegut, *Fates Worse than Death* (New York: Putnam, 1991), from which subsequent quotations are taken and identified in text parenthetically.
2. Kurt Vonnegut, *Fates Worse than Death* (Nottingham, U.K.: Bertrand Russell Peace Foundation [Spokesman Pamphlet No. 80], 1982). This individual sermon is reprinted on pp. 139–49 with the exception of some introductory material for the readership in England and congregation in New York.

CHAPTER SEVEN: A PUBLIC PREFACE FOR PERSONAL FICTION

1. Kurt Vonnegut, *Mother Night* (New York: Harper & Row, 1966), from which subsequent quotations are taken and identified in text parenthetically; this was the novel's first hardcover printing but its second edition, as *Mother Night* (copyrighted 1961), was first published as a paperback original by Fawcett Publications, Greenwich, Conn., in Feb. 1962.
2. Kurt Vonnegut, *Slaughterhouse-Five* (New York: Delacorte Press/Seymour Lawrence, 1969), from which subsequent quotations are taken and identified in text parenthetically.
3. Kurt Vonnegut, *Breakfast of Champions* (New York: Delacorte Press/Seymour Lawrence, 1973), from which subsequent quotations are taken and identified in text parenthetically.
4. Kurt Vonnegut, *Slapstick* (New York: Delacorte Press/Seymour Lawrence, 1976), from which subsequent quotations are taken and identified in text parenthetically.
5. Kurt Vonnegut, *Jailbird* (New York: Delacorte Press/Seymour Lawrence, 1979), from which subsequent quotations are taken and identified in text parenthetically.
6. Kurt Vonnegut, *Deadeye Dick* (New York: Delacorte Press/Seymour Lawrence, 1982), from which subsequent quotations are taken and identified in text parenthetically.
7. Kurt Vonnegut, *Galápagos* (New York: Delacorte Press/Seymour Lawrence, 1985).
8. Kurt Vonnegut, *Bluebeard* (New York: Delacorte Press, 1987).
9. Kurt Vonnegut, *Hocus Pocus* (New York: Putnam, 1990), from which subsequent quotations are taken and identified in text parenthetically.
10. Kurt Vonnegut, *Timequake* (New York: Putnam, 1997).

BIBLIOGRAPHY

Because this study's approach has been developmental, and so that Kurt Vonnegut's uncollected work can be seen in relation, the primary portion of this bibliography follows chronological order.

WORKS BY KURT VONNEGUT
[materials published before 1976 would have included the "Jr." after his name]

Novels

Player Piano. New York: Charles Scribner's Sons, 1952.
The Sirens of Titan. New York: Dell, 1959.
Mother Night. Greenwich, Conn.: Fawcett, 1962. New York: Harper & Row, 1966 (second edition, first hardcover publication, with a new introduction by the author).
Cat's Cradle. New York: Holt, Rinehart & Winston, 1963.
God Bless You, Mr. Rosewater. New York: Holt, Rinehart & Winston, 1965.
Slaughterhouse-Five. New York: Delacorte Press/Seymour Lawrence, 1969.
Breakfast of Champions. New York: Delacorte Press/Seymour Lawrence, 1973.
Slapstick. New York: Delacorte Press/Seymour Lawrence, 1976.
Jailbird. New York: Delacorte Press/Seymour Lawrence, 1979.
Deadeye Dick. New York: Delacorte Press/Seymour Lawrence, 1982.
Galápagos. New York: Delacorte Press/Seymour Lawrence, 1985.
Bluebeard. New York: Delacorte Press, 1987.
Hocus Pocus. New York: Putnam, 1990.
Timequake. New York: Putnam, 1997.

Collections of Short Fiction
[*indicates a nonfiction work]

Canary in a Cat House. Greenwich, Conn.: Fawcett, 1961.
    Contents and original publication:
    "Report on the Barnhouse Effect," *Collier's* 125 (February 11, 1950): 18–19, 63–65.
    "All the King's Horses," *Collier's,* 127 (February 10, 1951): 46–48, 50.
    "D.P.," *Ladies' Home Journal* 70 (August 1953): 42–43, 80–81, 84.
    "The Manned Missiles," *Cosmopolitan* 145 (July 1958): 83–88.
    "The Euphio Question," *Collier's* 127 (May 12, 1951): 22–23, 53–54.
    "More Stately Mansions," *Collier's* 128 (December 22, 1951): 24–25, 62–63.
    "The Foster Portfolio," *Collier's* 128 (September 8, 1951): 18–19, 72–73.

"Deer in the Works," *Esquire* 43 (April 1955): 78–79, 112, 114, 116, 118.

"Hal Irwin's Magic Lamp," *Cosmopolitan* 142 (June 1957): 92–95 (with the omission of its final sentence).

"Tom Edison's Shaggy Dog," *Collier's* 131 (March 14, 1953): 46, 48–49.

"Unready to Wear," *Galaxy Science Fiction* 6 (April 1953): 98–111.

"Tomorrow and Tomorrow and Tomorrow," *Galaxy Science Fiction* 7 (January 1954): 100–110, as "The Big Trip Up Yonder."

Welcome to the Monkey House. New York: Delacorte Press/Seymour Lawrence, 1968. Contents and original publication:

All stories from *Canary in a Cat House* with the exception of "Hal Irwin's Magic Lamp"; "Tom Edison's Shaggy Dog" is reprinted with the absence of its last line.

*"Preface," previously unpublished.

*"Where I Live," *Venture—Traveler's World* 1 (October 1964): 145, 147–49, as "You've Never Been to Barnstable?"

"Harrison Bergeron," *Magazine of Fantasy and Science Fiction* 21 (October 1961): 5–10.

"Who Am I This Time?," *Saturday Evening Post* 234 (December 16, 1961): 20–21, 62, 64, 66–67, as "My Name Is Everyone."

"Welcome to the Monkey House," *Playboy* 15 (January 1968): 95, 156, 196, 198, 200–201.

"Long Walk to Forever," *Ladies' Home Journal* 77 (August 1960): 42–43, 108.

"Miss Temptation," *Saturday Evening Post* 228 (April 21, 1956): 30, 57, 60, 62, 64.

*"New Dictionary," *New York Times Book Review*, October 30, 1966, pp. 1, 56, as "The Latest Word."

"Next Door," *Cosmopolitan* 138 (April 1955): 80–85.

"The Hyannis Port Story," purchased by *Saturday Evening Post* in 1963 but not published (due to President Kennedy's assassination).

"Go Back to Your Precious Wife and Son," *Ladies' Home Journal* 79 (July 1962): 54–55, 108, 110.

"The Lie," *Saturday Evening Post* 235 (February 24, 1962): 46–47, 51, 56.

"Unready to Wear," *Galaxy Science Fiction* 6 (April 1953): 98–111.

"The Kid Nobody Could Handle," *Saturday Evening Post* 228 (September 24, 1955): 37, 136–37.

"EPICAC," *Collier's* 126 (November 25, 1950): 36–37.

"Adam," *Cosmopolitan* 136 (April 1954): 34–39.

Dramatic Works

Happy Birthday, Wanda June. New York: Delacorte Press/Seymour Lawrence, 1971.

Between Time and Timbuktu. New York: Delacorte Press/Seymour Lawrence, 1972.

Work for Children

Sun/Star/Moon. New York: Harper & Row, 1980 (with illustrations by Ivan Chermayeff).

Collections of Nonfiction

[* indicates a fictive work, ** an interview]

Wampeters, Foma & Granfalloons. New York: Delacorte Press/Seymour Lawrence, 1974. Contents and original publication:

Bibliography

"Preface," previously unpublished.

"Science Fiction," *New York Times Book Review*, September 5, 1965, p. 2.

"Brief Encounters on the Inland Waterway," *Venture—Traveler's World* 3 (October/ November 1966): 135–38, 140, 142.

"Hello, Star Vega" [review of I. S. Shklovskii and Carl Sagan's, *Intelligent Life in the Universe*], *Life* 61 (December 9, 1966): R3, as "Hello, Star Vega, Do You Read Our Gomer Pyle?"

"Teaching the Unteachable," *New York Times Book Review*, August 6, 1967, pp. 1, 20 (with several paragraphs, including the ending, omitted).

"Yes, We Have No Nirvanas," *Esquire* 69 (June 1968): 78–79, 176, 178–79, 182.

*"Fortitude," *Playboy* 15 (September 1968): 99–100, 102, 106, 217–18.

" 'There's a Maniac Loose Out There,' " *Life* 67 (July 15, 1969): 53–56.

"Excelsior! We're Going to the Moon! Excelsior!," *New York Times Magazine*, July 13, 1969, pp. 9–11.

"Address to the American Physical Society," *Chicago Tribune Magazine*, June 22, 1969, pp. 44, 48–50, 52, 56, as "Physicist, Purge Thyself."

"Good Missiles, Good Manners, Good Night," *New York Times*, September 13, 1969, p. 26 (as "Topics: Good Missiles, Good Manners, Good Night).

"Why They Read Hesse," *Horizon* 12 (Spring 1970): 28–31.

"Oversexed in Indianapolis [review of Dan Wakefield's *Going All the Way*]," *Life* 69 (July 17, 1970): 10.

"The Mysterious Madame Blavatsky," *McCall's* 97 (March 1970): 66–67, 142–44.

"Biafra: A People Betrayed," *McCall's* 97 (April 1970): 68–69, 134–38.

"Address to the Graduating Class at Bennington College, 1970," *Vogue* 156 (August 1970): 54, 144–45, as "Up Is Better than Down."

"Torture and Blubber," *New York Times*, June 30, 1971, p. 41.

"Address to the National Institute of Arts and Letters, 1971," *Vogue* 160 (August 15, 1972): 56–57, 93, as "What Women Really Want Is. . . ."

"Reflections on My Own Death," *Rotarian*, May 1972, p. 24.

"In a Manner That Must Shame God Himself," *Harper's* 245 (November 1972): 60–63, 65–66, 68.

"Thinking Unthinkable, Speaking Unspeakable," *New York Times*, January 13, 1973, p. 31.

"Address at Rededication of Wheaton College Library, 1973," *Wheaton College Alumnae Magazine* 60 (February 1973): 15–17, as "Essay for the Wheaton Library"; and *Vogue* 162 (July 1973): 62–64, as "America: What's Good, What's Bad?"

"Invite Rita Rait to America!," *New York Times Book Review*, January 28, 1973, p. 31.

"Address to P.E.N. Conference in Stockholm, 1973," *Ramparts* 12 (July 1974): 43–44, as ". . . But Words Can Never Hurt Me."

"A Political Disease [review of Hunter S. Thompson's *Fear and Loathing: On The Campaign Trail '72*]," *Harper's* 246 (July 1973): 92, 94.

**"Playboy Interview," *Playboy* 20 (July 1973): 57–60, 62, 66, 68, 70, 72, 74, 214, 216, conducted by David Standish.

Palm Sunday. New York: Delacorte Press/Seymour Lawrence, 1981.

Contents and original publication (not including the new framing and connective commentary written by Vonnegut, and not including materials written by others):

"Dear Mr. McCarthy," not previously published.

"Un-American Nonsense," *New York Times Long Island Weekly*, March 28, 1976, sec. 21, p. 16, as "Banned Authors Answer Back."

"God's Law," previously unpublished.

"Dear Felix," previously unpublished.

"What I Liked about Cornell," previously unpublished.

"When I Lost My Innocence," submitted to *Aftonbladet* (Sweden), not previously published in English.

"I Am Embarrassed," not previously published.

"How To Write with Style," International Paper Company, May 1980, as a handout in their "Power of the Printed Word" program; also featured as a national advertisement in many magazines.

**"Self-Interview," *Paris Review* no. 69 (Spring 1977): 56–103, as "Kurt Vonnegut: The Art of Fiction LXIV."

"Who in America Is Truly Happy? [review of William F. Buckley Jr.'s *A Hymnal*]," *Politics Today*, January/February 1979, p. 60, as "The Happy Conservative."

"Something Happened [review of Joseph Heller's *Something Happened*]," *New York Times Book Review*, October 6, 1974, pp. 1–2, as "Joseph Heller's Extraordinary Novel about an Ordinary Man."

"The Rocky Graziano of American Letters," not previously published.

"The Best of Bob and Ray," in *Write If You Get Work: The Best of Bob and Ray*, by Bob Elliott and Ray Goulding. New York: Random House, 1975.

"James T. Farrell," not previously published.

"Lavinia Lyon," not previously published.

"The Noodle Factory," *Connecticut College Alumni Magazine*, Fall 1977, pp. 3–5, 42–43; *Mademoiselle* (August 1977): 96, 104–5, as "On Reading/Writing/Freedom."

"Mark Twain," *Nation* 229 (July 7, 1979): 21–22, as "The Necessary Miracle."

"How Jokes Work," not previously published.

"Thoughts of a Free Thinker," not previously published.

"William Ellery Channing," not previously published.

*"The Big Space Fuck," in *Again, Dangerous Visions*, edited by Harlan Ellison. Garden City, N.Y.: Doubleday, 1972, pp. 246–50.

"Fear and Loathing in Morristown, N.J.," not previously published.

"Jonathan Swift," not previously published.

*"The Chemistry Professor," not previously published.

"Louis-Ferdinand Céline," in *Castle to Castle*, *Rigadoon*, and *North*, by Louis-Ferdinand Céline. Harmondsworth, U.K. & New York: Penguin, 1975, as "Introduction" to each individual volume.

"Dresden Revisited," in *Slaughterhouse-Five*. Franklin Center, Pa: Franklin Library, 1978, as "A Special Message to Subscribers from Kurt Vonnegut."

"Palm Sunday," *Nation* 230 (April 19, 1980): 469–70, as "Hypocrites You Always Have with You."

Fates Worse than Death. New York: Putnam, 1991.

Contents and original publication (not including the new framing and connective commentary written by Vonnegut, and not including materials written by others):

Bibliography

"Preface," including a questionnaire submitted to the *Weekly Guardian* (Great Britain) but not previously published in the United States.

Untitled comments on his father, *Architectural Digest* 41 (June 1984): 30, 34, 36, as "Sleeping Beauty."

"Address to the American Psychiatric Association," not previously published.

Untitled comments on his sister, art, and interruptions, *Architectural Digest* 43 (May 1986): 170–75, as "Art/Great Beginnings: In Praise of the Incomplete."

Untitled essay on Jackson Pollock, *Esquire* 100 (December 1983): 549–54, as "Jack the Dripper."

Untitled comments, *Bluebeard*. Franklin Center, Pa.: Franklin Library, 1987, as "A Special Message to Subscribers from Kurt Vonnegut."

Untitled essay on Lake Maxincuckee, *Architectural Digest* 45 (June 1988): 27, 29, 31, as "The Lake."

"Introduction," in *Never Come Morning*, by Nelson Algren. New York: Four Walls Eight Windows, 1987.

Remarks to Hemingway Conference at Boise, Idaho, in *Blowing the Bridge: Essays on Hemingway and For Whom the Bell Tolls*, edited by Rena Sanderson. New York: Greenwood Press, 1992, pp. 19–25, as "Kurt Vonnegut on Ernest Hemingway."

Comments on his "Requiem," adapted from "The Hocus Pocus Laundromat," *North American Review* 271 (December 1986): 29–35.

Proposed testimony to the Attorney General's Commission on Pornography, *Nation* 242 (January 23, 1986): 65, 81–82, as "God Bless You, Edwin Meese."

"Address to the Graduating Class at the University of Rhode Island," not previously published.

"Preface," in *A Very Young Author and Photographer: Jill Krementz at Fifty*. New York: Privately printed, 1990.

Lecture on strategic bombing and its victims, *Smart* (June 1990): 73–79, as "Tough Question, Tough Answer."

Comments to an audience in the year 2088, advertisement for Volkswagen Corporation in issues of *Time* magazine, 1988.

Essay on relative freedoms, *Lear's* 1 (November/December 1988): 106–15, as "Light at the End of the Tunnel?"

Lecture on science and technology at Massachusetts Institute of Technology, not previous published.

Comments on New York City as a folk society, *Architectural Digest* 44 (November 1987): 76, 78, 80, as "Skyscraper National Park."

Untitled comments, in *Hocus Pocus*. Franklin Center, Pa.: Franklin Library, 1990, as "A Special Message to Subscribers from Kurt Vonnegut."

Essay on war preparations, *Nation* 237 (December 31, 1983/January 7, 1984): 681, 698–99, as "The Worst Addiction of Them All."

Sermon on threats to human life, in *Fates Worse than Death*. Nottingham, U.K.: Bertrand Russell Peace Foundation Spokesman Pamphlet No. 80; "Fates Worse than Death," *North American Review* 267 (December 1982): 46–49.

Address to Unitarian congregation in Rochester, New York, *The World: Journal of the Unitarian Universalist Association* 1 (January/February 1987): 4, 6–8, as "Love Is Too Strong a Word."

147

Essay on Mozambique, *Parade*, January 7, 1990, pp. 16–17, as "My Visit to Hell."
Address to translators, Columbia University, not previously published.
Essay on humor, *New York Times Book Review*, April 22, 1990, p. 14, as "Notes from My Bed of Gloom: Or, Why the Joking Had to Stop."
Essay on reading, *Kroch & Brentano Christmas Book Catalogue* (1990).
"Mass Promulgated by Me in 1985," *North American Review* 271 (December 1986): 29–35 as "Requiem: The Hocus Pocus Laundromat."
"My Reply to a Letter from the Dean of the Chapel at Transylvania University about a Speech I Gave There," previously unpublished.

Uncollected Short Fiction

"Thanasphere," *Collier's* 126 (September 2, 1950): 18–19, 60, 62.
"Mnemonics," *Collier's* 127 (April 28, 1951): 38.
"Any Reasonable Offer," *Collier's* 129 (January 19, 1952): 32, 46–47.
"The Package," *Collier's* 130 (July 26, 1952): 48–53.
"Poor Little Rich Town," *Collier's* 130 (October 25, 1952): 90–95.
"Souvenir," *Argosy*, December 1952, pp. 28–29, 76–79.
"The Cruise of the Jolly Roger," *Cape Cod Compass* 8 (April 1953): 7–14.
"Custom-Made Bride," *Saturday Evening Post* 226 (March 27, 1954): 30, 81–82, 86–87.
"Ambitious Sophomore," *Saturday Evening Post* 226 (May 1, 1954): 31, 88, 92, 94.
"Bagombo Snuff Box," *Cosmopolitan* 137 (October 1954): 34–39.
"The Powder Blue Dragon," *Cosmopolitan* 137 (November 1954): 46–48, 50–53.
"A Present for Big Nick," *Argosy*, December 1954, pp. 42–45, 72–73.
"Unpaid Consultant," *Cosmopolitan* 138 (March 1955): 52–57.
"The Boy Who Hated Girls," *Saturday Evening Post* 228 (March 31, 1956): 28–29, 58, 60, 62.
"This Son of Mine . . . ," *Saturday Evening Post* 229 (August 18, 1956): 24, 74, 76–78.
"A Night for Love," *Saturday Evening Post* 230 (November 23, 1957): 40–41, 73, 76–77, 80–81, 84.
"Find Me a Dream," *Cosmopolitan* 150 (February 1961): 108–11.
"Runaways," *Saturday Evening Post* 234 (April 15, 1961): 26–27, 52, 54, 56.
"HOLE BEAUTIFUL: Prospectus for a Magazine of Shelteredness," *Monocle* 5, (1962): 49–51, with Karla Kuskin.
"2 B R O 2 B," *Worlds of If*, January 1962, pp. 59–65.
"Lovers Anonymous," *Redbook* 121 (October 1963): 70–71, 146–48.

Uncollected Nonfiction

"Der Arme Dolmetscher," *Atlantic Monthly* 196 (July 1955): 86–88.
"Headshrinker's Hoyle on Games We Play [review of Eric Berne's *Games People Play*]," *Life* 58 (June 11, 1965): 15, 17.
"Everything Goes Like Clockwork [review of Friedrich Dürrenmatt's *Once a Greek . . .*]," *New York Times Book Review*, June 13, 1965, p. 4.
"Infarcted! Tabescent! [review of Tom Wolfe's *The Kandy-Colored Tangerine-Flake Streamline Baby*]," *New York Times Book Review*, June 27, 1965, p. 4.

Bibliography

"Second Thoughts on Teacher's Scrapbook [review of Bel Kaufman's *Up the Down Staircase*]," *Life* 59 (September 3, 1965): 9–10.

"The Unsaid Says Much [review of Heinrich Böll's *Absent without Leave*]," *New York Times Book Review*, September 12, 1965, pp. 4, 54.

"Don't Take It Too Seriously [review of *Prize Stories 1966: The O'Henry Awards*, edited by Richard Poirier and William Abrahams]," *New York Times Book Review*, March 20, 1966, pp. 1, 39.

"The Fall of a Climber [review of Richard Condon's *Any God Will Do*]," *New York Times Book Review*, September 25, 1966, pp. 5, 42.

"Money Talks to the New Man [review of Goffredo Parise's *The Boss*]," *New York Times Book Review*, October 2, 1966, p. 4.

"Reading Your Own," *New York Times Book Review*, June 4, 1967, p. 4.

"Deadhead Among the Diplomats [review of John Kenneth Galbraith's *The Triumph*]," *Life* 64 (May 3, 1968): 14.

"The Scientific Goblins Are Gonna Git Us [review of *Unless Peace Comes*, edited by Nigel Calder]," *Life* 65 (July 26, 1968): 8.

"Let the Killing Stop," *Register* (Yarmouth Port, Mass.), October 23, 1969, p. 3.

"Times Change," *Esquire* 73 (February 1970): 60; expanded as "Introduction," in *Our Time Is Now: Notes from the High School Underground*, edited by John Birmingham. New York: Praeger, 1970.

"Nixon's the One," in *Earth Day—The Beginning/A Guide for Survival Compiled and Edited by the National Staff of Environmental Action.* New York: Bantam, 1970, pp. 64–65.

"War as a Series of Collisions [review of Len Deighton's *Bomber*]," *Life* 69 (October 2, 1970): 10.

"The High Cost of Fame," *Playboy* 18 (January 1971): 124.

"Closed Season on the Kids [review of *Don't Shoot—We Are Your Children*]," *Life* 70 (April 9, 1971): 14.

"Foreword," in *Transformations*, by Anne Sexton. Boston: Houghton Mifflin, 1971.

Liner notes, Kurt Vonnegut Jr. reads *Slaughterhouse-Five*. New York: Caedmon Records, 1973, TC 1376, signed "Philboyd Sludge," a corruption of the "Philboyd Studge" Vonnegut used to sign the preface to *Breakfast of Champions*.

"A New Scheme for Real Writers," *New York Times Book Review*, July 14, 1974, p. 47.

"Writers, Vonnegut and the U.S.S.R.," *American PEN Newsletter* no. 17 (November 1974): [1–2].

"Conversations with Syd," in *Syd Solomon: A Retrospective Showing.* Sarasota, Fla.: Ringling Museum of Art, 1974, pp. 4–7.

"Tom Wicker Signifying [review of Tom Wicker's *A Time to Die*]," *New York Times Book Review*, March 9, 1975, pp. 2–3.

"Vonnegut on Trout," *Fantasy and Science Fiction* 48 (April 1975): 158.

"*Nashville*—A Shadow Play of What We Have Become and Where We Might Look for Wisdom," *Vogue* 165 (June 1975): 103.

"New York: Who Needs It?," *Harper's* 251 (August 1975): 3.

"Opening Remarks," in *The Unabridged Mark Twain*, edited by Lawrence Teacher. Philadelphia: Running Press, 1976.

"Only Kidding, Folks? [review of seven novels by Stanislaw Lem]," *Nation* 226 (May 13, 1978): 575.

"Cabinet Eavesdropping: Message of the Leaked Minutes," *Nation* 227 (September 30, 1978): 307, 310.

"The Birth of an Extra Edition," in *A Century at Cornell*, edited by Daniel Margulis. Ithaca, N.Y.: Cornell Sun, 1980, p. 66.

"Preface," in *The Writer's Image*, by Jill Krementz. Boston: Godine, 1980, pp. vii–x.

Three-page letter, mailed by the American Civil Liberties Union, on censorship with an appeal for donations.

"A Reluctant Big Shot [on Walter Cronkite]," *Nation* 232 (March 7, 1981): 282–83.

"Literature as Encouragement," *Index on Censorship*, June 1981, p. 19.

"A Truly Modern Hero [on Ignaz Semmelweis]," *Psychology Today* 15 (August 1981): 9–10.

"Stars and Bit Players [on liberalism and literary values]," *Nation* 233 (November 28, 1981): 580–82.

"The Most Beautiful Court in the World," *World Tennis* 29 (March 1982): 30.

"A Gorgeous Movie—An Audacious Political Act [review of the film *Reds* by Warren Beatty]," *Vogue* 172 (April 1982): 315–16.

"Letters to the Young [review of Ernest Callenbach's *Ectopia* and *Ectopia Emerging*]," *Nation* 234 (May 22, 1982): 621.

"An Appreciation," in *Bob and Ray: A Retrospective*, program for the Museum of Broadcasting, New York, exhibit of June 15–July 10, 1982, pp. [2–4].

"William Saroyan, 1980–1981," *Proceedings of the American Academy of Arts and Letters*, 2nd series, no. 33 (1982): 86.

"Homely Truths [commencement address]," *Dartmouth Alumni Magazine* 75 (June 1983): 32–33.

Letter to Erskine Caldwell, commemorative tributes, Dartmouth College Library Special Collections bound volume, August 8, 1983.

"The Idea Killers [on freedom of speech]," *Playboy* 31 (January 1984): 122, 260, 262.

"Imagine the Worst [on President Ronald Reagan]," *Mother Jones* 9 (October 1984): 26.

"Jimmy Ernst, 1920–1984," *Proceedings of the American Academy of Arts and Letters*, 2nd series, no. 35 (1984): 76–77.

"A Tribute [to Richard Brautigan]," in *Dictionary of Literary Biography Yearbook: 1984*, edited by Jean W. Ross. Detroit: Gale Research, 1985, pp. 168–69.

"From the Desk of Kurt Vonnegut [on PEN Congress]," *Mother Jones* 10 (January 1986): 26.

"Can't Prague Even Leave Jazz Alone?," *New York Times*, December 14, 1986, p. 28.

"Preface," in *The Seventh Cross*, by Anna Segher. New York: Monthly Review Foundation, 1986.

"To Allen," in *Best Minds: A Tribute to Allen Ginsberg*, edited by Bill Morgan and Bob Rosenthal. New York: Lospecchio Press, 1986, p. 282.

"Foreword," in *Varga, The Esquire Years: A Catalogue Raisonné*. New York: Alfred Van der Marck Editions, 1987.

"Afterword," in *Free to Be . . . a Family*, by Marlo Thomas. New York: Bantam, 1987, p. 172.

Bibliography

"What I'd Say If They Asked Me [hypothetical acceptance speech written for presidential candidate Michael Dukakis]," *New Republic* 247 (July 16–23, 1988): 53–54.

"Preface," in *Love Action Laughter and Other Sad Tales*, by Budd Schulberg. New York: Random House, 1989.

"The Courage of Ivan Martin Jirous," *Washington Post*, March 31, 1989, p. A25.

"Slaughter in Mozambique," *New York Times*, November 14, 1989, p. 27.

"Introduction," in *The Sirens of Titan*. Norwalk, Conn.: Easton Press, 1990, pp. vii–ix.

"Presentation to Paul Engle of the Award for Distinguished Service to the Arts," *Proceedings of the American Academy of Arts and Letters*, 2nd series, no. 41 (May 1990), 37–38.

"Frank Conroy: The Triumph of Arch," *Gentlemen's Quarterly* 60 (September 1990): 370.

"Heinlein Gets the Last Word [review of Robert Heinlein's *Stranger in a Strange Land*]," *New York Times Book Review*, December 9, 1990, p. 13.

Introduction to Italian edition of *God Bless You, Mr. Rosewater* (*Perle ai Porci*). Milan: Elèuthera, 1991.

Comment on television adaptation of Vonnegut's short stories, in *Welcome to "Kurt Vonnegut's Monkeyhouse,"* promotional brochure for cable television series, February 1991. Los Angeles: Atlantis Productions, 1991.

" 'Somewhere in ETO': Hoosiers in the European Theater of Operations [letter to his family written in 1945 from a POW repatriation camp in France]," *Traces of Indiana and Midwestern History* 3 (Fall 1991): 43–45.

Introduction to Italian edition of *Breakfast of Champions* (*La Colazione de Campioni*). Milan: Elèuthera, 1992.

"One Hell of a Country," *Guardian* (England), February 27, 1992, p. 21.

"Presentation to Sam Shepard of the Gold Medal for Drama," *Proceedings of the American Academy of Arts and Letters*, 2nd series, no. 43 (May 1992): 53–54.

"A Tribute to James Brooks," *Proceedings of the American Academy of Arts and Letters*, 2nd series, no. 43 (May 1992), 59–60.

[Comments on Jerzy Kosinski, in English, Polish, and French], in *Jerzy Kosinski: The Faces and Masks*, with photographs by Czeław Czaplinski. Łodz, Poland: Museum Aztuki, 1992, p. 130.

"Why My Dog is Not a Humanist," *Humanist* 52 (November/December 1992): 5–6.

Introduction to Italian edition of *The Sirens of Titan* (*Le Sirene di Titano*). Milan: Elèuthera, 1993.

"Preface to the 25th Anniversary Edition of *Slaughterhouse-Five*," in *Slaughterhouse-Five* (New York: Delacorte Press/Seymour Lawrence, 1994), pp. xi–xiii.

"Stuart Dybek," *Proceedings of the American Academy of Arts and Letters*, 2nd series, no. 45 (May 1994), 23.

"If I Knew Then What I Know Now . . . : Advice to the Class of '94," *Cornell Magazine* 96 (May 1994): 31.

"The Last Smoker in New York," *New York Times* special advertising supplement titled *NYChristmas 1994*, November 20, 1994, pp. 51–52.

Statement on Abbie Hoffman, Abbie Hoffman Tribute, New York, November 29, 1994.

"A Very Fringe Character," in *An Unsentimental Education: Writers and Chicago*, edited by Molly McQuade. Chicago: University of Chicago Press, 1995, pp. 236–42.

151

"Vonnegut and Clancy on Technology," *Inc. Technology* 17. iv [bonus supplement to *Inc.* 17, xviii] (November 14, 1995): 63–64, 66.

"Foreword," in *The Winner of the Slow Bicycle Race,* by Paul Krassner. New York: Seven Stories Press, 1996, pp. 15–16.

"Introduction," in *A Connecticut Yankee in King Arthur's Court,* by Mark Twain. New York: Oxford University Press, 1986, pp. xxxi–xxxiii.

Tribute to Allen Ginsberg, in "Touching America," by Greil Marcus, *Rolling Stone* no. 761 (May 29, 1997): 42.

SELECTED CRITICISM ON KURT VONNEGUT

Allen, William Rodney. *Understanding Kurt Vonnegut.* Columbia: University of South Carolina Press, 1991.

Broer, Lawrence R. *Sanity Plea: Schizophrenia in the Novels of Kurt Vonnegut.* Ann Arbor, Mich.: UMI Research Press, 1989. Second edition, expanded, Tuscaloosa: University of Alabama Press, 1994.

Bryan, C. D. B. "Kurt Vonnegut, Head Bokononist," *New York Times Book Review,* April 6, 1969, pp. 2, 25.

Giannone, Richard. *Vonnegut: A Preface to His Novels.* Port Washington, N.Y.: Kennikat Press, 1977.

Hicks, Granville. "Literary Horizons," *Saturday Review* 52 (March 29, 1969): 25.

Klinkowitz, Jerome. *Kurt Vonnegut.* London & New York: Methuen, 1982.

———. *Slaughterhouse-Five: Reforming the Novel and the World.* Boston: Twayne, 1990.

———. *Structuring the Void: The Struggle for Subject in Contemporary American Fiction.* Durham, N.C.: Duke University Press, 1992.

Lawrence, Seymour. "A Publisher's Dream," Summary 1, 2 (1971): 73–75.

Lundquist, James. *Kurt Vonnegut.* New York: Ungar, 1977.

Merrill, Robert, ed. *Critical Essays on Kurt Vonnegut.* Boston: G. K. Hall, 1990.

Muztazza, Leonard. *Forever Pursuing Genesis: The Myth of Eden in the Novels of Kurt Vonnegut.* Lewisburg, Pa.: Bucknell University Press, 1990.

Reed, Peter J. *Kurt Vonnegut, Jr.* New York: Warner, 1972.

Schatt, Stanley. *Kurt Vonnegut, Jr.* Boston: Twayne, 1976.

Scholes, Robert. *Fabulation and Metafiction.* Urbana: University of Illinois Press, 1979.

———. *The Fabulators.* New York: Oxford University Press, 1967.

———. *"Slaughterhouse-Five,"* New York Times Book Review, April 6, 1969, pp. 1, 23.

Wakefield, Dan. "In Vonnegut's Karass," in *The Vonnegut Statement,* edited by Jerome Klinkowitz and John Somer. New York: Delacorte Press/Seymour Lawrence, 1973, pp. 55–70.

Yarmolinsky, Jane Vonnegut. *Angels without Wings.* Boston: Houghton Mifflin, 1987.

BIBLIOGRAPHY

Pieratt, Asa B. Jr., Julie Huffman-klinkowitz, and Jerome Klinkowitz. *Kurt Vonnegut: A Comprehensive Bibliography.* Hamden, Conn.: Shoe String Press, 1987.

INDEX